Creating the
Virtual Classroom

Distance Learning
with the Internet

2

Creating the Virtual Classroom

Distance Learning with the Internet

Lynnette R. Porter

WILEY COMPUTER PUBLISHING

John Wiley & Sons, Inc.
New York • Chichester • Weinheim
• Brisbane • Singapore • Toronto

Executive Publisher: Katherine Schowalter
Editor: Theresa Hudson
Managing Editor: Mark Hayden
Text Design & Composition: Publishers' Design and Production Services, Inc.

Designations used by companies to distinguish their products are often claimed as trademarks. In all instances where John Wiley & Sons, Inc., is aware of a claim, the product names appear in initial capital or ALL CAPITAL LETTERS. Readers, however, should contact the appropriate companies for more complete information regarding trademarks and registration.

This text is printed on acid-free paper.

This publication is designed to provide accurate and authoritative information in regard to the subject matter covered. It is sold with the understanding that the publisher is not engaged in rendering legal, accounting, or other professional service. If legal advice or other expert assistance is required, the services of a competent professional person should be sought.

Library of Congress Cataloging-in-Publication Data:

Porter, Lynnette R.
    Creating the virtual classroom : distance learning with the
Internet / Lynnette R. Porter.
        p.   cm.
    Includes index.
    ISBN 0-471-17830-6 (pbk. : alk. paper)
    1. Distance education—United States.   2. Internet (Computer
network) in education—United States.   3. World Wide Web
(Information retrieval system)   I. Title.
LC5805.P67   1997
371.3'5—dc21   96-38065
                                                       CIP

Printed in the United States of America
10 9 8 7 6 5 4 3 2

About the Author

Lynnette R. Porter received her M.A. in English, with a specialization in technical writing, from Bowling Green State University, where she also received her Ph.D. in English, with specializations in technical communication, rhetoric, and composition.

She has been an active member of the Society for Technical Communication, for which she served on the board of directors as a director-sponsor. Additionally, she is a frequent speaker at the Society's regional and international conferences and has participated in several committees. She is a member of several other professional associations, including the Association for Business Communication and the Association of Teachers of Technical Writing.

She has been an associate professor at The University of Findlay in Ohio and also operates a consulting business. In her role as consultant, she has been a writer of everything from brochures and newsletters to manuals and proposals; an editor of two professional journals; and a technical/computer trainer.

Contents

viii ■ *Contents*

List of Illustrations

Preface

Distance learning is not a new subject, but it recently has come in vogue again. With the advent of new educational and training technologies and the need to meet the needs of learners in a fast-paced world, distance learning is becoming a necessity. In its best sense, it can help educate more people anywhere at any time. Our renewed interest in distance learning has the potential to change public perception of education and its ongoing importance throughout our lives.

For consistency, I use *distance learning* as the preferred term, instead of distance education, another common term. Although many educators prefer the latter term, I use *distance learning* to indicate instruction for both education and training.

The term *education* in this book includes elementary and secondary programs, continuing education and noncredit programs, and public and private colleges and universities; it refers to more traditional courses offered through accredited or licensed institutions. *Education* also implies knowledge that may be highly pragmatic, or simply "nice to know"; it includes theoretical as well as application-based information.

Training includes skill development and knowledge geared toward practical applications; although training may be offered by traditional educational institutions, it also is the province of private vendors, such as businesses specializing in customized training for individuals and corporations, and in-house training departments.

Distance learning involves both education and training; the emphasis varies with the types of courses being offered. Finally, I use the term *learner* to refer to anyone who takes a distance learning course. I realize that some "learners" may not actually learn anything, although they have taken a course. Nevertheless, I prefer this term to indicate persons who take distance learning courses, in part to emphasize the lifelong nature and importance of education and training.

I prefer to highlight the benefits of distance learning and some positive implications for educational change, although I indicate throughout the book that distance learning programs must be carefully designed and managed if they are to be effective for learners. The effectiveness of distance learning programs depends on their design and implementation; throughout this book you'll read some principles and suggestions for planning an effective course or program.

This book has been designed for educators, trainers, administrators, businesspeople, and the learners they hope to serve. It provides an overview of distance learning and the types of programs most commonly offered. Because I often emphasize online distance learning programs, most examples come from the World Wide Web (Web) and the Internet.

The book consists of the following chapters:

Chapter 1 Distance Learning in Today's Education and Training
Chapter 2 Types of Distance Learning
Chapter 3 Funding a Distance Learning Program
Chapter 4 Preparing a Grant Proposal
Chapter 5 Determining the Suitability of Distance Learning Courses
Chapter 6 E-mail, Faxmail, and Voice Mail as Distance Learning Tools
Chapter 7 The World Wide Web in Education and Training
Chapter 8 Teleconferencing and Desktop Videoconferencing
Chapter 9 Advertising Your Distance Learning Program
Chapter 10 Reconceptualizing Education and Training through Distance Learning
Chapter 11 International Educational Issues

Most chapters include descriptions of distance learning programs and courses, plus suggestions for implementing your own courses. Questions to help you plan your course or program and checklists also guide you.

As well, seven appendices provide lists of online and print resources to help you learn more about distance learning programs and to locate additional examples of programs and their materials. The appendices are these:

Appendix A Bibliography of Printed Sources
Appendix B Distance Learning Newsgroups and Mailing Lists
Appendix C Online Resources about Grants and Granting Opportunities
Appendix D E-zines about Distance Learning

Appendix E Instructional Web Sites
Appendix F Copyright, Patent, Trademark, and Intellectual Property Web sites
Appendix G International Distance Learning

As with any book including information about and from the Internet and the Web, many addresses and examples may change between the time the book is written, then used by readers. I have tried to update the samples and locations of electronic information up to the date of publication.

Distance learning is a challenge, for those who create the programs and those who participate in them. It offers us the potential to provide ongoing education to more people, but it also requires us carefully to evaluate our instructional methods and the technologies to establish communication among learners and educators/trainers. I hope you will use this book as one of many first steps toward developing more effective distance learning courses and programs.

Acknowledgments

In preparing this book I browsed several hundred Web sites, visited distance learning classrooms, attended conference presentations and meetings featuring educators and trainers experienced with distance learning, observed teleconferences, and discussed distance learning with colleagues through several mailing lists and newsgroups. Many people who provided insight into distance education were anonymous; I "met" them through their Web sites and e-mail messages. Nevertheless, I thank the many people whose work with distance education helped shape my perspective on this changing topic.

More specifically, I thank two reviewers who assisted in the manuscript preparation: Brandi Ross, for her helpful comments on an early draft of the book, and Bart Porter, for his insight and inspiration throughout the development of the book.

Distance Learning in Today's Education and Training

1

*D*istance learning has become a hot topic in the past few years, although it's far from being a new idea. Whether it's called distance learning, directed learning, assisted learning, distance education, or some other name, there is an obvious answer to the question, What is distance learning? It is educational or training information, including the instruction and experience that learners gain, although they are physically distant from the source of that information and instruction.

In practice, however, distance learning can be much more than this simple definition indicates. It can involve the use of new technologies, innovative materials, and interactive instructional methods. It can reach people of all ages and abilities who might otherwise find it difficult to further their education or get the training they need. It can help learners realize the importance of life-long education, whether for personal interest or career preparation and enhancement. Distance learning is not a panacea for all educational or training ills, but it does offer additional possibilities for educating and training more people than can be easily and efficiently accommodated in more traditional settings, such as in-house corporate training programs, public schools, and universities. In its broadest sense, distance learning can be very private or it can be highly formalized.

Distance learning is an important way for educational institutions, from public elementary and secondary schools to state-funded and private colleges and universities, to offer instruction to a new market of students. In the past, some potential "customers" have had difficulty fitting traditional courses into their schedules; they lived too far from the site offering the instruction or the costs were prohibitive for them to take the courses they wanted. If the instruction wasn't required, these students often didn't learn about that subject area. With more distance learning opportunities, educators can reach this market, benefiting both the educational institution and the learners it serves.

Businesses, too, frequently define distance learning in terms of training opportunities for their employees, who may be located far from corporate training centers or the home office. Travel costs, including the time needed for travel, limited the opportunities for training or retraining staff. In-house training now can refer to teleconferencing or desktop videoconferencing, as well as online education, so that corporate trainers can reach employees located anywhere in the world.

If the company needs to outsource training, it can hire consultants to develop distance learning materials and set up the equipment needed to distribute instruction, or it can pay for employees to take courses via distance learning programs, which may be offered through an academic institution or by a private business specializing in customized training.

Distance learning programs can be designed to meet any group of learners' needs. The technologies used in distance learning, the structure of a course or a program, and the degree of supervision for a distance learning course can be varied to meet a particular group's needs or interests. As well, vendors may specialize in one type of distance learning program, or they may offer courses showcasing a wide variety of subjects, technologies, and educational/training methods. The possibilities for designing a distance learning course are myriad, but the success of a program depends on effective planning to meet a market need for a course or a program.

WHAT ARE SOME STRUCTURAL DIFFERENCES IN DISTANCE LEARNING PROGRAMS?

Some distance learning programs offer highly structured courses, with deadlines for learners to be evaluated and standards by which participants' progress is measured. These courses may be offered by a business or a university or college, but they follow a schedule of courses. Many courses lead to a degree or certificate; learners who take one or several courses may be required to take a certain number of courses within a time frame in order to complete the program. Some courses may be offered only once during a scheduled term or a year, and the sequence of courses may be set so that there is a clear hierarchy of courses, from beginning to more advanced studies.

Vendors who provide structured distance learning environments may offer entire degree or certification programs "long distance." Others may require site visits to the vendor's primary location, attendance at proctored lecture or examination sessions, or completion of some courses at the home site; only a specified number of courses taken via distance education can be counted toward completion of a degree or certification program.

In other forms of distance learning, participants may take courses because they want to learn or are required to learn a new skill or subject area for their jobs, but they face no deadlines for mastering the subject and may not need or expect formal evaluation of their achievements. Some courses have a *proficiency* type of exam that learners can take at any time, as long as they can eventually show their mastery of a skill or a subject. Many private vendors (e.g., training companies) offer courses year-round, whenever an individual or a group expresses interest in a course. Some programs are customized for in-house use and can be offered whenever a company requests the vendor to supply training.

Even within these less-structured programs, the design of a single course still may be structured. Learners may have to complete a series of lessons or activities in a given sequence, although they have no time limitations for completing one unit or the entire course.

WHAT DEGREE OF SUPERVISION IS REQUIRED IN A DISTANCE LEARNING COURSE?

In some courses, the educators or trainers who prepare materials and direct the course are actively involved in working with learners. They may have been hired specifically to provide distance learning courses and to work with learners, or they may also teach or train learners in more traditional, face-to-face instruction on site, in addition to presenting one or two distance learning courses. In more highly structured courses, learners usually have more direct interaction with educators/trainers, who may evaluate the learners' progress and provide a final "grade" or other signifier that learners have achieved course objectives.

Courses that lead to a degree or a certification are monitored more closely than courses not taken for some type of credit. Many vendors are licensed, accredited, or otherwise evaluated as high-quality providers of instruction. To maintain their status, they carefully monitor distance learning courses, the educators/trainers, course materials, and learners' progress.

In other forms of distance learning, the course may be unmonitored, and the learners themselves have full responsibility for proceeding with the course and evaluating their mastery of a skill or subject. This type of distance learning is often appropriate for learners who don't require credit for a course, but simply need to master a skill or a subject area. For example, learners who want to learn to use a new software package may work with an online tutorial. They can learn at their own pace and access the materials at any time, in any order (although there is probably a preferred sequence of units indicated in the tutorial). Because no one monitors their progress, the learners have to check their own mastery of the subject, usually through practical applications of the activities they've completed in the simulation.

Distance learning courses with little or no formal interaction between the educators/trainers who designed the materials and the learners using them are more common in hobby- or interest-related courses. Even training courses may fit into the interest category, although learners may be motivated by the need to update their job skills in order to remain employed or employable.

WHO PARTICIPATES IN DISTANCE LEARNING?

Participants in distance learning include the people who create and disseminate the learning materials and the learners. Both categories of participants have specific needs and responsibilities. However, the line between those who need information and those who provide it is becoming blurred. Learners may also become educators/trainers or vendors, once they've gained more expertise or knowledge about a subject area. In the same way, for educators/trainers and vendors to remain current with technology and the subject matters they present, they also have to keep learning. They probably will learn a great deal from the "customers" who take their courses. The nature of distance learning encourages interaction among different groups of learners and educators/trainers, so that ideally, everyone benefits from the interaction and comes away from the experience with new skills and/or knowledge.

Distance learning is even more important today, when society is changing rapidly. Learners need to meet ongoing needs for education (the foundation of theory and facts needed for basic or advanced understanding of a subject area) and for training (specific task-related activities, built on a foundation of knowledge about a subject area). As society becomes technologically more sophisticated, the knowledge base changes; what is considered a "well-rounded education" changes with an expanded knowledge base. Therefore, the need for a good understanding, from basic concepts to advanced theories and applications, is important and ongoing for people who want to work in highly technical or scientific careers.

When society becomes more technologically sophisticated, it tends to become more streamlined, as tasks become automated or people's work is completed more efficiently. This streamlining in business and industry can lead to downsizing or job redesign, as some jobs completed by people become obsolete.

Streamlining at home, such as the use of more efficient appliances and the convenience of communicating through home computer centers (e.g., to pay the bills, order pizza, take an educational course, telecommute to a job), changes the concept not only of work, but also of play. People may take one of two approaches to streamlining on the homefront: Their work day never ends, because they now have the capacity to work at home at any time, or they have more free time, because they can accomplish more tasks *virtually*, instead of *in person*.

Streamlining, on the job and in our personal lives, reinforces the need for additional training, as well as the underpinning of education. We often need to understand why we do something (theory-related information) before we can understand how to apply the information or why we complete a task in a certain way. Whether the education and training are related to a personal interest—such as how to program the VCR, how to design a Web page, or how to invest in stocks—or career-related—such as updating job skills or learning to work with new equipment—they are crucial to personal and professional success. Distance learning is one way to help persons of all ages and backgrounds get the education and training they need to work and live more productively in a changing world.

Who should (or eventually will) participate in distance learning programs? Ideally, the answer is *everyone*. Although that may not be practical, the possibility for reaching more people through distance learning is greater than ever before, as is the need to educate, train, or retrain greater numbers of people.

VENDORS OF DISTANCE LEARNING COURSES OR PROGRAMS

Technological changes affect us all, whether we are primarily learners (or potential learners) or the people who provide the education or training. Because so many new subject areas need to be presented to a wider audience, there is seldom a lack of something about which to teach or train. With the explosion of Internet services, which are becoming available to more people daily, just about anyone can become a "vendor" of educational and training materials. That doesn't mean that everyone should become a vendor or that the quality of information made available to a wider electronic audience can be guaranteed—only that more people who haven't been in the education or training business now can get into that business.

More people, individuals, and companies or institutions, have the capability of transmitting and receiving information about a subject matter. However, that capability doesn't equal *distance learning*. For true learning to take place, vendors need to promote research into the needs of potential learners, provide access to the *appropriate* technologies for the types of distance learning courses and different subject matter, continually update the course content and technologies used to disseminate the information, and hire and support effective educators/trainers. (Throughout the book, you should assume that *a distance learning vendor* is one who takes distance learning seriously and is committed to providing accurate, effective information to the learners who will take a course away from the originating source of the course.)

Many businesses and educational institutions serve as vendors and provide distance learning opportunities. Some distance learning providers are traditional educational institutions, consortia of educational institutions and/or businesses, in-house training groups or departments, businesses that specialize in offering training to clients and individual customers, the government, grantors with an interest in distance learning, and individual consultants.

Individual Educational Institutions

Elementary, middle, and high schools offer distance learning programs to students within their districts or regions. Although some distance learning programs can be designed so that students in remote locations or those limited to home-based study, for example, can take a complete educational program away from the base school, most distance learning programs for young students involve a few courses that are not currently offered at the home school. For example, students may not be able to take a foreign language or an arts course in their school, and they can't easily travel to a site where the instruction can be provided in person. A distance learning course meets their needs, although it is only one component of the students' complete education.

Distance learning can be offered through an institution to provide adults with remedial or supplementary instruction. For example, adults may need to take a general equivalency diploma (GED) program to receive the equivalent of a high school diploma. The GED courses may be offered via distance learning so that more adults can participate in the program and receive the education (and verification of their achievement) that they need.

Universities and colleges, either public or private, also offer distance learning programs. They may provide a regular program of study or offer special events, such as teleconferences or online discussions. They may offer noncredit courses through a continuing education or adult education program, for example, to target learners not interested in a complete degree program. They may also provide for-credit courses or entire programs, possibly leading to a degree or certification.

Consortia of Educational Institutions and/or Businesses

Consortia are often created through the need to meet common interests and share resources. For example, several academic institutions with similar degree programs may share resources or collaborate to offer courses. The consortia may offer courses that complement, rather than only compete, with those offered by the individual institutions making up the consortia. Because the "business" of education is becoming more competitive, and many institutions are looking for ways to streamline programs, eliminate duplication of services within a region, and manage escalating costs, a consortium may be one way for administrators with similar programs to keep offering courses and to remain marketable. Working with, instead of against, the competition helps all academic institutions stay in business.

Other consortia are formed on the basis of their common geographical boundaries (e.g., within a state); the group may decide to allow certain institutions to offer specific courses on the Web or through teleconferences so that competition for learners is minimized and individual institutions can focus on developing high-quality distance learning programs for a specific part of the educational market. Again, cooperation among academic institutions can help ensure that all institutions reach a viable share of the market.

However, educational institutions are not the only ones that should band together to keep educational costs reasonable and to ensure that the learners who need courses or programs can find them. Consortia often create an alliance between educational institutions and private businesses. A common example is the collaboration of businesses in the telecommunications industry and academic institutions. The business may provide the technologies for disseminating educational information and leave the creation of distance learning materials to professionals in educational institutions. For example, a telecommunications company may become partners with a local college to develop a series of educational broadcasts. The telecommunications company provides the technology and broadcast expertise, whereas educators and learners provide the know-how to create effective educational materials and formats and the personnel to make the on-air presentations. These consortia use the expertise of individual businesses and educational institutions to develop integrated, effective distance learning programs.

The businesses gain a new market segment, because they can reach more learners (possible customers). Businesses also gain the prestige of working with academic institutions and assisting the community or region with educational and training activities; they gain the intangible benefit of a higher status. They also may gain a practical advantage by working closely with the research departments of universities and colleges, so that they can maintain a "cutting edge" knowledge base or learn first about scientific or technical advances.

Of course, the educational institutions also gain from the consortium. They may receive equipment and the expertise to install and maintain it—an important source of funding that many institutions need if they are to provide new technology to their students. They enhance their reputation by working with experts in the "real world" of applications and business, so they can gain more students who want to take courses or receive degrees from an institution that offers the best of academia and business.

Businesses (or Departments within Companies) That Need to Disperse Information In-House

Some businesses have training departments responsible for providing information in a variety of formats, including distance learning. In larger corporations, a separate division or a company with which the parent business has merged may provide the training.

In-house training programs, teleconferences, conference calls, e-mail, online (Web-based) simulations and tutorials, and other venues can promote distance learning activities within a company. These programs can be offered on a schedule or on a continual basis, so that employees can take the training they need when it is most convenient for their department.

In-house training can take place within a corporation at one site or it can be offered from the home site to satellite offices located anywhere in the world. The training can be offered so that all employees at any location can receive the same training within the same time frame or it can be offered at one location at a time.

Businesses That Provide Educational or Training Services to Clients, including the Public

Some vendors are in the business of marketing educational or training materials and services to clients, whether individuals or other companies. These vendors usually offer noncredit instruction, instead of university, credit-based courses, that may be career or interest-related. Because these vendors' sole business is training, they may be able to customize distance learning courses or programs to meet the needs of groups of learners, such as those within a client's company. They may offer different programs for individuals, alone or joined in groups with no other common bond than their need to take a course at this time. Usually, there's more flexibility in the type of distance learning programs offered by these vendors and they may offer the widest variety of subject matter.

Governmental Units That Study and/or Provide Distance Learning

Some governmental agencies or departments, such as Department of Energy or Department of Education, develop programs to study and evaluate distance learning. They may work with professionals in the private and public sectors to promote or create a specific program. They may provide the means, such as grants, to study distance learning further. Other governmental units work as businesses do to provide in-house distance learning for employees or clients.

Although the federal government often encourages or promotes distance learning initiatives, state or local governmental units may also offer similar programs or their own distance learning programs. For example, Indiana has a highly developed electronic network to link public schools within the state for distance learning programs. Federal, state, and local governmental units may provide funding, research grants, tax incentives, or other motivators to encourage distance learning research and applications.

Grant-Funded Projects and/or Grantors Who Want to Promote Distance Learning

Grantors, or those who provide funds or other types of support, promote distance learning in a variety of ways. By offering grants, they may promote a specific type of program, use of a specific technology, or development of specific materials. They may emphasize research or applications of research; they may encourage the development of a new educational or training tool or technology; they may provide the resources to offer distance learning programs to more learners. The type of grant varies with the grantors and their specific interests in distance learning.

Grantors may require collaboration among educational institutions and/or businesses or encourage individuals to develop innovative projects. This is another reason why developing consortia is a good idea; many grantors want to help support institutions or businesses that have already sought ways to collaborate and share technologies, methods, and resources.

Individual Consultants, Tutors, Information Designers, Teachers, and Other Entrepreneurs

These entrepreneurs provide distance learning opportunities on their own, similar to the services provided by vendors that are larger businesses. Individuals may market their materials or services to a variety of clients and offer specialized areas of expertise. Although most consultants involved with distance learning offer their services full time, some educators and trainers may work part time to design materials and offer courses or to provide their expertise to businesses and institutions that want to offer distance learning programs.

Although most consultants offer distance learning courses for a fee, some individuals have designed free courses, usually for the Web. These interest-related courses are often about the Web and designing information for it. For example, a popular "free" course (although the documents and graphics within the site are copyrighted and should not be reproduced without permission) explains how to use hypertext markup language (HTML) to design a Web page. Other individuals who have designed software or written more extensive documentation may offer a free course to whet potential customers' interest in more advanced or elaborate courses, documents, or products that can then be purchased.

LEARNERS WHO TAKE DISTANCE LEARNING COURSES

The learners who participate in distance learning programs have a variety of educational needs. Some may only be interested in a one-time course or teleconference; others may want to complete a degree program or meet long-term educational requirements, such as those for certification or high school equivalency. Learners may be part of a group completing the same program at the same time or they may work alone at their own pace. The range of learners who use distance learning programs is wide.

Adult Learners

Often termed *nontraditional students*, adult learners may work part time or full time, or they may be currently un- or underemployed and want to develop more marketable skills. Their work and personal schedules vary widely, and they bring a variety of life and work experiences and expectations to a distance learning program.

These learners may need specialized training to keep up with current job demands or they may be looking for more general education. Their motivations range from personal interests to job pressures. They may be interested in only one program or type of material, or they may want to pursue long-term educational needs.

Adult learners also represent a variety of learning styles. Some may find that traditional education methods, such as lecture and discussion, are not the best ways to help them learn. Many may prefer hands-on activities, self-directed question-and-answer sessions, observations of a task being performed or a process as it takes place, and graphics instead of text as a primary style of document. The interactive capabilities of some distance learning technologies, especially those available through the Internet, therefore, may be more attractive to adults. Because distance learning should and usually does involve multiple media to present course information, adults may like distance learning courses better than traditional classroom-based courses or in-house training sessions conducted in a laboratory.

Children and Youth

Some younger learners, for one reason or another, may not be able to meet the educational requirements of their state or home institution. Other children and youth may be physically unable to participate in educational programs offered in traditional classrooms or they may be geographically isolated from educational institutions. Even students who attend a public or private school may need distance learning courses to supplement the amount or type of instruction available at their home schools. Distance learning thus provides these learners with the needed instruction.

Regular courses for children may be provided, so that students learning from home or within a classroom can complete a formal program of study. For example, students who need to complete a course may be able to take it by watching closed-circuit television broadcasts; one teacher can instruct many classes at the same time across long distances. Students whose districts cannot afford to provide that course or whose teachers lack the credentials or expertise to offer the instruction can thus receive the same instruction they would have from a teacher in the classroom.

Special tutoring programs, preschool programs, or supplemental courses can also be offered to younger students. These programs may be part of a required educational program or they might be highly recommended to give students additional practice or information to assist them within their regular program.

People at a Distance from an Educational Center

Those who live in rural areas, where specific educational or training programs may be unavailable or difficult to access on a regular basis, can benefit from distance learning. People who need international access to information also find distance learning appealing; information accessible through the Internet, for example, can link people and resources anywhere in the computerized world.

Distance learning programs can train employees who may not have the time to travel to the home office or a central location for training. Travel costs may be prohibitive for some companies or branches. Distance learning offers companies the option of training employees anywhere at any time, whether they work in rural or urban locations.

People Who Have Difficulty Attending Classes or Programs Regularly

Adults whose work and personal schedules don't permit them to attend classes scheduled by a university in their area can take distance learning courses at their convenience. Adults or youth who suffer from a temporary or permanent illness or condition that prevents them from participating in other types of educational programs can receive similar instruction at home or in another setting. Persons with different abilities, which may make it difficult to participate at the same pace or in the same way as other learners in a classroom, may participate fully by using specially designed materials that enhance their learning.

In short, distance learning can be an effective method of education or training for almost everyone. It promotes the sharing of information and experiences, so that the people who design and provide the materials and the people who use them can learn from each other. Distance learning, if used wisely, can provide additional educational opportunities to persons of all ages, from all backgrounds, with different abilities, different interests, and different needs, almost anywhere in the world, at almost any time.

WHAT ARE THE BENEFITS OF DISTANCE LEARNING?

As if the implied benefits in the previous statement aren't enough incentive for educators, trainers, and learners to want to participate in distance learning programs, there are other benefits, too. One of the greatest changes in our perception of learning comes from the possibility of easily accessed education and training throughout life. Because educational programs are becoming available at reasonable costs, through a variety of media and institutions, and with flexibility in scheduling to meet many different learners' needs, lifelong learning is not only possible, but becoming accepted as a requirement for actively participating in the modern world. Distance learning helps make lifelong learning possible and attractive to more people.

For example, a businesswoman who already has one degree but wants to learn more about a specific subject area in order to enhance her likelihood of advancing professionally may want to take one or two classes during the year. She isn't interested in a degree program, but she needs a high-quality course that will meet her professional interests and aptitudes. Distance learning offers her the possibility of continuing her education within her schedule.

In contrast, a young professional who has been in the workplace for two years and has a bachelor's degree now finds that he needs a master's degree for career advancement. He doesn't want to leave his employment to enroll in a two-year master's program and his work schedule includes evening and weekend hours, making it difficult to work full time and participate in a traditional degree program. Distance learning allows him to complete a degree program, whether from a local university or an institution anywhere in the world.

Employees in an automotive repair shop need to know about the latest computerized maintenance tools so that they can be competitive with workers in other businesses. During breaks and after work, their employer encourages them to take training mini-courses to learn about the latest technology and practice with simulations before they work on someone's car. A couple want to further their hobby interests by collaborating with other artists on a few projects; they'd like to share information and learn from each other. They don't have to learn more because of job pressures or the possibility for career advancement; they're interested in learning more because they enjoy working with pottery. Distance learning courses meet their needs to further their interests, as well as enhance their careers.

Learners who participate in distance learning programs may receive some or all of the following benefits: They may learn independently, at their own pace, in a convenient location, at a convenient time, about a greater variety of subjects, from a greater variety of institutions or educators/trainers.

Learn at Their Own Pace

Learners can take a course during a traditional term or training session, or they can take their time to complete learning activities. They can go over materials many times or proceed quickly and use materials during the day, after work, during breaks, in the middle of the night, or at regularly scheduled intervals—whenever is convenient for them and the provider of the information. They can learn during predetermined time segments (such as an hour-long discussion or a 15-minute teleconference) or participate for as long or as little as they need, for as many times as is appropriate for them to gather information or master a skill or concept.

Learn in a Convenient Location

Depending upon the medium or media being used to provide materials or experiences, distance learning can take place in many convenient locations. For example, teleconferences may link two or more sites and videotapes of the session may also be viewed later at home or in the workplace. Learners at home or at work can access Web-based information or use the Internet to send and receive e-mail, work with mailing lists, and download bulletin board notices. Cable television broadcasts, either closed-circuit or wide-area transmission, can be received at home, in the office, or in a public setting (e.g., a library, an airline terminal). At a simpler level of distance learning technology, printed materials might be mailed, then used anywhere that can be reached by surface mail.

The variety of distance learning media helps ensure that people who want to take a course can take one conveniently, wherever they are located. Because distance learning spans many technologies that can reach virtually (or virtually reach) nearly everyone in the world, learners may find that anyplace can be a learning environment. For example, they may not prefer to study at the beach, but they can.

Learn about Topics That May Not Be Covered in Courses or Programs Offered in Their Area

Many universities, colleges, businesses, and independent consultants may offer educational and training programs within a geographic region. These information providers may specialize in certain programs or they may be "generalists" that offer a wide variety of introductory programs.

Because most institutions try to develop their niche within the marketplace, they usually emphasize one or more subject areas or types of programs, such as being known for a master's program in occupational therapy. Those potential learners living in a geographic region where the specializations fail to match their interests or educational needs need to look outside the region for a high-quality specialty program. Distance learning can help learners find a number of programs specializing in their areas of interest, even if the programs aren't offered in their geographic region.

Participate in the Programs of Universities, Colleges, Businesses, and Other Groups That Offer High-Quality or High-Prestige Programs without Having to Relocate

Within each discipline or profession, some institutions are noted for their high-quality training or educational programs. Participating in high-quality, specialized programs through distance learning can enhance learners' professional standing and provide them with exactly the type of training or education they'll need on the job.

Learners who want to "attend" a school whose name is instantly recognized as a prestigious institution now can take at least some courses without having to relocate near the institution. For example, learners who want to take a course from Harvard University may be able to participate through courses offered on the World Wide Web. Although the experience may never compensate for being a part of the student body on the Harvard campus and learners are not guaranteed a degree from Harvard by participating in distance learning courses, nevertheless, they can benefit from their association with a high-quality institution noted for its academic excellence.

In the same way, learners may want to work with a "name" instructor within a company, institution, or discipline. It may not be practical for learners to go where the expert works, but distance learning can make the expert or his or her materials available to a wider audience.

Learn according to Their Preferred Mode of Learning

Everyone has a learning preference. Some people are active learners; others are more passive. One benefit of distance learning is the variety of materials available to meet everyone's learning preference at least some of the time.

For example, some people are hands-on learners, who learn best by doing. Hands-on learners might prefer using online, CD, or interactive video simulations of tasks they'll need to complete later. Virtual reality may be a big part of their educational experience.

Some people learn best by discussing their ideas aloud with peers, to sort through the information and get feedback from other people. Discussion and news groups probably will be preferred by learners who need to discuss their ideas with a group. These learners might enjoy e-mail, as well as teleconferences or interactive broadcasts, to help discuss materials with others.

Other, more traditional learners may prefer lecture and notetaking methods to gather information. They may prefer to read and think about material before applying it, and prefer to work with an instructor who provides lectures, notes, handouts, and reading assignments. These learners may like to participate in teleconferences, read information stored on the Internet, peruse databases on CD or online, and download their assignments to a printer.

For learners who prefer graphics to prose, the Web, as well as video and broadcast, offers a wealth of diverse materials. Film, animation, sound effects, music, voiceovers, static (nonmoving) and moving graphics, photos, drawings, schematics, and 3-D virtual environments are some formats through which they might learn best.

The degree of interactivity required by individual learners can be matched with the type of technology and course. Some media are more interactive, and some subject areas require more direct learner involvement. Distance learning courses, if they're well designed, offer learners a wide range of choices, so that they can find the right mix of interaction and learning style to enhance their individual capacity to learn or be trained.

Practice Working with Different Technologies

As learners work with broadcasting technologies, computers, CD players, videotape recorders, and other educational technologies, they not only learn about their subject areas, but also have practice working with a variety of interactive technologies. They become fluent with rapidly changing technical areas and receive a broader picture of the many media and technologies that are used to provide them with materials and learning experiences. One of the great benefits of distance learning is that learners not only gather information and experiences relating to their primary area of study, but also pick up additional skills and knowledge related to the technology. The more advanced the technology, the more learners can absorb simply by working with it. This benefit may be especially important to companies who want to train their employees for more technical job tasks or for students in academic institutions who want to work with computer- or broadcast-related technologies in their careers.

Direct Their Learning

One of the most important benefits may be that learners can direct their learning. Most learners need and want a guide, whether an institution through its requirements and policies, or an individual educator, who may provide tutoring, mentoring, and counseling, in addition to serving as an instructor. However, the learners themselves must take responsibility for participating in programs, completing assignments, gathering information, and developing skills.

As learners have more materials made available to them in exciting, innovative ways, they're more likely to want to learn more and learn on their own. Instead of having an educator tell them where to access information, what to do, and what to locate, learners are more likely to share with educators what they've found and how much information is available. They're also more likely to continue their education and training on their own, even when they're not taking a distance learning course.

One of the important highlights of distance learning is the sense of sharing between the educators and those being educated, the trainers and those being trained. The educators and trainers become facilitators in a learning environment, and they learn from their students. Education is no longer the privilege of a few; it is no longer something to possess. It is an ongoing process through which everyone benefits and gains experience and knowledge.

WHAT IS THE FUTURE OF DISTANCE LEARNING?

Educational institutions, companies, and consortia of businesses and/or educational institutions enthusiastically describe distance learning opportunities in their promotional literature and Web sites. Distance learning can be used by educational institutions, such as public or private schools from preschool through graduate programs. It can provide materials in a single medium or multiple media and in different formats to meet different learners' preferences in learning styles, needs, and abilities. It offers learning opportunities to people anywhere the technology can reach, at any time, and usually for a reasonable cost. Distance learning can bring people together to discuss ideas and share information, and it has the potential for being a highly efficient, effective, innovative form of education and training.

The future of distance learning depends primarily on the creative use and development of new technologies and their regulation. As learners become more aware of distance learning and the potential to continue developing knowledge and skills more easily and conveniently, the need for new materials and presentation media should continue to increase.

Changes in the Use of Educational Tools

As more tools become available, more variety in educational and training methods can be expected. Education and training don't rely on the acquisition or use of technological tools; after all, one-on-one discussions and demonstrations between an educator and a learner are very low-tech, but effective means of sharing information and encouraging learning and skill development. Nevertheless, with an increase in the number of ways people can communicate and information can be transmitted and received, materials in different formats can enhance the learning/training process and better meet people's different needs and preferences.

Telecommunications tools lead the way in newer technology; some learners will undoubtedly choose one distance learning course over another because it involves the use of one type of tool instead of others. Projected technologies that can be implemented in distance learning courses include pagers and holster phones, so that learners and/or educators/trainers can be reached anywhere, any time, to answer questions or provide information. Voice mail, pager messages, and faxmail can be sent to or from just about anywhere—directly to a hand-held unit, a car, plane, or home computer system. The miniaturization of communications equipment makes it easier to talk or leave messages.

Home-based computer systems are predicted to connect a variety of electronic devices, such as VCR, personal computer, TV, and phone/fax. Working, receiving an education or training, paying bills, talking and seeing others during communications, and accessing all types of multimedia information, for work or pleasure, can take place at home. One electronic number, instead of separate numbers for a phone, fax, and e-mail, for example, can be assigned to a person, so that many different types of communication can be sent to that person. These anticipated changes in the telecommunication industry involve the use of new tools and the linking of currently available electronic communication networks and devices. Although this communication can be invasive, it also can help more people work together, for education and training, as well as any other activity. Making these tools available cost effectively to more people, however, will be another challenge.

Changes in the Ways We Think about Education and Training

The big change involved with distance learning won't come from the materials or the media, however, although innovative education tools and approaches will certainly be exciting. The biggest change should come with the public's view of traditional learning institutions, especially those of higher learning.

Even at the K through 12 level, however, distance learning has the capability of radically changing the face of traditional education. As more students enter traditional public or private schools, classrooms are overcrowded, and educators and administrators are hard pressed to provide new technology and/or enough access to it to be worthwhile. Some schools, for example, limit computer use to a half hour per week, per student, simply because there are too many children and too few computers. Depending upon the school district and its funding base, some schools can afford to expand the number and types of educational programs and facilities to meet growing demands. Schools with more money can afford to build new buildings, upgrade equipment, and hire more teachers. Schools with less money have to make do, possibly with outmoded facilities and a reduced number of teachers.

Distance learning programs can't solve all these, and other, problems facing K through 12 school systems. But distance learning can provide yet another option to be explored. Sharing programs through computer or broadcast networks, for example, can broaden the number of courses offered across school districts. In-home educational programs can assist with overcrowding in traditional classrooms. Of course, making the distance learning technologies available, either at home or in classrooms, is a monumental challenge; nevertheless, distance learning is one option to explore in meeting the nation's education crisis.

Beyond K through 12, there most likely will be more competition among business and traditional educational institutions for adult learners. If a company hires a young person fresh from high school graduation and offers that person high-quality in-house education programs, with, of course, the implied promise of advancement within the business once the learner has mastered the appropriate skills and knowledge, why should that learner attend a traditional university? If adults already in the workforce need to develop new skills or receive an advanced degree, why shouldn't they shop around at several institutions worldwide or decide to take the appropriate courses from commercial vendors, consultants, or companies, instead of going to the local college? As the number and variety of educational opportunities grow, the percentage of learners opting for a traditional two- or four-year degree program may dwindle significantly.

As learners understand that the educational and training processes are not short term, but lifelong, they may develop different expectations for and appreciation of the *learning* experience. If additional education and training are expected and offered painlessly and cost effectively, more learners will probably choose to continue meeting their career- and personal interest-related needs for new knowledge and skills. They may actually enjoy learning and choose to take more courses and participate in more educational or training activities, instead of meeting requirements for a job or a degree. Education may again be perceived as something worthwhile to *do*, instead of serving only as a measure of something one is expected to *have*.

More educational and training opportunities can theoretically be made available to more people through distance learning courses. Unlike some forms of education (e.g., university or college degree programs, certification programs) and training (e.g., specialized programs only offered to employees of a company), distance learning can make education and training affordable to more people. Because university or college education is expensive, it is often out of the reach of the people who should benefit from this level of education. Because training and retraining is often costly, displaced employees, persons who lack a high school diploma or proof of similar academic coursework, and incarcerated persons, for example, may not have access to the instruction they need to become employed. Distance learning programs are one way to provide education to the masses.

Changes in the Mission of Traditional Academic Institutions

Where does that leave today's colleges and universities? For many learners, the "college experience" is an important reason to attend classes as a full-time or a part-time learner. Working with other learners, being part of a total educational environment, and collaborating closely with academic mentors will still be valuable to many learners. Some institutions, as well, offer intensive programs to immerse students in educational experiences, such as co-ops, internships, work-study programs, and such specialized areas of study as those for foreign languages. When full-time concentration on education is necessary, a traditional approach may very well be the best.

Universities have traditionally provided learners with the opportunity to think and visualize not only what they want to be, but what is possible. Research and the development of creative ideas are encouraged in academia, and these valuable contributions to society shouldn't be minimized. Support for these academic endeavors frequently benefits society in the long run.

Learners who want a well-rounded education may opt for a more traditional experience, too. A liberal arts education is likely to continue to be easier to obtain at a traditional institution instead of taking courses only through distance learning. In fact, for learners who want a bachelor's or a master's degree, some on-campus coursework will continue to be a necessity. Even if learners spend most of their time off-site, taking classes through distance learning programs, at least some of their time should be spent at the home institution. Learners may need to visit campus for initial enrollment, participation in some required courses, and testing, for example.

Nevertheless, the role of the traditional academic institution is changing; colleges and universities will have to compete with a growing number of other educational providers or vendors. This trend should promote more collaboration among business, industry, and academia to provide high-quality, innovative education. It should also help improve the quality of instruction and the sharing of important resources to avoid unnecessary duplication of services.

The collaboration should go beyond a business-academic partnership. As the costs for resources climb, many institutions can't keep up with the latest technology or provide the best facilities. A smart move for many institutions offering similar programs will be to share resources instead of competing with each other for learners. Sharing resources and offering complementary, not purely competitive, programs will be especially useful for smaller institutions, private schools, and colleges and universities within the same region.

Because distance learning provides more flexibility for learners in the ways and times they learn, they should develop more interest in lifelong learning. Our society demands that citizens develop new skills as the marketplace changes and as society becomes more technologically sophisticated. As people of all ages and abilities realize the need to learn is ongoing, they'll look to new, cost-effective providers of the skills and knowledge they want.

Changes in the Ways Academic Institutions Think of Themselves

As an educator and a trainer, I've often despised the way academicians are portrayed by the media as "eggheads" or lofty idealists who have little notion of what work is like in the "real world." Working in an academic environment differs in many ways from working within a business office or at an industrial job site, yet it is also similar in that it is a business. Nevertheless, the "business" of education is more than just an assembly-line process of bringing in students to attend classes, creating evaluations of students who meet objectives, and providing a piece of paper indicating attendance at the institution, if not mastery of subject areas and development of skills.

Administrators and educators should understand their mission, and their obligation, to provide high-quality instruction and to create an environment conducive to learning, whether that takes place on-site or in a *virtual classroom*. Some institutions may be virtual universities or colleges, existing for all practical purposes only in cyberspace.

The instructors affiliated with a virtual institution may be located within other businesses or academic institutions, or they be consultants working from home or their own office. The administrative staff may be located within a small office and there may be no real campus. In their Web sites, some vendors of distance learning programs are playing with the concept of a virtual university that has a virtual campus, existing only in the imaginations of the people working with the online university. These vendors sometimes describe their "virtual swimming pool," for example, or other fanciful sites that make the "on-campus" life attractive to distance learners. Although this information is humorously done tongue-in-cheek, the point it makes is important: Learners taking courses through a virtual college or university can perceive that institution in any way they like, as long as they receive the education or training they need.

One of the problems with the perception of traditional academic institutions has been that some administrators and educators choose to disassociate themselves from "business" concerns. For example, administrators and educators must determine how their limited resources will be used. Should the institution build an expensive real library building, housing paper documents and multimedia? Or should the funds be used to provide more networking capabilities for learners and faculty, so that online library resources are used instead of hardcopy documents on campus? Should the institution support the hiring of new faculty, requiring additional office space and support resources, among other needs? Or should the money be allocated for "faculty" who work part time leading distance learning courses for the institution and full time elsewhere? How much should the institution invest in new technologies and which technologies will best meet the needs of learners and the institution? Should the emphasis be placed on distance learning, on-campus programs, or a combination? These types of business decisions must be made, and quickly, so that institutions can plan their future and the ways that they'll meet the current and upcoming educational challenges.

Because distance learning offers more opportunities for learners to work with a variety of vendors, traditional institutions must recognize their need to compete with companies, institutions, and individuals who previously didn't or couldn't offer high-quality instruction. Just like other businesses, educational institutions may have to downsize their programs, reduce the number of faculty, and find ways to cut costs and share resources. Although this may be especially frightening to some faculty and administrators, the trend for evaluating educational institutions and reworking them to meet new challenges is ultimately healthy. Thinking in business terms and trying to make institutions efficient doesn't mean that courses have to be taught impersonally or offered in an assembly-line fashion. One of the reasons learners will choose to attend academic institutions in the future, instead of working with another vendor, is because of a university's or college's unique atmosphere, created by its unique collaboration of administrators and educators, and its setting and "tone" of instruction. The personal touch shouldn't be lost when educational institutions also understand that they must be efficient, effective vendors of educational services, whether working from a real campus or a virtual environment.

A common practice that is coming under fire is tenure. Although tenure allows faculty members a guarantee of academic security and the freedom to teach courses as they see fit, it also can encourage some faculty to become mired in the ways they've always taught courses or used technology. If tenure is eliminated, there is more competition among educators who want to keep their jobs or find new jobs. Eliminating tenure may also give institutions the option of eliminating some jobs and reducing the number of faculty needed to teach courses.

The business of education not only involves changing perceptions of faculty, but of subject matter. As society changes, there is less likelihood of having an accepted *body of knowledge* considered the canon for a particular discipline or job. The body of knowledge is expanding and changing; it's nebulous, not fixed. Educators as well as learners have to exchange information in an effort to keep up with the most relevant pieces of information they need for their jobs and life in general. To keep current, educators should be required to update their skills and knowledge, to learn with and from their learners. They need to establish firmer links with representatives from businesses and industries as they prepare course content and work with the technologies needed to create an effective learning environment, whether within a traditional classroom or in cyberspace.

SUMMARY

Distance learning doesn't provide all the answers to the education and training dilemmas facing us today. In fact, it raises several more questions about the types of education and training that are needed and desirable. It has the capability of changing the way we view education and training on a global level, as well as on a personal one. Distance learning offers several alternatives to our traditional concepts of learning, but more importantly, it has the potential to excite and enrich all of us as learners and educators. The format of instruction, methods of receiving and sending information, type of evaluation, ways to participate, cost, quality of instruction, and schedule for participating in courses vary among distance learning programs. Nevertheless, distance learning is and will be a primary means of education and training well into the next century.

Types of Distance Learning

Distance learning incorporates many different technologies, which range from something as simple as a mailed document to the more elaborate technologies of computers and broadcast media. Each type of distance learning can be effective and can help create a virtual classroom; however, different types of programs are especially well suited to different audiences and situations.

Although distance learning is not new, recently it has become more popular because of the Internet and World Wide Web—but distance learning programs involve more than the use of computers. Distance learning programs may involve hardcopy documents, audiotapes, videotapes, disks, CDs, broadcasts, and e-mail, for example, used alone or in combination. The history of distance learning is an illustration of the rise in popularity and common usage of different technologies, but the future of distance learning depends on the ways newer technologies can be used most effectively to provide high-quality education and training to more people at a reasonable cost.

Before you plan a distance learning course, you should have a good idea of the range of technologies you might employ. Seldom will you choose just one method of sending and receiving information; most distance learning programs involve several ways to connect learners and educators/trainers. However, you usually have one primary means of presenting information, with secondary methods used to supplement course materials or establish communication among course participants. Knowing your options is a good first step in planning your distance learning course. The next sections describe some common forms of distance learning.

CREATING A VIRTUAL CLASSROOM

A *virtual* classroom should not be much different from a *real* classroom or training room—at least, not in the ways that count. An effective classroom does the following:

- It provides the tools that learners need when they need them. If it's not possible to have all the tools in the classroom, an effective educator/trainer explains where the tools can be easily located.
- It creates an expectation for and an environment conducive to learning.
- It brings together educators/trainers and learners to share information and exchange ideas.
- It allows learners the freedom to experiment, test their knowledge, practice completing tasks, and apply what they've discussed or read about.
- It provides mechanisms for evaluating performance.
- It provides a safe haven in which learning can take place.

A virtual classroom is no different. Educators/trainers who plan to establish a virtual classroom, using whatever technologies are appropriate for their course and learners, should create an effective learning environment that meets the previously listed descriptors.

Providing Tools for Learners

The virtual classroom must contain the tools needed for the course and the ability to receive and send information among learners and educators/trainers. For example, if learners will read documents, the documents should be accessed online from the Web site. If learners need additional documents that can't be placed online within the course's Web site, educators/trainers must provide links to other sites where the information is stored. They may need to send documents through the mail or list bookstores where learners can purchase the required materials.

If, instead, a distance learning course involves a teleconference, any materials referenced during the teleconference should have been sent to learners seeing the teleconference from another site. The teleconference room itself must be equipped with the necessary technology to make sure that all learners, whether in a remote location or at the originating site of the teleconference, can receive all the information. Overheads, graphics, online documents, demonstrations, and so forth, should be easily seen on screen so that learners can take notes, ask questions, or refer to materials already in their possession.

In some courses, educators/trainers offering a distance learning course may need to provide some tools to create the "classroom." Software, for example, or passwords and codes, are necessary for learners who will work with a simulation or need to gain access to information stored on the network.

Creating an Expectation for Learning

Distance learning courses can be as difficult, important, and effective as in-person classes or training sessions. But to receive the same status as in-person courses, distance learning classrooms must create within learners and educators/trainers the same expectation that learning will occur and that the course is serious business. "Serious" doesn't mean dull or uninteresting; it does mean that learners will complete the coursework and meet their responsibilities with the same intensity that they would in a regular classroom. Educators/trainers treat the distance learning course with the same amount of preparation and treat individual learners with the same degree of courtesy and interest that they would in a regular classroom.

Setting course objectives, explaining the purpose and design of the course, developing high-quality materials, and making sure that learners and educators/trainers can communicate with each other at certain points in the course are important ways of creating an expectation for learning.

Bringing Together Learners and Educators/Trainers

Learners and educators/trainers may seldom (or never) see each other during the course; they may never have the opportunity to meet in person. Nevertheless, an effective classroom is the place where learners and educators/trainers create a community of sharing. Writing e-mail messages back and forth can establish a personal link among participants in a course, as can participation in a mailing list, a newsgroup, or a multiple-user domain (MUD). Through a teleconference or a desktop videoconference, participants can see and/or hear and/or speak with each other, to create a more personal form of communication. Even a Web site can create a personal atmosphere through a friendly, interesting design of the site and individual pieces of information linked within that site. Also, the use of a mailto: link so that learners can send e-mail directly to instructors can encourage learners to ask questions or make comments and requests while they work at the site.

When educators/trainers use more than one medium to create a virtual classroom, the sense of community among learners and instructors is enhanced. The more ways to communicate with each other and develop a sense of the people behind the programs, the more personal the education or training.

A virtual environment may never take the place of being in the same room with other learners or instructors, but the careful selection of instructional media and design of ways to communicate with each other can go a long way in bridging the distance among participants.

Creating the Space for Experimentation and Application

Education and training involve more than listening to someone talk about a subject or reading and discussing materials. Theoretical background is important, but so is application. In effective classrooms, learners have the opportunity to apply what they learn. In a regular classroom, they may complete workshop activities, conduct an experiment in a lab, demonstrate the correct way to complete a task, or make a group presentation to express their ideas.

The virtual classroom should be designed to allow learners similar types of practice and sharing activities. For example, a teleconference or a desktop videoconference can be used for group or individual speeches and presentations. An online simulation, with appropriately designed feedback for acceptable and incorrect actions or choices, can allow participants to act out what they've learned, role play, conduct an experiment, or complete a task. For example, after reading about and observing how to enter information about patients into a hospital database, learners may practice entering data, accessing the database, and modifying records. The simulation should include feedback, so that if learners enter the wrong type of information or incorrectly code entries, they receive a message indicating the correct procedure and type of information. Virtual classrooms should provide activities as well as referential information. They should help learners develop both skills and knowledge appropriate to the course.

Evaluating Performance

In addition to the immediate feedback provided through simulations, for example, other ways of evaluating learners' performance should be built into the course. The classroom environment might include sites where learners can ask questions and receive answers, take practice or real examinations and receive comments about the accuracy of their responses, and otherwise measure how well learners are doing. Some forms of feedback can be very personal; educators/trainers may write e-mail messages, add comments to assignments and return them to learners (e.g., as attachments to e-mail, through surface mail, by fax), discuss performance on the phone or during a teleconference or videoconference, and so on. Some forms of feedback can be mechanized, such as online comments that pop up on-screen during a simulation or a self-scoring online quiz. Whatever evaluation methods are included in the course design, learners should always have an objective measure of their progress.

Creating a Safe Haven

Learners need the freedom to experiment, to make incorrect assumptions and choices, to succeed and showcase what they've learned, and to interact with others, free of anxiety. An effective classroom is the place where learners feel free to express themselves in appropriate ways, to take risks so that they can learn more, to share their ideas, and to ask questions. The virtual classroom can provide that safe haven for learners to interact with each other and take the risks they need to learn more. It should allow them the opportunity to question instructors and other learners, and to test their ideas and skills in nonthreatening ways.

Educators/trainers who develop a virtual classroom can create a "safe" atmosphere in several ways. They can establish protocols for using the technology (e.g., providing equal access to resources, ensuring that no one can tamper with another learner's or the educator's/trainer's materials) and for communicating with each other (e.g., "no flame" rules for e-mail messages, guidelines for netiquette, procedures for talking in turn during a teleconference or videoconference). Through their instructional materials, educators/ trainers can encourage questions and comments. Creating a safe haven involves establishing and maintaining professionalism among all the course's participants and valuing the contributions of each member of the virtual class.

TYPES OF DISTANCE LEARNING COURSES

The virtual classroom can be created with any type of technology, simple or sophisticated. Some courses and subject areas are better suited to some distance learning technologies than others; some institutions or businesses prefer designing only one or a few types of distance learning courses. When you plan to develop a distance learning course, you have several options. The following sections highlight some common types of distance learning courses.

CORRESPONDENCE COURSES

Although distance learning currently is receiving a great deal of publicity in education and corporate training circles, it is not a new method of delivering information. Correspondence courses and independent studies have been used for years to provide mail-order education that learners can complete wherever and whenever it is easiest for them.

Early correspondence courses allowed learners to write to request course materials, which were then mailed. The learners read textbooks, booklets, and other instructional materials at their own pace, although there was usually a specified time frame when materials needed to be received from learners for some type of evaluation. The learners completed assignments and took examinations (which sometimes were proctored at another site to ensure that the learners did their own work without inappropriate study aids or assistance). Completed materials were then returned to the institution that originally sent the materials. *Graded* materials returned via mail completed the cycle.

Correspondence courses today may offer more diverse materials than the printed documents sent to and received from learners in the past. Today's courses can involve videotapes, audiotapes, CDs, disks, and documents, depending on the types of materials that best present information about a certain topic. However, the "correspondence" part of the course remains much the same. Learners request information, which is sent by mail. Of course, faxed documents and e-mail can also play a role in this correspondence, but mail is still a cost-effective feature of these types of distance learning courses.

The effectiveness of this type of distance learning depends on the learners. Participants who do not do well with the first set of materials they receive may have to re-do assignments or take another examination before going on to the next set of materials, for example. Because learners work on their own, they may have trouble grasping difficult concepts or they may not understand the significance of one piece of information that really is a linchpin for understanding later information. Some learners need occasional guidance as they complete materials. However, learners who thrive on independence and are motivated by a genuine interest to know more about a subject or to develop a new skill often do better in a distance learning course. They can work quickly and make more progress in a short time than they would if they took a classroom-based course.

In *ungraded* courses that learners may take because they're interested in a subject, not because they need high school, college, or university credit or job-preparation training, participants may simply move from one set of materials to the next, even though they have not mastered the previous level of knowledge or skill. Although the participants are using materials quickly, they really aren't learning the subject matter. Again, the individual learner is responsible for mastering the subject matter.

Those learners who want to understand the materials will read them until they understand the topic or they'll seek assistance to help clarify confusing areas. Motivated learners will take their time with assignments and exercises, so that they develop their skills and relate what they've studied to practical applications. As with any type of instruction, including classroom-based courses or in-house training sessions, the effectiveness of correspondence courses, in the past and today, depends on individual learners' interests, ability to learn well on their own, and design of the educational materials.

Correspondence courses may be created by degree- or credit-granting institutions or businesses that evaluate learners' level of achievement. For example, adults who want to gain the equivalence of a high school diploma can take correspondence courses to prepare them for taking the GED examination. Other institutions or individual private vendors offer correspondence "classes" to help people prepare for a new career; university, college, high school, or equivalence credit usually aren't offered for these correspondence classes.

The home page of one degree-granting institution specializing in correspondence courses is presented in Figure 2.1. It provides a new look at an older distance learning technology.

As with any educational or training endeavor, participants should check out the amount and the quality of the instruction being offered. Similarly, as every university does not provide the type of learning experience an individual may need, so every distance learning center does not offer the method of instruction, subject matter, or amount of interaction individual learners may need to learn through a correspondence course. The quality of correspondence courses, as any other type of course, varies. The resulting education often depends upon individual learners' initiative and ability to work well on their own. Learners who are highly motivated and need the flexibility of studying and practicing when it is convenient for them are best suited for correspondence courses.

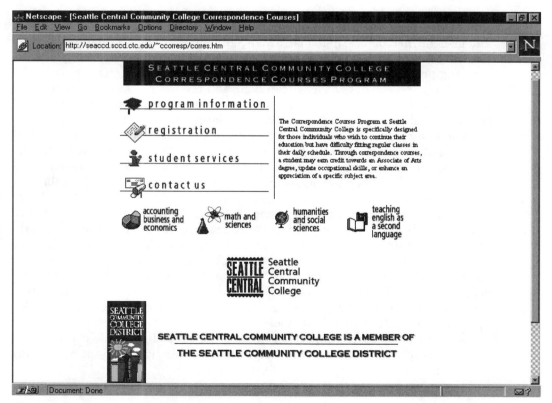

Figure 2.1 Seattle Central Community College Web site.

http://seaccd.sccd.ctc.edu/~ccorresp/corres.htm
© 1996 Seattle Central Community College Correspondence Courses Program

Audiotapes, Videotapes, CDs, and Other Audiovisual Aids in Distance Learning Courses

When audiocassette recorders and players, and later, videocassette and CD recorders and players became common at home, in the office, and even in the car, providers of correspondence courses took advantage of these media. In addition to offering print materials sent through the mail, many institutions mail audio- or videocassettes or CDs to supplement their educational programs. Taped lectures, discussions, simulations, demonstrations, and other instructional methods help more learners participate in distance learning.

Those learners who are more visually oriented and do not learn best by reading especially benefit from correspondence courses that incorporate different media into the instruction. The mechanics of receiving the materials, using them and participating in the course, returning materials to be evaluated (and often the tapes, too), then receiving feedback about one's performance remain the same.

However, the learning curve improves for most learners, as they are drawn into the learning process, because audiovisual materials allow learners to view and/or hear instructors, demonstrations, and simulations. The materials offer a more personal touch, which helps learners feel less isolated throughout the learning process. Even though they may not be able to talk directly with educators/trainers, learners at least can hear and see them. They gain additional information by picking up on nuances of inflection and body language, for example, and can feel a part of the virtual classroom.

Some subject matter is better taught when learners can see as well as read about it. Learning how to repair machinery is difficult when learners only read about the process and look at still graphics. They can learn much more easily when they see someone performing the process and explaining what is being done.

Although reading materials provide core information in terms that learners can understand, viewing demonstrations, watching simulations, and otherwise becoming visually engaged with the information enhances learners' ability to recall the information. Visual information also clarifies what may have been difficult concepts to read and only mentally "see." Because more people are very familiar with the process of watching television, and indeed get much of their everyday information from TV, videocassettes in particular have become useful educational tools.

Audiovisual aids are important in many forms of distance learning. Their use in correspondence courses has helped to keep this type of distance learning more commercially viable in the Information Age.

BROADCAST EDUCATION

Correspondence courses, no matter which media are involved, haven't been the only form of distance learning in the past 30 years. For many years, closed-circuit television programs have brought prerecorded or live instruction into classrooms within a building (whether a school or an office) or within a city school system. Public broadcasting, and some commercial, radio, and television stations have provided courses on a regular schedule, so that educators in classrooms could tune in at predetermined times. When the programs are broadcast to a wider audience, those learners who take a course for credit may be required to complete and submit assignments and receive feedback from an educator; some broadcast courses may be highly structured and offered as part of a university's or a college's regular course offerings. The University of Alaska's Anchorage telecourses are one illustration of broadcast programs (see Figure 2.2).

Of course, children's programming, such as *Sesame Street*, and how-to pro-

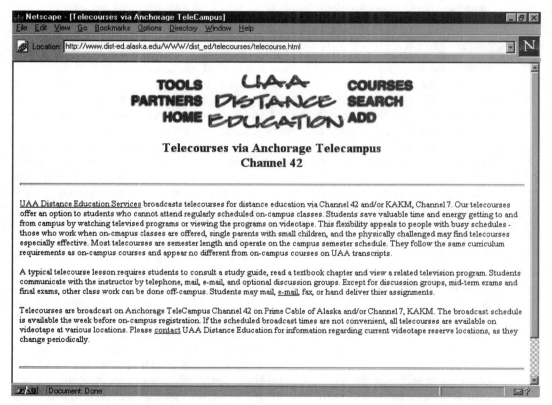

Figure 2.2 University of Alaska, Anchorage Web site.

http://www.dist-ed.alaska.edu/WWW/dis_ed/telecourse.html
© University of Alaska

grams like *This Old House* or *The Frugal Gourmet* can be thought of as distance learning programs, too. The instructional and educational materials are broadcast, but the learners aren't officially tested or evaluated to see what they've learned. Throughout this book, however, only formal distance learning programs, not those available for public broadcast or by purchase of videocassettes or audiocassettes for home use, will be described.

TELECONFERENCES AND DESKTOP VIDEOCONFERENCES

Teleconferencing is important not only in business communication and in-house or consortium meetings, but also for education in general. Many universities, colleges, and high schools, for example, use teleconferencing to link classrooms at great distances or to connect classrooms with businesses or organizations. One educator can reach many more learners at one time and the participants at every site can hear, see, and discuss, just as they would face-to-face. Cameras within the educator's room can zoom in to provide close-ups of a demonstration, for example, and transparencies, handouts, photographs, and other visual information can be highlighted on a TV screen.

Teleconferencing allows educators and trainers to present information shown on television screens in a remote location, so that participants can see what's taking place at the site originating the transmission and interact with people at the originating and linked sites. Broadcasts like this are the most common form of teleconferencing today, but software and hardware have made desktop conferencing possible and increasingly more affordable and user-friendly.

Desktop videoconferencing can link participants working at standalone computers to see and hear each other. Because individual computers are used, each unit must be equipped with a camera to show who's working at that computer. In addition, depending upon the software and hardware used for the videoconference, participants may be able to send e-mail to each other during the videoconference and share online documents.

Learners may use desktop videoconferencing from their home or office; they don't have to travel to a predetermined site to participate in the teleconference, which can certainly be a benefit. The quality of desktop videoconferencing depends on the type of equipment and software used; low-end technology may not give participants the quality they would like or that a teleconference can provide. However, the costs of teleconferencing may place it out of reach for individual learners or small businesses and academic institutions.

In both teleconferencing and desktop videoconferencing, individuals or groups of learners can be linked to a discussion and see the presentation of educational or training materials in real time. Teleconferences can provide instruction to individuals or several groups of learners at one time; videoconferencing can link individuals (with limits as to the number of participants who can be linked at one time).

When teleconferencing or desktop videoconferencing is used in distance learning, the course may be highly structured, so that participants meet at a specified time and location. A whole course may be conducted through teleconferences or videoconferences. In addition, periodic use of teleconferencing or videoconferencing can enhance a correspondence course or other form of distance learning.

Teleconferencing and videoconferencing can be used to offer the best of on-site education or training and independent study. For example, learners may work on their own to master concepts and complete assignments, but periodically they can discuss topics, ask questions, view demonstrations, and otherwise participate with a group. Thus, learners work alone at their own pace for much of the course, but they also become part of a group of learners taking a course at the same time.

The University of Calgary's home page and a sample course listings screen for one institution offering distance learning courses through teleconferencing are provided in Figures 2.3 and 2.4.

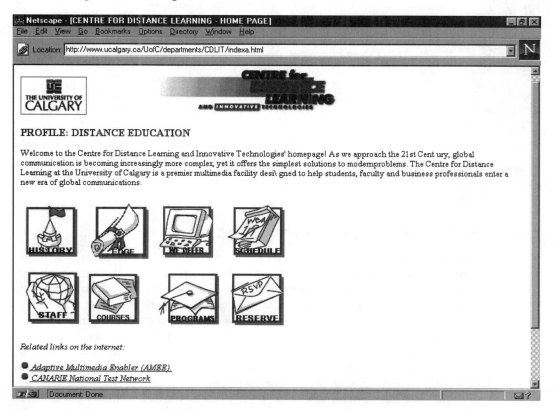

Figure 2.3 Centre for Distance Learning, University of Calgary Web site.

http://www.ucalgary.ca/UofC/departments/CDLIT/indexa.html
© Center for Distance Learning, The University of Calgary, 1996

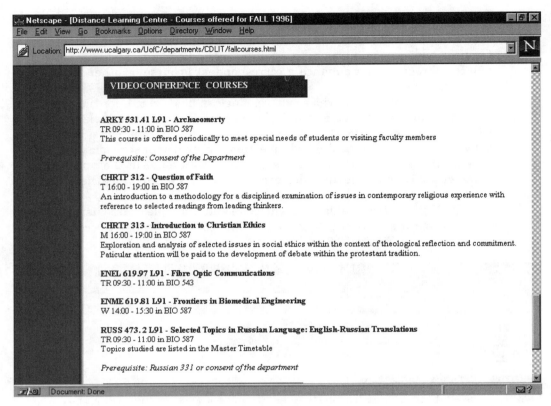

Figure 2.4 University of Calgary's videoconference courses.

http://www.ucalgary.ca/UofC/departments/CDLIT/indexa.html
© Center for Distance Learning, The University of Calgary, 1996

COMPUTERIZED EDUCATION AND TRAINING

Distance learning may involve short distances, as well as thousands of miles, within a building or around the world. Some correspondence courses require learners to purchase disks, whether floppy disks or CDs, as part of their educational materials. In-house training programs often provide customized online tutorials or programs on disk to help learners increase their knowledge and skill level at their own pace. This type of instruction frequently relies on standalone personal computers, although some companies and schools set up local area networks (LANs) to offer customized tutorials, demonstrations, quiz banks, and so forth, for employees or learners.

Computer-based training (CBT) and computer-aided instruction (CAI) became popular more than a decade ago, as more companies and educational institutions installed computer equipment. Because more employees and learners have access to computers, CBT or CAI offers *lab* options for training and education.

Learners, for example, may be expected to complete several disk-based or online assignments to supplement the discussion and lecture provided in a traditional classroom or training center. Practice activities, interactive assignments (often with immediate feedback provided through the computer program), and supplementary audiovisual materials let learners work at their own pace and repeat activities until the information is mastered. Employees often learn new skills or update work-related knowledge through CBT or CAI. They may participate in training sessions away from the office or they might be required to spend their spare time or flextime in the office using disks or online programs.

These materials, like any others that can be sent through the mail, can also be used in correspondence courses. Computerized educational tools can be purchased commercially (just check the amount of educational software for children and adults on the market). Just as they use broadcast materials, learners also may use computer programs as part of a regimented educational or training program or choose to use them because they want to learn more on their own.

THE INTERNET AND THE WORLD WIDE WEB

With the constantly increasing popularity of the Internet, distance learning has taken on new meaning. The Internet is an international network that links one computer to another. Unlike a LAN, the Internet is a wide area network (WAN), one so large that virtually any computer anywhere in the world can be linked to others. Learners' computers have to be physically connected to other computers; most often this connection is made via a modem, using telephone lines to transmit and receive information.

The modem can be internal or external. An internal modem comes built into the computer; a cord from the phone fits into a slot in the computer to make the phone line connection. An external modem most often is a small box that connects cords from the phone and the computer to make the connection between the two. However, as the technology changes, modems linking users by telephone lines are only one method of connecting computers to networks.

People who want access to the Internet need more than a modem or another device to make the connection. Computer users also need access to a server. The server allows Internet access, often in addition to other computer services. It connects a group of individual computers to the Internet and allows information coming through the Internet to be filtered back to the individual computer.

Once learners have subscribed to, or signed up for, a free or purchased Internet provider, they gain access to the educational materials and services designed for the Internet and World Wide Web (WWW). E-mail, or electronic mail, allows one person to write messages to an individual or a group; this tool can be used to update the "correspondence" part of correspondence courses. Electronic bulletin boards and mailing lists link individuals to more information and other people interested in similar topics. Online chat rooms promote discussions. Very simply, primarily written communication tools can enhance distance learning programs.

Perhaps the most exciting part of the Internet is its multimedia and hypertext capabilities. The Web provides information in many different formats. Of course, text is still a popular way to transmit information, but the Web also presents information in sound bites, such as music, voice, or special effects. Graphics may be still photographs, drawings, cartoons, diagrams, tables, or other artwork, but they also may be moving, such as animation or video.

Hypertext links allow learners to move from one piece of information to a related piece of information. A link might be an underlined word or phrase, an icon or a symbol, or a picture, for example. When a link is selected, usually by clicking a mouse on the link, the user sees another piece of information, which may be electronically stored on another computer thousands of miles away. Hypertext links may take viewers to a thematically related piece of information within the same document or Web site, or to information found at another site.

Because of the interactive, multimedia capabilities of the Internet, and especially the Web, distance learning is gaining popularity with new groups of learners, educators, and trainers. Educational and training materials can be stored on a Web site so that learners anywhere have access to the information at any time. There is a greater potential for sharing information through the Internet than through other means of transmitting and receiving information.

When the Internet is used in distance learning courses, learners can also gain that personal touch by sending e-mail messages to their instructor or to other learners. Chat rooms and mailing lists can connect groups of learners to discuss a topic and share ideas. Assignments can be sent electronically instead of through the mail and feedback can be provided more quickly. Materials from learners can be added to the Web site to share with others taking the same course and new information can be added quickly to the Web site. The use of electronic media in distance learning has turned a tried-and-true method of instruction into a hot commodity.

Athabasca University's home page and course descriptions illustrate another approach to online distance learning. Because so many vendors now offer online courses, the courses shown in Figures 2.5 and 2.6 represent only a small part of the range of courses available online, as well as the design of Web pages.

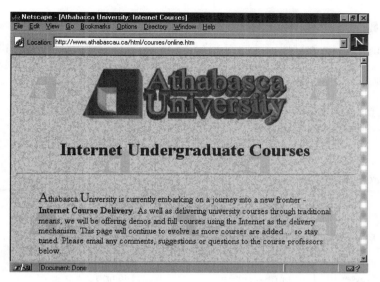

Figure 2.5 Athabasca University's Internet undergraduate courses.

http://www.athabascau.ca/html/courses/online/htm
© Athabasca University 1996

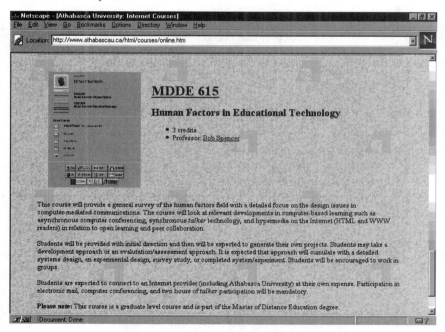

Figure 2.6 Online course description, Athabasca University.

http://www.athabascau.ca/html/courses/online/htm
© Athabasca University 1996

DESIGNING AN EFFECTIVE DISTANCE LEARNING PROGRAM

As you design a virtual classroom, you need to keep the needs of your audience in mind, as well as the practicalities of the types of courses you plan to offer, the requirements placed on the course because of its subject matter, and the types of technology to which you have ready access. Table 2.1 compares different types of distance learning you might consider as you design a single course or an entire program.

Table 2.1 Options for Distance Learning

Method of Distributing Instruction	Considerations for Appropriateness	Cost Items for Vendor and/or Learner
Surface mail correspondence	Older method of distribution Slower method of distribution May include print, video, audio, and disk materials May be easily copied Little interaction with educator/trainer	Printing/reproduction Mailing
Audiotape	Limited to instruction that can be heard May not be useful to learners with special needs May be easily copied Little interaction with educator/trainer May be used by individual or group at same time	Recording talent Recording of master soundtrack Duplication of tapes Mailing or delivery (possible)
Videotape	May be easily copied Little interaction with educator/trainer May be used by individual or group at same time Involves more senses	Recording talent Taping/editing of master copy Duplication of tapes Mailing or delivery (possible)
E-mail correspondence	Potentially faster method of distribution Limited to learners with access to e-mail May include attached documents and graphics May be distributed to many learners or a single learner at once Can promote more and more frequent communication among learners and educators/trainers	Access to computer and e-mail

Web site	Potentially faster method of distribution	Access to computer, Internet, and Web browser
	Limited to learners with access to the Web	
	May include hypertext and hypermedia materials	Development and maintenance of site, with associated user fees
	May be accessed by many learners or a single learner at once	
	May include e-mail (mailto:) links	
	Involves more senses	
	Can be updated frequently	
	May require security to limit access to learners	
	Limited instantaneous interaction between learners and educators/ trainers	
Cable television or closed circuit programs	May be accessed by many learners or a single learner at one time	Recording talent
		Studio recording time
	May be limited in the times and places for broadcast	Air time
	May be videotaped for later use	
	Involves more senses	
	Limited interaction between learners and educators/trainers	
Teleconferencing	May involve one learner or a group of learners (preferably) at one time	Teleconferencing capability, including monitors, cameras, fiberoptic cable connections, etc.—a specially equipped classroom
	May be limited in the times and places for the teleconference	
	May be videotaped for later use	
	Involves more senses	
	Allows one-way or two-way audio or audio-video communication between learners and educators/ trainers	
Desktop videoconferencing	May involve one learner or a group of learners (preferably) at one time	Videoconferencing capability, including computers and software for sending and receiving multimedia information and being connected to a LAN or a WAN
	May be limited in the times and places for the videoconference	
	Involves more senses	
	Allows one-way or two-way audio or audio-video communication between learners and educators/ trainers	

SUMMARY

Distance learning can only be effective when there's a good match of material and media; even then, the course's effectiveness depends on how well the combination of material and media meet the target audience's needs. Good distance learning programs require careful planning; the more carefully crafted the course, the more likely it is to meet the educational needs of learners. In later chapters, you'll read more about designing distance learning courses, based on careful research and planning. Before you begin planning a specific course, however, you also should understand some basics of funding your courses and programs.

Funding a Distance Learning Program

3

Distance learning programs can be expensive, especially if you're starting with little equipment and big dreams. Although distance learning can be accomplished with lower costs and less technology, most vendors (including educational institutions as well as businesses and individual entrepreneurs) who want to offer distance learning programs like to work with online (computer-based) information, videoconferencing, or teleconferencing, for example, instead of surface mail correspondence or audiotape.

A business or an academic institution that plans to offer a distance learning course or program should be prepared to support the course(s) with annual line items to their budget. Start-up costs for high-tech distance learning programs can be expensive and the vendor must be able to get the course started before revenues from learners come in. Once the course or program is operational, the costs for keeping the technology current, developing new materials and updating courses, and marketing the courses still must be figured into the annual budget. Executives and administrators who want their organization to become a distance learning vendor must be prepared to support the program, without skimping, from its inception.

Before you start developing a distance learning course, you should investigate the types of technology you intend to use and determine what it will cost to start a course or program and what the projected costs will be to offer the course X number of times over X time frame. Knowing what it will cost to offer the ideal program, then determining how the "ideal" can be translated into "practical and effective" or locating additional sources of funding, are crucial to the success of a distance learning program.

Even if you decide to use lower-cost technologies, the distance learning program needs to be budgeted carefully so that quality is never sacrificed for speed of delivery or number of learners served. The cost of the technology shouldn't be the determining factor in which types of distance learning courses you offer, but cost-benefit analyses are certainly important in determining if you can offer the courses you want. To make sure that you can offer high-quality distance learning courses, using the type(s) of technology best suited for the course and to meet your learners' needs, you usually need to find sources of funding beyond those your institution can provide.

When you plan a distance learning program, or even a single course, you therefore must become familiar with finding sources of funding and carefully plan the costs for current and future distance learning projects. Common ways of funding a distance learning course include:

- Charging fees for distance learning courses or special *distance events*
- Increasing the number of learners for each course
- Decreasing the costs for each course
- Finding short-term or long-term partners to share the costs of offering distance learning courses
- Receiving grants

You might need more than one approach to funding a project. The combination of funding methods you choose depends upon the extent of your program, your business's or institution's level of technology and interests in distance learning, and the number and types of courses you want to provide.

FEES FOR DISTANCE LEARNING PROGRAMS

One good source of at least some funds for distance learning comes from the buyers of the academic or training service: the learners (or the employers who pay for their education or training). Although some examples of distance learning found in this book were developed by nonprofit agencies and are offered free to people who want to learn about a particular topic, most distance learning courses are fee-based. Whether individual learners pay for the course on their own, companies pay in-house or outside vendors for employees to receive additional training, or organizations or associations pay for career preparation for clients, someone pays for the cost of instruction.

However, in addition to the standard fee for taking any type of training or educational course, people taking a distance learning course may pay a special fee to help offset the costs of the technology. This fee should not be prohibitive, but it can help pay the costs of designing and offering the course, as well as help fund additional costs, such as postage, needed by distance learners more than on-campus or in-house learners.

Some types of distance learning are more expensive and special fees may be assessed for occasional *special events*. For example, if learners at three different sites want to participate in a teleconference, each group at a site may pay a one-time fee to participate in the teleconference. Some professional associations and organizations periodically promote national teleconferences so that persons in remote sites can listen to, if not speak with, a panel of participants in the originating site. A teleconference from a national business conference might be offered to any site that has the equipment to downlink the broadcast, for instance. Learners who want to see the broadcast may be asked to pay a one-time fee in order to sit in on the session.

Depending upon the type of distance learning being offered, learners also may be expected to have their own equipment, such as a television and videocassette player if they want to participate in a videotape-based course or a personal computer with the required software and modem to access online information. In lieu of paying higher fees or special fees to take a distance learning course, the vendor's costs may be offset when learners provide their equipment or purchase special software, for example, so they can participate in the course.

But distance learning programs often cost more than vendors can reasonably charge learners for the service. Start-up costs before the first learners can take a course need to be covered before the program can get off the ground; ongoing upgrades to technology may require more funds than can be expected to be covered by learner fees.

INCREASING THE NUMBER OF LEARNERS

Within a traditional classroom, the ratio of educators/trainers to learners usually shouldn't be higher than 1:15 for an effective course. In workshop or demonstration courses, the ratio between instructors and learners may need to be lower, perhaps no higher than 1:10. You've probably participated in sessions where the ratio is much higher and learning still took place. However, to be most effective, one educator/trainer should work with a limited number of learners.

In distance learning, the ratio increases, sometimes tremendously. Depending upon the type of technology used to create the virtual classroom, the course might have a very high number of learners for one educator/trainer. In fact, that's why many companies and institutions like distance learning: It requires fewer instructors to meet the needs of many more learners. Nevertheless, there will be a limit to the number of learners you can reach in one course.

When you plan the fee structure for your course, you should anticipate the greatest possible number of learners you can accommodate within one course.

You should have a contingency plan so that when the optimum number is reached, you don't have to turn away people who want to take the course now. You might need to have another educator/trainer lead another section of a course, have assistants work with the day-to-day administration tasks (including, for example, answering e-mail messages, updating the Web site, making copies of materials to be sent to learners, preparing mailings), or create additional materials or access codes to materials.

To increase the number of learners taking a course at one time, you may also have to develop a marketing strategy to get out the word about your course. Advertising a course and promoting your institution's or company's distance learning capabilities should be part of a vendor's ongoing work. (That's why part of your annual budget for a distance learning course should include the cost items associated with marketing and promotion.)

DECREASING THE COSTS FOR EACH COURSE

As you plan a distance learning program, determine how many courses can be offered in a given time frame and how many courses can use the same technologies. Also, determine which equipment needs to be purchased and which can be leased, rented, or borrowed, for example. You also need to know if you really need the latest technology, or if you're only buying bells and whistles that provide glitz but little substance to the course content or the method of communicating with learners. A thorough analysis of what your business or institution has and what is needed for the courses you plan to offer can help you decide where you can streamline costs and where you should invest more heavily.

For example, it won't be cost effective to purchase the equipment needed for teleconferencing if you only plan to offer a course via teleconferencing once or twice, or only for a few weeks or months of the year. You might lease, rent, or borrow the required equipment if you plan a limited number of teleconferences.

On the other hand, if you plan to offer a slate of teleconference-based courses, and this technology is best suited to meet learners' needs and the courses' design, then the start-up and maintenance costs may be reasonable for the type of distance learning program you envision.

If you don't need as high-tech a solution, you might work with the existing technology and reduce start-up and maintenance costs. For example, you may already have Internet capabilities and need to budget the costs of designing, maintaining, and updating Web sites. Of course, you'll still have expenditures as you develop more interactive information and work with multimedia online, for example, but these costs will be less than those of upgrading other types of technologies. If most of your distance learning courses will involve the Internet (e.g., Web sites, e-mail, mailing lists, bulletin boards, MUDs), you can effectively and cost efficiently manage to offer several courses at one time. Much of the core information (e.g., documents, samples, simulations) may not need to be updated each time the course is offered, but the design of home pages and linked information may need to be updated frequently. Your budget can reflect how much new technology you'll need and how much information can be reused between courses and each time the course is offered.

FINDING SHORT-TERM OR LONG-TERM PARTNERS

Most vendors find it necessary to work, at least occasionally, with partners. Consortia of businesses and academic institutions, for example, can work together on a short-term or a long-term basis to develop distance learning programs and avoid duplicating courses and services.

You might look for short-term partners to help you start up a distance learning program or to offer a specific course. Short-term partners may also be used to provide the technology you need for a special event, such as a one-time teleconference or broadcast. Short-term partners may also be interested in special research projects, like those involving grants.

Long-term partners may invest in new technology with you and share in its use. Your business may provide ongoing support for certain courses or programs and in turn receive assistance from learners and educators/trainers, who provide their expertise to your employees. In addition, some academic institutions specialize in research and development (R&D); the products or theories developed through R&D can be offered first to your business. Educational institutions can benefit from the assistance of businesspeople, who can provide insight into career and workplace trends, offer technical assistance, and provide equipment or funding.

Finding partners is one of the best solutions to the funding problem. Partnering helps you promote distance learning programs and activities and makes more people in the community or region aware of your courses. It gives you a broader support base, as well as access to expertise that your business or institution might not have. It also shows potential grantors that you're actively seeking ways to fund and promote your distance learning program—that you're a serious vendor who should be considered for grants.

Figure 3.1 provides some questions you should consider as you investigate costs for current or upcoming distance learning courses. By using these questions as part of a budget checklist, you can determine how you can most cost effectively offer one or several distance learning courses. After you review these questions and have a better idea of what your current funding base is, you might choose to investigate grants as another source of partially funding your distance learning initiatives.

Questions about the Course's Fee Structure

- How much does the learner pay for a course taught on site?
- How much will it cost to provide materials and administer the course for each distance learner?
- How many learners are from one company and how many are individuals?
- How many special events are planned for this course and how much will they cost?
- What is a reasonable cost for this course and how does it compare to similar courses offered by other vendors?

Questions to Determine the Best Number of Learners per Course

- What is the total cost to our institution/company to offer this course?
- What are the learner:total cost ratio and the best educator:trainer ratio for this course?
- How many people can be accomodated by the technology and what are the technological limitations?
- What are the technical requirements for each learner (e.g., what type of software or hardware)?
- How many people have indicated interest in the distance learning course?

Questions to Determine if You Can Decrease the Costs for Each Course

- How can the technology along with educators/trainers work more efficiently within and among the courses?
- How can administrative costs be reduced?
- Which courses can share technologies and resources?

Questions about Partners for Your Distance Learning Program

- Who are potential partners within the community, region, company, from business, industry, or academia?
- What can we offer our potential partners and who will provide these resources?
- What potential partners have worked with distance learning programs in the past?
- How can we categorize our partners (e.g., short-term or long-term projects)?

Figure 3.1 Questions to determine the appropriate (nongrant) types of funding for your distance learning program.

GRANT FUNDING

Grants offer several good possibilities for partial funding of a distance learning program. Also, receiving grants from several grantors who agree to fund separate parts of the program is an effective means of paying for distance learning projects. However, grantors will also want to know that other sources of funding have been investigated and that cooperative agreements among people representing industry, local and national businesses, individual investors, and academia have been considered, if not confirmed.

Grantors don't plan to fund a project indefinitely. They like to know that the seed money or current support they provide will help keep the program going until other funding sources can take over the project. No matter how attractive the grant or supportive the grantor, at some point you'll have to find other sources of funding for your project.

Good distance learning is often a blend of different groups who can offer some pieces for the whole puzzle, such as technology, a waiting audience, or well-developed educational or training resources. Finding partners for a distance learning venture is necessary to fund a program and keep it running as the market grows and changes.

Finding Grantors

Many grantors provide resources for vendors or consortia who plan distance learning programs. Your job is to locate the best potential grantors for your project and to find several grantors who might be able to fund different parts of your program or provide follow-up funding once other sources of funding have been used. In developing a grant proposal, first discover who offers grants that will meet your needs, then learn how you can show grantors that your project meets their needs, too.

Although you frequently are not allowed (and ethically should not anyway) to submit identical proposals to more than one grantor simultaneously, you can submit proposals to different grantors, if each grantor might fund a different part of your project. For example, one grantor may offer equipment grants; another may want to invest in innovative technology, but not the equipment itself; and still another may grant funds for the development of courses about a specific subject.

Grantors make awards periodically, but their cycles for soliciting, accepting, and reviewing proposals and selecting recipients take place throughout the year. Some companies may begin a new awards cycle following the beginning of a new fiscal year on July 1; other grantors may have a starting date of January 1, to coincide with the calendar year's beginning. Some grantors work on a cycle of only a few months, but others may take a year or two to determine who will be funded.

Some grantors fund projects on cycles, so that a Phase 1 project may involve funding of the research and planning for projects that may be funded (but are not automatically guaranteed to be funded) in Phase 2. A Phase 2 project may involve a separate granting process, requiring another grant proposal, and the entire process may take place a year or two after the Phase 1 projects have been funded.

Finally, some grantors have open-ended granting periods. They fund projects that meet their needs and preferences as those projects are proposed. If these grantors fail to find a project that piques their interest during a granting period, they may not fund any projects for that period. On the other hand, if they receive five proposals for worthwhile projects that match their interests and priorities, all five projects may be funded during the same granting period.

Looking for grantors must be an ongoing task if you want to fund your program. If you're the person or part of the team in charge of soliciting funds, you regularly must search for new grantors, keep up-to-date with the activities of current or previous grantors, and develop a process for researching funding, applying for grants, and following up after awards have been made. Seeking funding can be a full-time job. To make sure you know all you can about a potential grant and grantor, you'll need to contact representatives of the granting agencies, as well as read their printed and online information.

Print Sources of Information about Grantors

Where can you start to look for grantors? Several printed publications provide the latest solicitation notices, descriptions of funded projects, and announcements of upcoming grant programs. Weekly, at least, you should consult several sources of information about grants and grantors. These sources include, but probably won't be limited to the following:

Directories
Newsletters
Bulletins and brochures
Government publications and offices

Local libraries should provide copies of government sources and may, as well, offer a variety of newsletters, bulletins, and brochures. Printed sources, such as copies of the *Federal Register*, are available via subscriptions as well as at the local library. Locating and using these sources can be as inexpensive or expensive, convenient or inconvenient as you choose; the cost in your time for searching and reading these sources regularly should determine the sources to which you regularly subscribe and those you read periodically. As you work with print sources, check the date to ensure that you're working with the most recently published information.

Directories

Numerous directories describe grantors; specific directories offer information about granting opportunities within different subject areas, such as the sciences, arts, and humanities. Since your distance learning program may span several different subject areas, your search may include the use of different directories.

Although each publisher develops a specific format for a directory, most directories provide a great deal about each grantor: name, address, telephone number, fax number, e-mail address, Web site location, date of the institution's or agency's founding, relevant financial information, type of support provided (e.g., money, equipment), types of projects preferred, amount of awards, number of awards, any limitations or restrictions, application information, contact persons, and time frame for the solicitation and award.

Newsletters

In-house and outside newsletters often list grant-solicitation notices and provide announcements of awards. Foundations, corporations, the research and development (R&D) departments of companies and universities, professional associations, and even individuals publish newsletters at various intervals (e.g., quarterly, five times a year, monthly, weekly). Some articles may describe hot topics for future projects or may even include suggestions for submitting grant proposals. To learn how to get on the mailing lists or to subscribe to newsletters in your areas of interest, contact professional associations, university or collegiate research offices, and governmental and nonprofit agencies.

It's a good idea to peruse the periodicals section of the local library to locate additional newsletters. Reading current issues, even of periodicals not directly related to your areas of interest, help keep you aware of what different professional organizations and businesses are doing and who is offering grants.

Bulletins and Brochures

Bulletins may look like booklets or newsletters. The information in these bulletins is similar to that found in newsletters, but bulletins are usually shorter than newsletters and may contain only updated information about previously published grant notices or award announcements.

Grantors, especially government-related grantors, who want to promote a new grant program or offer a series of related grants may publish brochures to explain their programs and provide assistance in preparing proposals. Brochures answer the most frequently asked questions about a grant program; they are written to help potential proposal writers understand the process of submitting a proposal and then, when a proposal is accepted, of completing the project to meet specifications.

Government Publications and Offices

Each agency or department at every level of government may have brochures, booklets, information sheets, news releases, application forms, and compliance regulations for a host of grants. Learn about regularly published governmental documents, such as the *Federal Register*, a printed and online document that lists granting opportunities and describes any changes to the granting process. To make sure that you have all the available information about a granting opportunity, call, write, or send a fax to the grantor to request any additional publications.

Online Sources of Information about Grantors

Many electronic notices are updated more frequently than printed notices sent to other publications, such as professional journals or newsletters. If you use the Internet and the Web in your search, you can find individual grant notices within descriptions of companies, governmental organizations, and nonprofit organizations. By conducting an online database search (through gopher searches, for example), you can locate the complete text of governmental documents, from the federal level down to local agencies, or solicitation notices from other public and private grantors.

Some databases, such as GrantsNet (Figure 3.2), specialize in providing information about grants, grantors, and grantees. Other online resources, such as the Funding Sourcebook (Figure 3.3), also help link you to governmental, public, and private sources of funds. As you find these specialized databases relating to grants or your areas of education/training, you should add a bookmark to your browser. Keeping up with the latest grant information and regularly searching the databases should be an ongoing part of your work as a potential recipient of grants.

More grantors than ever provide information simultaneously in print and online media. Because the Web is becoming such an important medium for getting out the latest information, many private as well as public-agency grantors maintain Web sites. The site may include links to refer potential grantees to information about philanthropies, public funding, and specific grants.

If a grantor works with hard copy and soft copy, you should keep up with both versions of the information. Many grantors also maintain a frequently asked questions (FAQ) link, contact information (including a mailto: link), and descriptions of upcoming grants. Grantors may also provide descriptions of currently funded projects and samples of award-winning proposals.

Governmental agencies are typical grantors who provide information both in print and electronically. For example, the *Federal Register* is published several times a week and is also available online. The online version contains the same information as the print document, but the key information is linked so that you can easily find the notice or agency of greatest importance for your research.

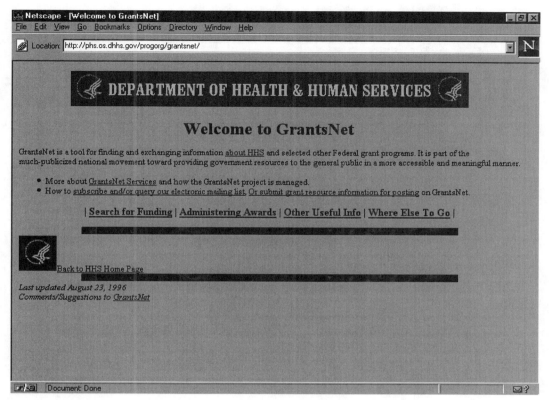

Figure 3.2 Department of Health and Human Services (GrantsNet).
http://phs.os.dhhs.gov/progorg/grantsnet/
© Department of Health and Human Services 1996

In addition to using standard references, like the *Federal Register*, you can locate new sources of grant information by conducting searches through Yahoo, AltaVista, Excite, Magellan, InfoSeek, and other Web search engines. New grantors and Web sites related to grants are being added to the Web each week. Also, information about the status of grants and changes to processes or forms are listed online much faster than in print. You should search the Web at least weekly to learn what's new.

Other Internet services can provide you with updates, too. Mailing lists are another source for finding electronic newsletters and e-zines; you can ask members of the list about the online publications they read and how to subscribe or find them. Bulletin boards also might provide a quick list of upcoming proposal deadlines, descriptions of new grant opportunities, and announcements of Web sites with grant information. Keep in mind that although many

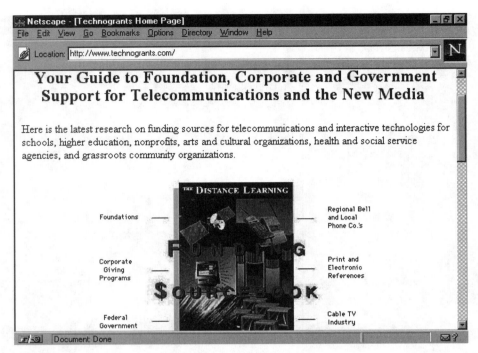

Figure 3.3 The Distance Learning Funding Sourcebook.

http://www.technogrants.com
© technogrants 1996

sources of information are provided free on the Internet, some organizations only allow you to download large texts if you subscribe to a service they offer or purchase the right to download particular information.

Appendix C lists Web sites with information about grants, grant writing, and grantors. You can use these sites, with their related links, as a starting point to locate online information.

DETERMINING WAYS TO MEET THE GRANTOR'S NEEDS

When you've determined which grantors can offer you the types of funding you need for your distance learning program, you then have to determine how you can convince each grantor that you have a worthwhile project that meets their need. Association with your distance learning program may offer a grantor several things: prestige associated with your project, direct advertisement (especially on a Web site) of the grantor's affiliation with and support of your project, use of your project as a demonstration or example to other educators or trainers, and use of the technology, materials, and resources developed through the grant-funded project.

Grantors may have different short-term and long-term needs for these tangible and intangible benefits of funding your project. Short-term projects may meet a grantor's immediate need for a product or a service or may help the grantor publicize its organization or interest in a particular project. Long-term needs may require ongoing research to study and attempt to solve a problem or to conduct projects that may take several years before tangible needs (such as the use of technology developed during the project) may become available. Your distance learning project may be able to meet both short- and long-term needs, but most grantors require you to submit separate proposals for projects meeting different types of needs or projects that will be completed at different times.

This type of preparation is necessary before you write a grant proposal. Before you begin to write a proposal, you need to know as much as possible about the grantor who will receive your proposal. You also should know about other sources of funding, both to supplement your current distance learning project and to fund additional projects. Keeping up with trends in grants, understanding the granting process, and making contacts with potential grantors are important first steps in the proposal-writing process. They also are important as part of your ongoing efforts to elicit support for your distance learning programs.

SUMMARY

Vendors budget not only the costs of sending information to learners, making information available to learners and potential customers, and receiving information from learners. They must plan the costs of upgrading the technology used in their programs. They hire and retain educators and trainers to develop and update course materials and work with learners during (and often before and after) the course.

Vendors also maintain the programs and look ahead so that they can keep meeting learners' current and future educational needs. They advertise and promote courses and programs. They also complete administrative tasks, like registering learners, taking fee payments, and providing the information learners need to start the course. Although people receiving the educational or training programs pay fees that go toward these items, the customers can't pay for the entire service.

Of course, the company or institution offering the distance learning program invests in their business, too. Distance learning programs should be ongoing line items in the budget. Realistically, this part of an annual budget can be expected to increase in costs as the distance learning programs gain popularity and are expanded to meet learners' growing needs. However, even this source may have its limitations.

That's why vendors or people who plan to offer distance learning courses often must look for additional outside sources. Charging special fees to learners who participate in special events (e.g., a teleconference) or take a distance learning course, increasing the number of learners served, decreasing the costs of the course, and finding short-term or long-term partners to share costs are all good ways to offset the costs of a distance learning program. However, one popular form of funding a distance learning program is through grants. Although federal grants are one source of equipment, money, or other resources, other grantors provide resources, too. Private businesses, public agencies, and even individuals may be in the grants business. When you look for ways to fund your distance learning program, you should investigate all these options. Chances are, you'll want to apply for grants to help you keep costs to learners in line and to keep the quality of your distance learning programs high.

Preparing a Grant Proposal

4

Preparing a grant proposal involves more than writing a paper or an electronic document. The writing process is the result of planning, as you read in Chapter 3. You first must understand who the grantor is and what the grantor wants. Then you can determine how your distance learning program or course can uniquely meet the grantor's needs. Before writing the first words of the proposal, you must have a clear objective for your distance learning program, a plan for creating and evaluating the program, and a thorough understanding of the grantor and the proposal-submission and evaluation processes.

WRITING A GRANT PROPOSAL

Usually, you submit hard copies (sometimes several) of the required forms for a grant application, as well as the proposal. Sometimes you can send a preliminary electronic proposal by filling out online forms and summarizing the information that later will be included in a more formal hardcopy document. Other grantors only require submission of an electronic grant proposal first; if your proposal is selected for further consideration, you may be asked to supply more information or write a hardcopy proposal. Always check the grantor's solicitation notice, whether in hardcopy or online, to learn where to get copies of the required forms and how to fill them out. If you fail to comply with the grantor's specifications, your proposal will not be accepted. Also, by studying the solicitation notice and understanding the grantor's requirements, you learn how much information you need to provide in the proposal and how the information must be formatted.

Before you write the proposal, analyze exactly what the grantor is looking for and how your proposed project can meet that need. The solicitation notice provides much of that information directly; you read about the criteria for acceptable projects and proposals. However, the style in which the solicitation notice is written and the keywords used to describe what the grantor is looking for also indicate what you should emphasize in your proposal and the tone and language you should use.

Before you write a proposal, you also need a clear understanding of the problem to be solved or the need that your project will help meet, and how limited or broad your project will be. Knowing exactly how your distance learning project, or a part of it, meets a grantor's needs or preferences for funded projects is an important part of persuading a grantor to support your project.

For example, if you're writing a proposal only to solicit equipment that will be used in a distance learning project, your focus must be on ways that this equipment will help meet a need or solve a problem. You must persuade the grantor that your project is more worthy or timely than other projects and that the equipment is necessary to solve an educational or training problem or meet a need. If you later write a proposal to a different grantor to solicit funds to develop materials for a specific course, your focus in that proposal will be on the way the course's information meets a specific need or helps solve a specific problem.

When you write a grant proposal, in electronic or paper format, you show not only that you have a worthwhile distance learning project, but that you're helping improve education or training by meeting a specific need or helping to solve a problem. You illustrate through the style, tone, and content of your proposal that you have the capability to complete the project and make a difference. You also show that you understand the type of projects the grantor prefers to support and can work with the grantor to improve the quality, frequency, or variety of educational and/or training distance learning programs.

SOLICITATION NOTICES AND SELECTION CRITERIA

First read the solicitation notice to learn about a grantor and begin to study the types of projects that grantor hopes to fund. A solicitation notice highlights what the grantor needs and expects, not only from the project to be funded but also from the grantee. Solicitation notices spell out the granting process; they list deadlines, provide addresses where you can request forms and supporting documentation about the grant or the grantor, and note contact people. They describe the granting process and the procedures needed to apply for a grant. Before you write even a draft of your proposal, study the solicitation notice so that you understand the grantor and determine how your project can uniquely provide the type of service or product that the grantor is looking for.

In addition to providing practical information you need to make sure your proposal is in compliance with the grantor's requirements, solicitation notices also give you broad hints about the style and language grantors expect to see in your proposal. For example, a solicitation notice that uses highly technical language implies that the grantor is looking for someone who is familiar with that level of terminology and can use it accurately in the proposal. That doesn't mean that your proposal should be filled with jargon. It does mean that you should write the proposal for an audience who understands the technical terminology and will be able to tell if you know the vocabulary.

The word choice in the solicitation notice can also indicate the grantor's interests. Repeated or emphasized words provide clues to the grantor's primary interests. By studying the solicitation notice, you can determine keywords that you'll also want to use in your proposal.

Grantors may publish solicitation notices online and in hardcopy. Many foundations, corporations, and nonprofit associations use the Internet as a primary means of listing their grant notices, although they also provide hardcopy forms and receive paper-printed proposals. The *Federal Register*, both online and in print, and print directories of grantors also can provide you with sample solicitation notices. Figure 4.1 shows you the BellSouth Foundation's first few chunks of online information in a solicitation notice.

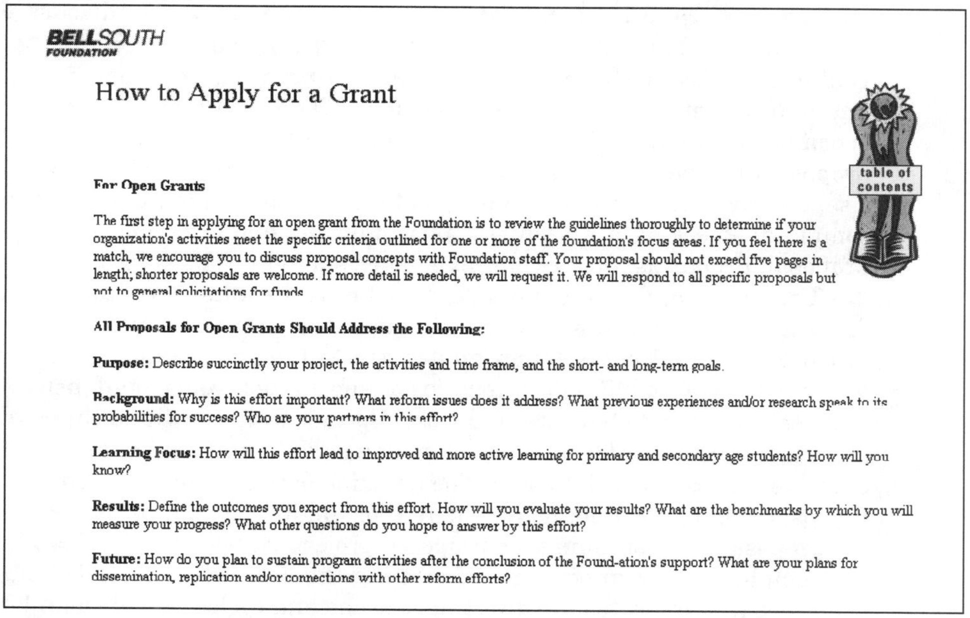

BELLSOUTH
FOUNDATION

How to Apply for a Grant

table of contents

For Open Grants

The first step in applying for an open grant from the Foundation is to review the guidelines thoroughly to determine if your organization's activities meet the specific criteria outlined for one or more of the foundation's focus areas. If you feel there is a match, we encourage you to discuss proposal concepts with Foundation staff. Your proposal should not exceed five pages in length; shorter proposals are welcome. If more detail is needed, we will request it. We will respond to all specific proposals but not to general solicitations for funds.

All Proposals for Open Grants Should Address the Following:

Purpose: Describe succinctly your project, the activities and time frame, and the short- and long-term goals.

Background: Why is this effort important? What reform issues does it address? What previous experiences and/or research speak to its probabilities for success? Who are your partners in this effort?

Learning Focus: How will this effort lead to improved and more active learning for primary and secondary age students? How will you know?

Results: Define the outcomes you expect from this effort. How will you evaluate your results? What are the benchmarks by which you will measure your progress? What other questions do you hope to answer by this effort?

Future: How do you plan to sustain program activities after the conclusion of the Found-ation's support? What are your plans for dissemination, replication and/or connections with other reform efforts?

Figure 4.1 BellSouth Foundation: How to apply for a grant.

http://www.bsf,org/bsf/grantguide
© BellSouth Foundation 1996

Category: Which of the BellSouth Founda-tion's focus areas, priorities and strategies does your project address?

Cost: What is your projects total projected cost? How much of this are you requesting from the Foundation? What other sources of funding have you received or are you pursuing? (Include a separate budget page which may be in addition to the five page proposal.)

Additional Information Required:

- BellSouth Foundation Proposal Cover Sheet (located in the back pocket)
- evidence of tax-exempt status
- brief background information about the organization and the persons involved

Please submit the original proposal plus one copy. DO NOT SEND video or audio tapes, photographs, artwork or other bulky materials. If brochures are necessary to explain an integral part of the project, please submit only one copy.

Open Grants Deadlines

All proposals MUST BE RECEIVED by February 1 (March 1 in 1996) or September 1 to be eligible for consideration during the spring or fall grant cycles, respectively. We will make and announce our decisions by the end of April and November.

Figure 4.2 BellSouth's Grant guidelines, continued.

http://www.bsf,org/bsf/grantguide
© BellSouth Foundation 1996

The first paragraph explains the process of applying for an open grant, step by step. Note language such as, "we encourage you to discuss proposal concepts with Foundation staff." This broad hint should tell you that, once you're clear about the project you want to propose, you should contact the Foundation's staff and talk over your ideas. The length of the proposal is also specified: fewer than five pages, but again, note the language that "shorter proposals are welcome." The emphasis suggests that you should write a precise, clearly stated proposal that gets to the point without being choppy or incomplete. The length statement also indicates one criterion for a successful proposal; proposals longer than five pages should not be submitted.

The Purpose, Background, Learning Focus, Results, and Future (the future funding section) sections ask specific questions that you must answer in your proposal. This outline of topics guides you to the organization of the proposal. Figure 4.2 shows additional categories of information you should include in your proposal, including Category and Cost. Specific forms, such as the cover sheet, and other required information that explains additional criteria for having an acceptable proposal are also listed. The deadline notice is always important; if your proposal is late, it cannot be considered for funding, no matter how well-written the proposal or outstanding the proposed project. Notice the use of capital letters that emphasize the importance of meeting the listed deadlines. The number of deadlines also indicates the granting seasons and cycles for this foundation and gives you an idea of when you should prepare proposals for submission.

The general information for open grants was provided in the first chunks of information. Other types of grants, RFPs (requests for proposals) and invi-

---

For RFP Responses or Invitational Grants

If your organization is selected to respond to an RFP or to receive an invitation to participate in a BellSouth Foundation program, we will contact you. We will explain the proposal submission process and deadlines for the particular program at that time.

General Criteria for Selection

The Foundation receives many more requests than it has resources to fund. Proposed programs which are submitted for review must address one or more of the categories outlined on the previous pages. Proposals most likely to receive a favorable review are those that:

* have an impact in Alabama, Florida, Georgia, Kentucky, Louisiana, Mississippi, North Carolina, South Carolina and/or Tennessee;
* focus on learning outcomes;
* lead to comprehensive, systemic change;
* have a broad and positive impact on diverse populations, with special attention to racial and other minorities and to students at risk;
* involve collaborative partnerships;
* link learning to work opportunities and workplace requirements;
* use technology to forge new connections, even when technology is not the primary focus of the program;
* demonstrate the capacity to gain continuing support and to link with other reform efforts;
* will result in dissemination of lessons learned and in replication of successful practices;
* are most likely to produce measurable results.

Figure 4.3 BellSouth's Grant guidelines and general selection criteria.

http://www.bsf,org/bsf/grantguide
© BellSouth Foundation 1996

tational grants, have other guidelines, which are described in Figure 4.3. Your proposal for this foundation should meet each of the bulleted items in the selection criteria. You would be wise to follow this list and use the same or similar language when describing your proposed project.

Most grantors list some restrictions for the type or number of proposals and projects they support. Figure 4.4 indicates this foundation's restrictions on projects and uses of funds. If your project covers any of these areas, you should research other grantors.

The proposal review process is further described in the solicitation notice. It tells you when it is appropriate to contact the program manager, who reads and selects proposals, and how and when you'll be contacted if your proposal is accepted.

Figure 4.5 is the concluding, pragmatic information you need to submit requests for further information and the proposal. The Foundation accepts hardcopy or electronic proposals, and the online form is provided at the Web site listed. The e-mail address for submitting information is also listed.

Grantors may also provide guidelines and forms online, so that once you've read the solicitation notice, you know how to meet the grantor's criteria for the project and the proposal. The table of contents (Figure 4.6) of the online grant guidelines highlights the kinds of information found on the Web site. Background information that you should read before you submit a proposal, in order better to understand the grantor and the foundation's priorities, and online forms are provided at the site.

Restrictions

The BellSouth Foundation does not make grants for:

- capital or building campaigns;
- endowment funds or campaigns;
- general operating expenses;
- education product development;
- equipment acquisition, except as a small or incidental part of a larger program;
- scholarships, financial aid and scholarship funds;
- single discipline curricula, unrelated to comprehensive school reform;
- individual study, research or travel grants;
- charitable dinners or fund-raising events;
- programs that are primarily recreational;
- programs that have an impact outside of our nine southeastern states;
- any organization that discriminates on the basis of race, creed, gender or national origin.

The Proposal Review Process

All proposals are reviewed by the Program Manager. If we determine that your proposal is not a match for our program, you will receive a letter declining funding early in the process. If your proposal appears promising, our full staff will begin an intensive review. In some cases, we will defer a proposal to a later funding cycle for further consideration. Please refrain from calling during the review process to check the status of your proposal. We will contact you if we need further information.

Figure 4.4 BellSouth's Grant guidelines and restrictions.

http://www.bsf,org/bsf/grantguide
© BellSouth Foundation 1996

Open Grant proposals and other communications should be sent to:

> Program Manager
> BellSouth Foundation
> 1155 Peachtree Street, N.E., #7H08
> Atlanta, Georgia 30309-3610
> 404-249-2396
> Fax 404-249-5696

To submit your proposal electronically.

- use online form at http://www.bsf.org/bsf
- e-mail to grants.manager@bsc.bls.com

E-mail proposals must be in the ASCII text format and have the words "grant proposal" in the subject field of the message

E-Mail BellSouth Foundation | Reports | Grants & Proposals

Communication Center | Links | Beyond the Foundation

BELLSOUTH *Copyright Notice*

Copyright 1996

Figure 4.5 BellSouth's Grant guidelines submission information.

http://www.bsf,org/bsf/grantguide
© BellSouth Foundation 1996

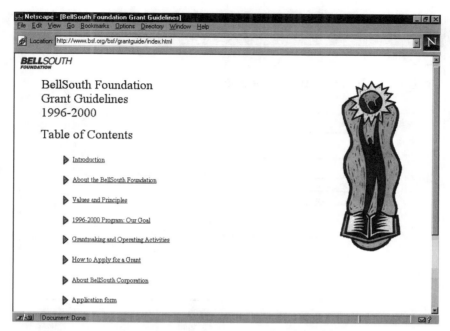

Figure 4.6   BellSouth's Grant guidelines table of contents.

http://www.bsf,org/bsf/grantguide
© BellSouth Foundation 1996

Figure 4.7 is the first partial screen of information you must complete when you submit an online proposal to the foundation. The form indicates the criteria for selecting proposals by leading you through the amount and types of information you need to provide. The text boxes indicate the amount and type of information you need to provide as identification of your proposal and business or institution.

Other types of information are requested on the form (see Figure 4.8). The clickable radio (round) buttons help you easily meet two criteria set by the Foundation. The default values for Yes indicate the Foundation's required or preferred response to each item. A scrollable text box allows more space to describe your organization's purpose. Whereas other text boxes limit the amount of information that can be submitted, the scrollable text box allows you the freedom to describe your organization at length. However, keep in mind that you should be as clear and precise as possible, even when you're allowed to submit longer descriptions in this type of text box.

Figure 4.9 shows other scrollable text boxes, indicating where you're expected to elaborate. Future funding and other avenues of support for your project require more description, as does the proposed project. The electronic form guides you to writing the proposal. By filling in the boxes or selecting items,

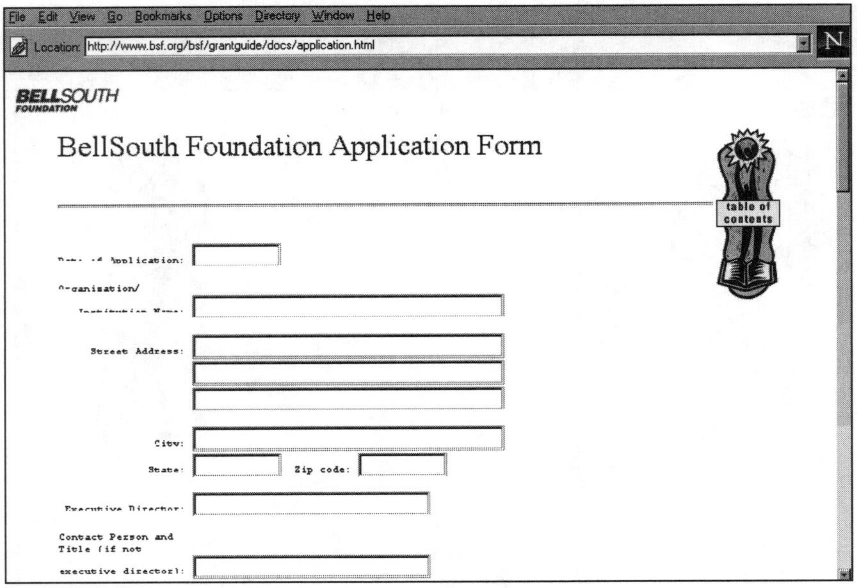

Figure 4.7 BellSouth's online application form.

http://www.bsf,org/bsf/grantguide
© BellSouth Foundation 1996

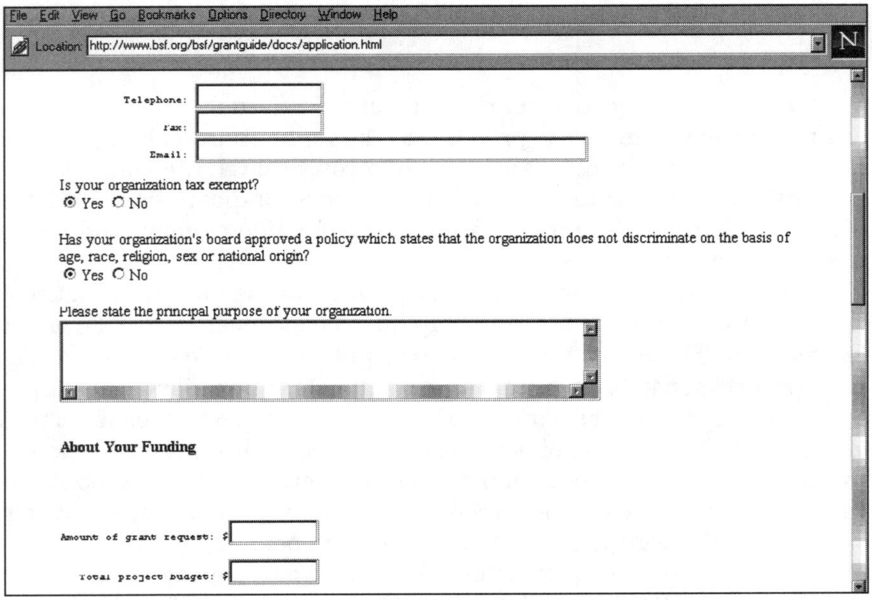

Figure 4.8 BellSouth's online application form, continued.

http://www.bsf,org/bsf/grantguide
© BellSouth Foundation 1996

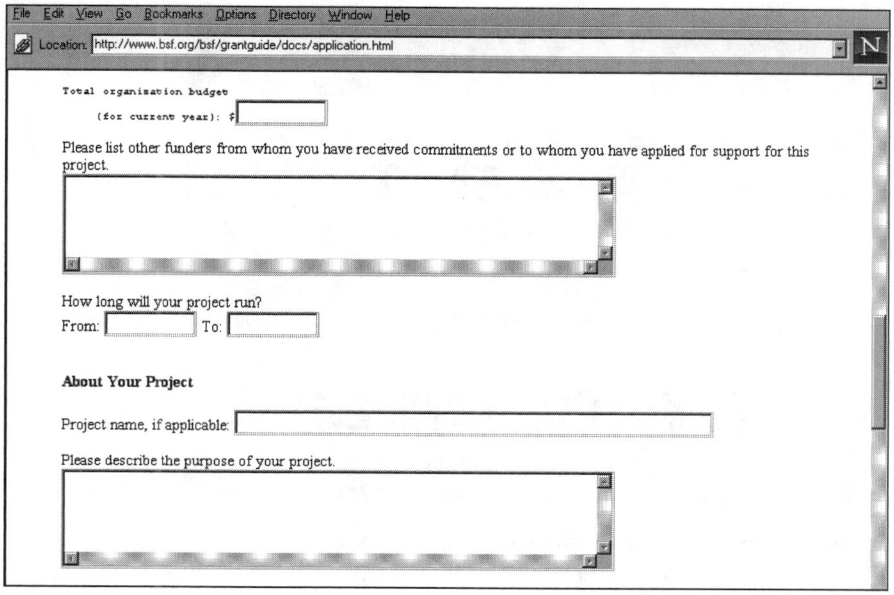

Figure 4.9 BellSouth's online application form, continued.

http://www.bsf,org/bsf/grantguide
© BellSouth Foundation 1996

you provide exactly what is required. The organization and formatting requirements are easy to meet when you submit an electronic proposal; however, your proposal usually doesn't have the space or length for you to elaborate. You need to be direct, without being cryptic, when you write an electronic proposal. Meeting the selection criteria and specifications may be easier in an electronic proposal, but the writing must be crisp and precise, even more so than in a multiple-page hardcopy proposal.

Other grantors provide similar information, but in different formats online. The Intelenet Commission, for example, is another grantor that is thorough in describing itself, its granting opportunities, and specific grant programs. The home page (Figure 4.10) consists of links about the Commission and its services, including the Intelenet Grant Program. One related site from this home page provides an announcement of a second round of funding, with links to information about the Commission, programs, and grants. Figure 4.11 introduces the program and provides updates through an online memorandum targeting school superintendents in Indiana.

Much of the text information provided at the Intelenet Commission's Web site can be downloaded and shared among administrators who want to apply for a grant. The online documentation resembles the hardcopy versions of solic-

Figure 4.10 Intelenet Commission's home page.

http://www.ai.org/intel/index.html
© Intelenet Commission 1996

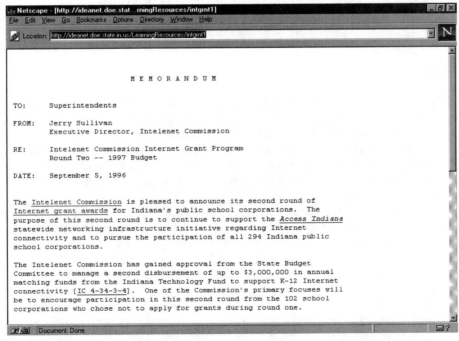

Figure 4.11 Intelenet's Memorandum.

http://ideanet.doe.state.in.us/LearningResource/intgrnt1
© Intelenet Commission 1996

itation notices and application guidelines. For example, Figure 4.12 highlights a multiscreen description of the grant program, including the purpose of the grants, eligibility requirements, technical specifications for the project, specifications of documents filed with the Commission, types of support provided by the grantor, and a statement describing the proper use of the grant (e.g., not as a matching fund grant). A later section describes the process for submitting the grant. A series of links at the end of this area of the Web site can connect users to online forms, guidelines, and information about other agencies.

The online application form for transport services, which can be downloaded to a printer, is part of the grant application (see Figure 4.13). Another online form that can be easily printed, completed, and returned in hardcopy is the application form for submitting a one-time grant (see Figure 4.14). The Commission's Web site provides all the information proposal writers need, as well as links for more information. Because many school administrators may prefer (or may have more access to) methods of preparing hardcopy proposals, the forms are suitable for downloading, printing, and sharing, as well as completing with a typewriter.

Still another complete package offered by a grantor is that provided by the Wisconsin Advanced Telecommunications Foundation and Educational Technology Board. Figure 4.15 illustrates the grantor's guidelines. The granting cycle is clearly indicated as one of the first chunks of information and potential proposal writers can note the deadline dates and begin planning their proposals well in advance of the next due date. The application forms were designed to be downloaded into two commonly available word processing packages, and the grantor understands that school systems may not have the latest versions of software. The downloadable formats of guidelines and forms can be read by older versions of the word processing software.

The Web site's table of contents provides direct links to information about the proposing organization's requirements and responsibilities, as well as descriptions of the granting (and appeals) process. Other links lead to contacts for technical assistance and more information about proposals, including sample forms. One form, the cover sheet, is shown in Figure 4.16. Note that the sample appears online, but the form to be filled out and returned is downloadable to a word processing software. Potential proposal writers can first view the form as they browse the Web, but they then need to download the information when they prepare to submit the proposal.

Each grantor has its own style in presenting Web information, but each also provides a wealth of resources and information about the grant proposal-writing process. As you read more solicitation notices, you'll become familiar with each grantor's language and style, as well as requirements. Reading first to note compliance requirements, which you must follow exactly or your proposal won't be considered for funding, then to understand the grantor and the nuances of language indicating areas of preferred support and projects being emphasized, give you the background information you need to write the proposal.

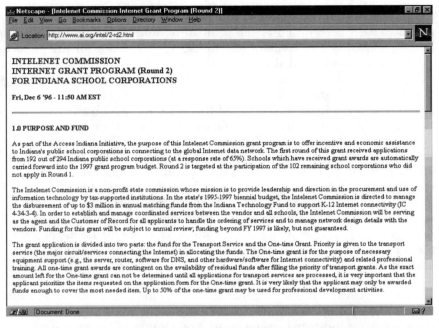

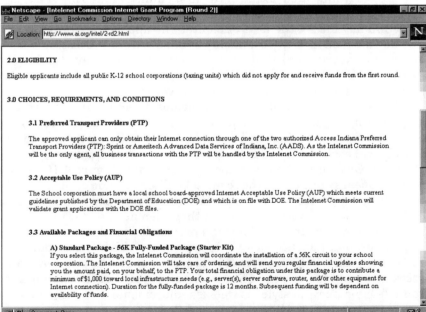

Figure 4.12 Intelenet's Grant Program.

http://www.ai.org/intel/2-rd2/html
© Intelenet Commission 1996

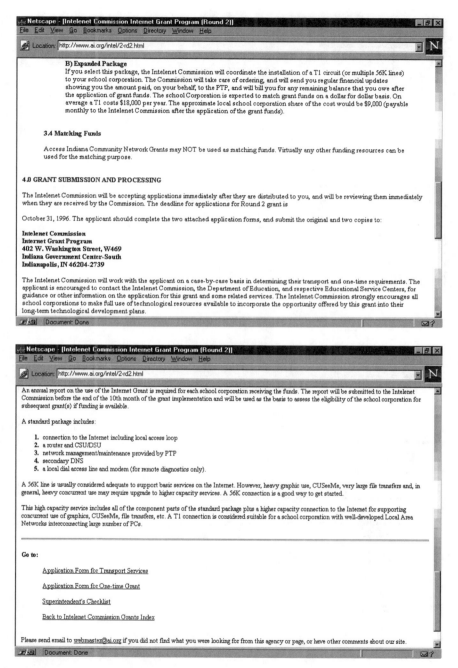

B) Expanded Package
If you select this package, the Intelenet Commission will coordinate the installation of a T1 circuit (or multiple 56K lines) to your school corporation. The Commission will take care of ordering, and will send you regular financial updates showing you the amount paid, on your behalf, to the PTP, and will bill you for any remaining balance that you owe after the application of grant funds. The school Corporation is expected to match grant funds on a dollar for dollar basis. On average a T1 costs $18,000 per year. The approximate local school corporation share of the cost would be $9,000 (payable monthly to the Intelenet Commission after the application of the grant funds).

3.4 Matching Funds

Access Indiana Community Network Grants may NOT be used as matching funds. Virtually any other funding resources can be used for the matching purpose.

4.0 GRANT SUBMISSION AND PROCESSING

The Intelenet Commission will be accepting applications immediately after they are distributed to you, and will be reviewing them immediately when they are received by the Commission. The deadline for applications for Round 2 grant is

October 31, 1996. The applicant should complete the two attached application forms, and submit the original and two copies to:

Intelenet Commission
Internet Grant Program
402 W. Washington Street, W469
Indiana Government Center-South
Indianapolis, IN 46204-2739

The Intelenet Commission will work with the applicant on a case-by-case basis in determining their transport and one-time requirements. The applicant is encouraged to contact the Intelenet Commission, the Department of Education, and respective Educational Service Centers, for guidance or other information on the application for this grant and some related services. The Intelenet Commission strongly encourages all school corporations to make full use of technological resources available to incorporate the opportunity offered by this grant into their long-term technological development plans.

An annual report on the use of the Internet Grant is required for each school corporation receiving the funds. The report will be submitted to the Intelenet Commission before the end of the 10th month of the grant implementation and will be used as the basis to assess the eligibility of the school corporation for subsequent grant(s) if funding is available.

A standard package includes:

1. connection to the Internet including local access loop
2. a router and CSU/DSU
3. network management/maintenance provided by PTP
4. secondary DNS
5. a local dial access line and modem (for remote diagnostics only).

A 56K line is usually considered adequate to support basic services on the Internet. However, heavy graphic use, CUSeeMe, very large file transfers and, in general, heavy concurrent use may require upgrade to higher capacity services. A 56K connection is a good way to get started.

This high capacity service includes all of the component parts of the standard package plus a higher capacity connection to the Internet for supporting concurrent use of graphics, CUSeeMe, file transfers, etc. A T1 connection is considered suitable for a school corporation with well-developed Local Area Networks interconnecting large number of PCs.

Go to:

Application Form for Transport Services

Application Form for One-time Grant

Superintendent's Checklist

Back to Intelenet Commission Grants Index

Please send email to webmaster@ai.org if you did not find what you were looking for from this agency or page, or have other comments about our site.

Figure 4.12   Intelenet's Grant Program, continued.

http://www.ai.org/intel/2-rd2/html
© Intelenet Commission 1996

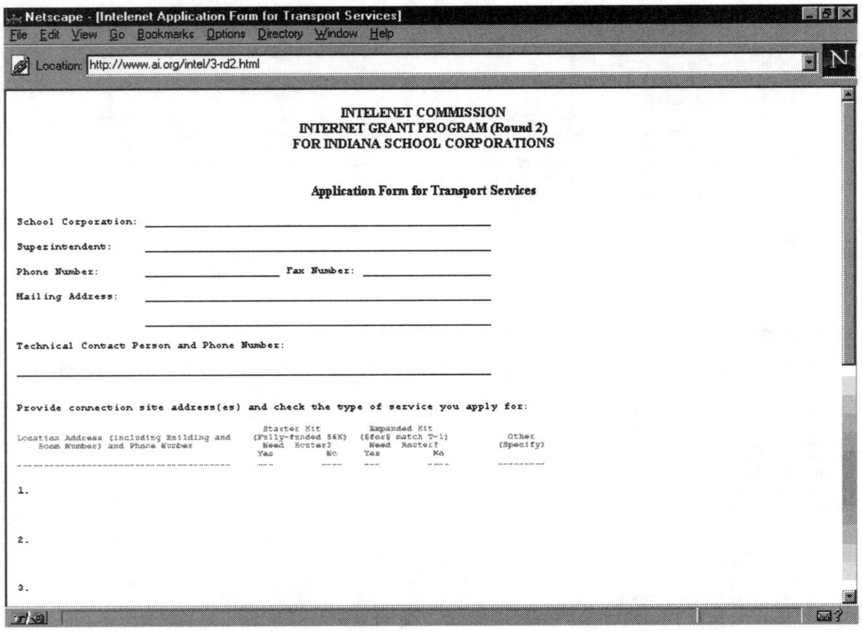

Figure 4.13 Intelenet's application form for transport services.

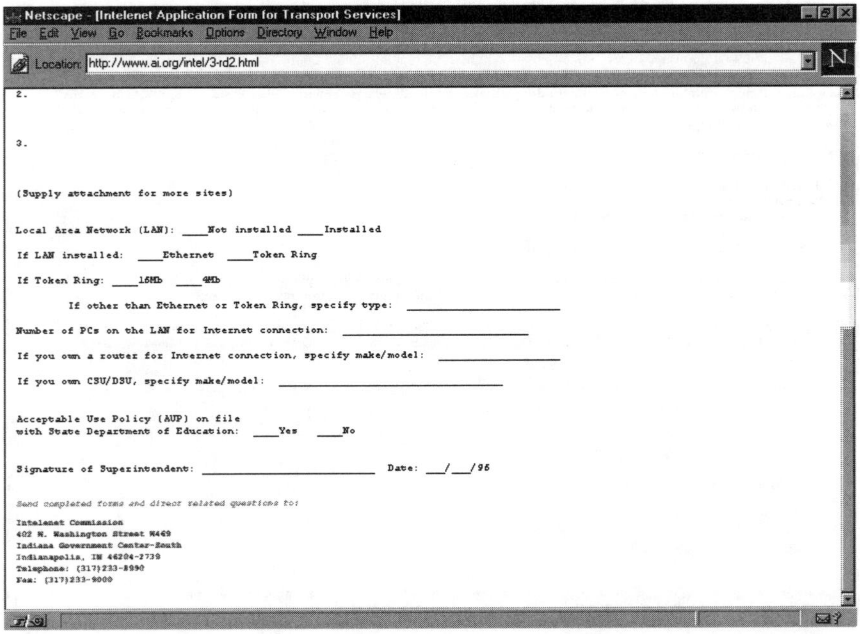

http://www.ai.org/intel/2-rd2/html
© Intelenet Commission 1996

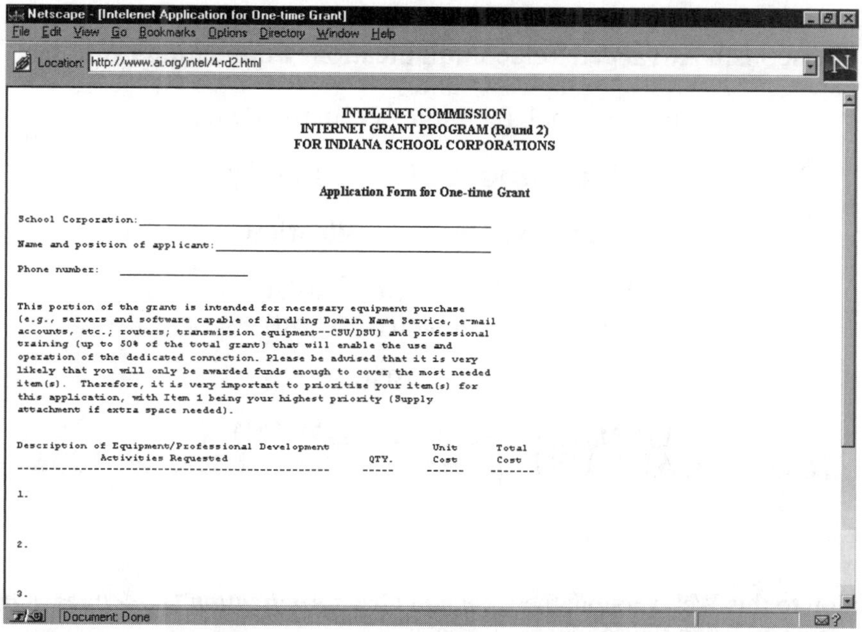

Figure 4.14 Intelenet's application form for a one-time grant.

http://www.ai/org/intel/2-rd2/html
© Intelenet Commission 1996

PARTS OF A TYPICAL PROPOSAL

The solicitation notice describes what grantors are looking for and how you can write your proposal to explain how you'll meet their needs and expectations. Grantors always want to know what you're going to do. When you write a grant proposal, your description must accurately detail the tasks that will be completed, including how they'll be accomplished, by whom, when, and where. You have to write measurable objectives or milestones for the project and convince the grantor that the project will be monitored and evaluated at the completion of specific tasks or on a mutually agreeable timeline. Grantors need to know that you can do what you propose to do and that your project will succeed on time and within budget.

Although each grantor prefers the proposal to follow its guidelines, you most often are asked to include the following types of information in your proposal. The organization and headings for these sections vary among grantors, but you should be prepared to write information about each of these areas: a problem or need statement, a rationale for the project and a description of its significance (e.g., why your project, instead of another project, should be funded

Wisconsin Advanced Telecommunications Foundation (WATF)
and
Educational Technology Board (ETB)

1996 Funding Cycles Only

Common Grant Application

Guidelines and Forms
(to be periodically revised)

May 6, 1996

APPLICATION DEADLINES:
JUNE 14, AUGUST 30, and NOVEMBER 29, 1996

NOTE:

In addition to this Web version, the *Common Grant Application Guidelines and Forms* are provided in the following formats:

Cover Sheet Form and Project Budget Form (WordPerfect ver.5.1)
Cover Sheet Form and Project Budget Form (MS Word ver. 2.0)

Because of their layout, the Web versions of the **Cover Sheet Form** and **Project Budget Form** are included only for information purposes. To get the actual formatted versions, select one of the options below:

Cover Sheet Form and Project Budget Form (WordPerfect ver.5.1)
Cover Sheet Form and Project Budget Form (MS Word ver. 2.0)

The WATF/ETB Grant Application Guidelines and Forms are posted as a public service to the WI Dept of Public Instruction's Web site in cooperation with the WATF and ETB. Any questions regarding the WATF and ETB grant process or program should be directed to: Todd M. Penske, Executive Director, Wisconsin Advanced Telecommunications Foundation and Educational Technology Board. For grants awarded in the first round of WATF grants, see the WATF press release.

Posted May 6, 1996. Expires November 29, 1996.

Figure 4.15 Wisconsin Advanced Telecommunications Foundation and Educational Technology Board's guidelines and forms.

http://www.state.wi.us/agencies/dpi/www
© Wisconsin Advanced Telecommunications Foundation and Educational Technology Board 1996

Contents
Contents

TABLE OF CONTENTS

- **Grant Program Description**
- **Eligible Applicants**
- **Eligible Applicant Priority Consideration**
- **Eligible Projects**
- **Anticipated Cash Funds and In-Kind Contributions Available**
- **Application Procedures**
- **Application Cover Sheet**
- **Grant Funding Restrictions**
- **Grant Application Deadline**
- **Wisconsin Public Records Law**
- **False, Misleading, or Omitted Statements**

Evaluation Criteria

1. **Applicant (Organization) Overview**
    ◊ **Problem/Opportunity Definition**
    ◊ **Project Goals and Objectives**
    ◊ **Project Design**

2. **Applicant Qualifications**
    ◊ **Project Management**
    ◊ **Project Evaluation**

3. **Partnerships and Community Support**
    Potential to Serve as a Model

4. **Applicant Financial Resources/Project Budget**
    - **Matching Funds Requirement**
    - **Withdrawal of Application**
    - **Review and Selection Process**
    - **No Obligation for Future Funding**
    - **Appeals Process**
    - **Technical Assistance**
    - **For Further Information, Contact**
    - **Cover Sheet Form** [for informational purposes only]
    - **Project Budget Form** [for informational purposes only]

Wisconsin Advanced Telecommunications Foundation
and
Educational Technology Board

Cover Sheet Form and Project Budget Form

NOTE:

Because of their layout, the actual **Cover Sheet Form** and **Project Budget Form** are provided below for informational purposes only. If you will be submitting a grant, please download the actual formatted **Cover Sheet Form** and the **Project Budget Form** using one of the formats shown below. You can also contact Todd Penske for the printed forms.

Cover Sheet Form and Project Budget Form (WordPerfect ver.5.1)
Cover Sheet Form and Project Budget Form (MS Word ver. 2.0)

COVER SHEET FORM Today's Date: _____

_____

Legal Name of Organization Telephone Number Fax Telephone Number

---

Figure 4.16 Wisconsin Advanced Telecommunications Foundation and Educational Technology Board's cover sheet.

http://www.state.wi.us/agencies/dpi/www
© Wisconsin Advanced Telecommunications Foundation and Educational Technology Board 1996

now), project objectives, your methods to meet these objectives, the materials needed to meet the objectives, a timeline, a description of the facilities and/or equipment needed to complete the project or that are already in place (that other competing proposal writers may not have available to them), a list of the personnel who will work on the project and their credentials, methods of evaluating the project, and a budget.

In addition to these sections, you may need to provide attached documentation to support what you've written in the proposal. For example, you may be asked to provide resumes for the key personnel involved with this project, a literature review of the research conducted to develop your methods, or a financial statement for your institution.

Problem or Need Statement and Rationale

Within this section you prove that a problem or need exists and that you understand how your project can help solve the problem or meet a short-term or a long-term need. You might refer to keywords the grantor used in the solicitation notice; in that way you indicate that you're familiar with the grantor's needs and assessment of the situation that needs to be changed.

This section must be persuasive and clear. You must show that you have a good grasp of the current situation and the project you're proposing can improve that situation. Whether the project is a practical application (e.g., providing specialized instruction to rural students who cannot otherwise meet a state education requirement) or theoretical research (e.g., a study of the effectiveness of using a monthly teleconference to train new elementary teachers), you need to indicate that there is a significant problem or need that must be addressed now, and your project is a sound, well-organized, cost-effective approach to meeting that need or solving that problem.

As part of this section or as a separate section, you may be expected to provide a rationale for your project, based on your assessment of the need or problem. Many distance learning projects are worthwhile, but only some can be funded at this time. You need to convince the grantor that your project is timely and should receive a higher priority than other worthwhile projects that could be funded as well at another time.

Objectives

Persuasive objectives help indicate the significance of your project; objectives must be specific, measurable tasks that show what you will do and how you will do it. Objectives often describe the number of people who will be affected by the project, the areas of improvement in existing programs, and ways to test the project's feasibility. Objectives must be written clearly and precisely so that the grantor understands how your project meets the criteria for funded projects and indicates your ability to do exactly what you write that you can do.

This section also helps grantors understand how you will be held accountable for the project. For example, when you write that your Web-based course will be taken by 50 people in a four-month time frame, you have set up an expectation to be met. You and the grantor now have a way to measure your achievement.

Methods, Materials, and a Timeline (Plan of Work)

Depending upon the grantor's preferred format for the proposal, methods, materials, and a timeline may be separate sections or they may be combined into a detailed plan of work. However you're asked to format the information, you have to provide grantors with a complete picture of the distance learning project they're expected at least partially to fund. They'll want to know the details of your approach, including the tasks, the materials used for each task, and the time each task will take. The resulting outline provides a blueprint for the project, so that the grantor knows when the project will begin and end, which tasks need to be accomplished in a sequence or simultaneously, what will be used to accomplish each task, and when completed tasks can be expected. Your progress can be measured by the way you follow this blueprint.

A methods section explains how you will meet your objectives, because several different tasks are probably going to be required to meet the larger objective. Each task must be described as a small, manageable step on the way to meeting an objective. It provides a logical order for the project, from start to finish. When the methods are so clearly detailed, and no steps seem vague or left out, grantors understand that you've analyzed the project and completely understand what is required to complete the project successfully. A precisely written methods section builds your credibility as a project manager and highlights the feasibility of the proposed project.

If you plan to use special materials (but not facilities or equipment), you can describe the materials and resources you'll use at each step in the project. Again, this section can build your credibility by showing grantors that you have the materials or know how to use the appropriate resources needed throughout the project.

By identifying the starting and ending times for each task in the project, you've created a schedule or a timeline. Grantors learn the starting and ending dates for the project and can see how long each task will take. They can see if the workflow is not only logical but cost-effective, when some tasks can be completed at the same time. A timeline indicates which tasks will take longer and when progress can be expected.

Facilities and Equipment

Facilities may entail nothing more than a building, but they may mean a building with special requirements, such as soundproofing for recording broadcasts or certain cable or wiring specifications. You may also need specialized equipment to complete the tasks. Therefore, in a facilities and equipment section, you describe what you need to use to complete the project.

In this section you persuade grantors that you own or have access to the facilities required to complete the project. If your organization is part of a consortium sharing facilities and equipment, you can explain how this special coalition allows all participants access to facilities and technology that other (competing) grantees may not have or be able to lease or buy cost effectively. If your proposal is an equipment or facilities proposal, you'll explain why you need the equipment or facilities, which will be funded by the grantor, to accomplish your objectives.

Personnel Qualifications

A personnel qualifications section may or may not be required. If you're not specifically asked about the people who will complete each task and have responsibility for different parts of the project, you might include a brief description of the personnel and their qualifications in the methods section.

Most technical proposals require you to list the key personnel who will manage one part or several tasks in the project. You provide the information that will persuade the grantor that you have the required workforce for the project, including the appropriate experts or experienced employees who have worked on similar projects. If you're going to work with outside consultants or contractors, you should also specify who these people are and what they will be expected to do throughout the project.

Grantors often like to see documentation of the credentials you've described in the body of the proposal. They may require you to supply resumes or copies of certifications, for example, in an appendix or as an attachment. Follow the grantor's specifications about how much or little information is needed.

Evaluation

All grantors expect that you, an outside auditor or consultant, and/or the grantor's representative will evaluate the project. Some projects require only a final report or demonstration. Other projects are evaluated on the basis of new technology or innovative programs that were created to be shared with others; the final evaluation is the sharing of new information or resources through demonstrations, presentations, or publications. Other grantors prefer to receive a series of audits and/or progress reports to check on the project at certain milestones. If you're fiscally responsible and meet your deadlines, your project is deemed a success.

You might be required to submit evaluations at regular intervals, such as each month or quarter, or you might instead be asked to comply with requirements at the completion of each major task described in the methods section or task plan. Read the solicitation notice and proposal format guidelines to determine what type of evaluation is appropriate for the grantor who will receive your proposal.

Cost or Budget

The cost or budget section explains how you'll spend the grant money. It shows that you can accomplish your tasks on time with the materials, facilities, equipment, and personnel you described previously in the proposal. This section also shows that you've accurately estimated costs and have a thorough understanding of the project's requirements.

Although a lump-sum, or total amount, budget may be required in some proposals, the most common type of budget is the line-item budget. Each item with its cost is spelled out in a line-item budget. For example, if you write a line-item budget that includes travel costs, not only will you be asked to provide a total for all travel items, but you must spell out who will travel, when, where, and how. The number of miles traveled by car multiplied by the amount charged per mile, for example, might be only one line in a long list of travel items. Accommodations, tips, meals, per diem rates, and any other travel expenses covered in the project must be broken down in the list, in addition to the specific travel items, such as airline or train tickets. Every big cost item (e.g., personnel, travel, equipment, materials) must be broken down into several subsidiary cost lines to explain how the money will be spent. The line-item budget also shows the grantor that you've accounted for every possible cost related to the project. The budget is only one part of the proposal, but it is a crucial section.

Some grantors fund only part of a project, but they still want to see a complete budget to get a better understanding of their (and others') commitment and degree of support for this project. Other grantors may want only an itemized inventory for their part of the funding.

Even if the grantor only will fund certain items, you often need to list additional funding sources to indicate other grantors or businesses who have agreed to help support the project or who have been solicited for funding. You may be required to list sources of future funding in a separate section in the proposal.

When you write a proposal, you usually list all direct and indirect costs that will be associated with the project, even if you'll only be asked to describe certain costs for the grantor or determine a total cost. Direct costs include expenses for personnel, materials, and equipment, for example. In addition, you may be faced with indirect costs, usually for administration of the grant once it's received. For example, some academic institutions require a *handling* or *processing* fee of 10 percent minimally to administer the grant. When you estimate the project's costs, you need to consider direct and indirect costs.

If you fail to estimate an expense, you either have to find other sources to pay for it or have to do without. The budget submitted in the grant proposal most often will be the basis for the amount of the award; usually you can't increase the budget after an award is made. If your budget is too low, you may not be able to complete the project, even though you were funded. If your budget is too high, the grantor may decide to fund less costly but similar projects or may think that you could cut some unnecessary expenses. A cost section must be accurate, but it must also show financial responsibility and good management.

An itemized (line-item) budget should list all proposed expenditures, such as travel, phone calls, supplies, equipment rental, and postage. Items that have a direct cost (i.e., you buy the service or consumable supplies) include the following:

■ Administrative operations, such as services for photocopying and Internet connections
■ Consumable supplies, such as paper, disks, videotapes, and software
■ Equipment, including purchase, lease, rental, maintenance, and repair
■ Facilities, including purchase, lease, rental, and (usually) utilities
■ Fees (e.g., consultants or contractors, building permits, licenses, copyright use)
■ Travel (e.g., lodging, meals, mileage, airfare, train fare, parking)

The Wisconsin Advanced Telecommunications Foundation and Educational Technology Board's online project budget form (Figure 4.17) is a good example of a formal cost sheet that should be downloaded and completed. The form first requires statements about committed and pending funding sources. Some items (e.g., private foundations, corporations) must be itemized. The next subsection involves the organization's earned income and some items must be itemized. Information about sources of funding and income must be outlined first, before the project's anticipated expenses are listed. Again, the number of items to be accounted for is extensive (e.g., audioconferencing hardware and software, consulting fees, insurance, Internet access, staff training and development, supplies). The Other category requires an itemized list of additional expenditures. Many grantors require this level or greater of budget planning and the amount of the award is based on the information provided on the cost forms. Even if a grantor doesn't require you to submit an itemized budget, it's still a good idea to prepare one, so that you clearly understand each area of income and outflow for your proposed project.

Grantors like to know that they're getting the most for their funds. Sometimes you may need to provide a brief cost-benefit analysis to show how cost-effective your project is and how the benefits relate to the overall cost.

Keep in mind that you usually get only one chance to submit a proposal to a grantor during an award cycle. Each item in the proposal must be precise, accurate, and clearly stated. This is especially true in a cost or budget section. Before you submit the proposal, double check the figures, including the total, for accuracy. If grantors discover a computation error, they may assume that you'll be as careless with the award as you were with your proposal. Your management of the proposal-submission process, including the preparation of a budget, indicates the quality of your project management.

PROJECT BUDGET FORM

Project Budget Period:

From: _____ To: _____

FUNDING SOURCES:	Committed	Funding	Comments
1. Grants-Contracts-Contributions:			
Federal/State Government			
Municipal/County Government			
Private Foundations *(Itemize)*			
Corporations *(Itemize)*			
Individuals			
2. Earned Income *(from events, publications and products only)*			
3. Membership Income			
4. User Fees			
5. In-Kind Contributions *(Itemize)*			
6. Operating Budget, Cash, Tax Levy			
7. Other *(Itemize)*			
8. **TOTAL FUNDING** *(Add all lines in each column)*			

Figure 4.17 Wisconsin Advanced Telecommunications Foundation and Educational Technology Board's project budget form.

http://www.state.wi.us/agencies/dpi/www
© Wisconsin Advanced Telecommunications Foundation and Educational Technology Board 1996

PROJECT EXPENSES	Amount Requested from WATF/ETB	Amount of Proposer's Cash Match	Amount of Proposer's In-Kind Match	Amount of Telecom. Provider's In-Kind Contribution
1. Audioconferencing Hardware/Software				
2. Cable/Wire (Fiber, Copper, Coaxial)				
3. Consultant/Professional Fees				
4. Insurance				
5. Instructional Materials				
6. Internet Access				
7. Labor Services				
8. Local/Wide Area Network Hardware/Software				
9. Local/Wide Area Network Peripherals				
10. Maintenance and Repair Services				
11. Marketing and Communications				
12. Membership Dues				
13. Personal Computer Hardware/Software				
14. Personal Computer Peripherals				
15. Printing/Photocopying				
16. Post/Courier Delivery				
17. Rent				
18. Room Design (Acoustics, Furniture, Lighting)				
19. Staff Training and Development				
20. Supplies				
21. Telecommunications Network Usage				
22. Telephone/Fax (Local/Long Distance) Service				
23. Travel				
24. Videoconferencing Hardware/Software				
25. Other *(Itemize)*				
26. TOTAL EXPENSES *(Add all lines in each column)*				

Future Funding

You may expect your project to continue past the initial funding period and need grant support just to get the project off the ground. Once the project has been successful—for example, your organization has developed a Web site and electronic course-related materials—you no longer need special funding to maintain and expand the online courses.

Some projects, however, will require additional support indefinitely, beyond what your organization or consortium can provide. If you plan to use future funding to keep a project operational, you should describe the sources you're investigating or the sources that have pledged future support. Current grantors like to know that, if appropriate, the project will be financially sound in the future and the good work they've helped begin will continue after the award has been used.

Sources of future funding may be specified in the budget information (as in Figure 4.17) or you may be asked to complete a separate section detailing the sources of future support. Follow the grantor's required format when you write your proposal.

MEETING A GRANTOR'S REQUIREMENTS

The amount and types of required information may vary among grantors, but the previously described sections are typical in proposals about distance learning. As you've learned, some forms and requirements are available in hardcopy only; some grantors prefer that you work with online forms and still others provide and accept information in hardcopy and softcopy formats. Similar information is provided in either format, although online forms tend to be shorter and require a direct, brief style. Hardcopy proposals usually allow you (if not require you) to provide more elaborate descriptions of your objectives, methods, and personnel.

If you have questions about the grant or the proposal, you should contact the grantor to ask your questions. Until the deadline for submission, or a date after which the grantor has specified that you should not call or write, grantors will discuss your proposal and the specifications with you. As you've seen in some solicitation notices, grantors often encourage questions and provide many links to resources that can help you prepare your proposal.

SUBMITTING THE PROPOSAL

Grantors adhere to deadlines and specifications—period. If you fail to meet a deadline or follow the instructions, your proposed project may not even be considered, much less awarded funding. Before you submit the proposal, double check the specifications one more time to ensure that you're providing complete information in the way that the grantor requested it. Read the proposal again to ensure that the style, language, and punctuation are correct, precise, and consistent. Check the number of copies and make sure that the appended materials are in order. Completing a final check helps ensure your compliance with the grantor's specifications.

A benefit of filing an online proposal or completing online forms is that the submission can be instantaneous; therefore, you don't have to worry about mailing the proposal or making multiples copies. For example, the sample proposal in Figure 4.18 was designed for an online form. It shows the limited amount of information that had to be submitted electronically, but it reflects the proposal writer's previous planning (especially with the budget, so that the correct amounts could be listed on the online form). The BellSouth online form you saw earlier in this chapter provided the outline for Figure 4.18.

FOLLOWING UP ON THE PROPOSAL

When you are awarded funding or support, follow the grantor's guidelines for receiving the award, conducting the project, and evaluating it. Periodically check with the grantor to provide updates and progress reports, and to ensure that all requirements are being met.

If, for some reason, your proposal was denied funding or support, check with the grantor to learn why the award was not made. Sometimes the grantor received so many worthwhile proposals that it became difficult to select just one to receive the grant; your project may be funded in the next granting period or you may be encouraged to submit the proposal again. If the grantor questioned an item or found that you did not comply with guidelines, you might discuss the proposal to determine how you can ensure compliance and improve the proposal for a future submission.

Some proposals are only partially funded. Check with the grantor to learn why full funding was not awarded. Again, the grantor may have decided to fund several projects partially, instead of fully funding only one.

Following up after you've heard from the grantor not only helps you develop a good working relationship with the grantor and ensure current or future funding for your projects, but it also helps you learn about the proposal-writing process and how to improve your proposals. Always follow up on the proposals you write, so that you can better guarantee your success in writing the next proposal.

Some grantors describe their appeal process in their Web site information or hardcopy documents. They know that they can't fund all worthy projects and they encourage you to explain why you should have at least partial funding if your proposal initially isn't selected. This is one way that grantors can help you understand how to improve your proposal, provide information that may have been missing in the original submission, or prepare a new proposal for the next granting cycle.

Date of Application: August 1, 1996

Organization/
Institution Name: ABC Consolidated School System

Street Address: 1234 Main Street

City: Any City

State/zip code: SC   12345-6789

Executive Director: Dr. Joan Doe

Contact Person
(if not director):   N/A

Telephone: 555-555-5555

Fax: 555-555-0000

Email: jdoe@abc.css.edu

Is your organization tax exempt?   Yes

Has your organization's board approved a policy which states that the organization does not discriminate on the basis of age, race, religion, sex or national origin?   Yes

Please state the principal purpose of your organization.

ABC Consolidated School System consists of 15 elementary and secondary schools in the greater Any City, SC, area. We serve more than 20,000 students in our school system. Our system meets all state and national education standards.

About your Funding

Amount of grant request: $XX,XXX.XX

Total Project Budget: $XX,XXX.XX

Total organization budget
(for current year) $XXX,XXX.XX

Please list other funders from whom you have received commitments or to whom you have applied for support for this project:

We have a commitment for $X,XXX.XX from the Educational Improvement Corporation in Any City, SC. In addition, we have applied for grant funds for follow-on funding from [federal agency XYZ] for $X,XXX.XX. This grant is for _____ only, and does not conflict with the proposal currently being submitted to BellSouth.

How long will your project run?

From September 1, 1997 to June 1, 1998

continued

Figure 4.18   Information for the online proposal form.

About Your Project

Project name, if Applicable:

Work Simulation Database

Please describe the purpose of your project:

The Work Simulation Database will allow elementary and secondary students to learn more about 50 careers in the sciences and technological employment areas. These careers involve employment requiring a wide range of skills and educational backgrounds, from apprenticeships to advanced degrees. Students can use the database to locate average salaries, educational requirements, and typical job descriptions for each career. Each career will also be presented through an interactive simulation, so that students can "job shadow" persons/characters at work. Each career segment will require students to complete an interest inventory after they work with the simulation and read the career materials. This interest inventory can be downloaded to a disk or printout so students can keep track of their career interests and the skills and knowledge they need to prepare for a career.

The database will be created and maintained through a collaborative effort among teachers, administrators, career counselors, and area business people in the school system and surrounding region. We will keep track of each student's use of the database and compile quarterly reports to determine if use of the database increases students' use of career materials in the home school. We also will keep track of the number of students who use the database, which career segments are accessed most often, and the ways teachers use the database with other career-development activities.

The database encourages students to use computer technology to access the database. Because the database is located on the Web, students can use any platform to work with the database. However, because the site requires a subscription code to access the information, only students within our school system will be able to use the database at this time.

The information is presented in several formats including, documents, pictures, charts, tables, and cartoons, as well as the hypertext links leading to other resources and the simulation, to meet different learners' needs. The simulations involve animation and video, as well as hypertext links so that students can interact with the simulation. They can answer and ask questions and observe (or "job shadow") people or characters as they perform typical job tasks for that career.

Students who are unable to attend classes in their home school, but who work at home or with tutors will have access to the Web site. Students with different abilities can access the information in the format that is easiest for them to use.

Therefore, the database makes career education information available to all students within our school system. Students can learn about careers by accessing information in the format that is easiest for them to use. They can visit the database as many times as they'd like and spend as much time as they want within a segment. Once they have learned about a career and interacted with the simulation, they can take an interest inventory that will help them to determine whether this career would be a good match for them. This comprehensive program offers students in all schools the same opportunity to learn about a variety of the fastest growing careers in our state and to understand how to prepare for a career that interests them.

Always follow up with grantors, even if your proposal wasn't selected at first. You show your level of commitment to your project and can receive information to help you prepare the next proposal. Also, you and the grantor get to know each other better. Of course, throughout the proposal-writing process, you should be thorough in your preparation and consult with the granting agency when you have questions (at least during the time frame when questions are encouraged). However, if your proposal is not successful, you shouldn't write off your efforts. Keeping in touch with grantors, whether through a formal appeals process or informal follow up, is an important part of the granting process.

SUMMARY

Writing proposals should be an ongoing process, especially if you're writing to support distance learning projects. Think of your project as many separate parts, which may be supported in different ways. Some grantors want proposals about technology or will support purchases of equipment or the installation of networks, for example. Others prefer to fund educational or training initiatives and will only support the development of curriculum or the establishment of a new course or program. Because different grantors can help you develop and support a distance learning program, your proposal-writing processes should take place throughout the year. You should always be searching for new grants and grantors, as well as continually researching your program's needs and strengths, so that you know not only what you need, but what you have to offer.

The proposal-writing process requires precision and meticulousness. The best proposals are the result of ongoing preparation, so that you know who to approach, what the grantor is looking for, what you uniquely offer to this grantor, and how to manage the project. Writing a proposal takes time—you need to allow adequate preparation time.

As you begin to fund distance learning projects, you'll write several proposals to different grantors. You may become much more familiar with the writing process, but you should never be complacent. Each proposal should be unique and suit the needs of a particular grantor.

When you write your first few proposals, you may want to check with potential grantors more frequently to ensure that you're providing all the required information in the required format. Many grantors provide online guidelines for writing a proposal or offer suggestions or samples to follow as you prepare the proposal.

Appendix C lists online sources of information about grantors and grants, including the "how to" information for preparing a grant. Although this list is not complete, because more Web sites are being offered online every week, it provides you with a good starting point to find information about proposal-writing online. You can also check with grantors to learn if funded proposals can be downloaded or read online. Some grantors make previously funded proposals available to writers who plan to submit a proposal during the next granting period.

Determining the Suitability of Distance Learning Courses

5

Some types of courses are more naturally suited to successful distance learning. Some educators or trainers are better suited to presenting information in a distance learning course and some learners thrive in a distance learning program. In other cases, the course is better presented one-on-one or in-person than through distance learning. Yet there are those educators, trainers, and learners who find this type of education difficult. The appropriate educational or training method must carefully be matched with the needs and interests of the people who present the course and those who take it. Each course must be carefully evaluated to see if it's suitable for a distance learning environment.

Distance learning is a wonderful method of providing high-quality education or training to people in widely separated geographic areas, often at their own pace and available at convenient, if sometimes untraditional, times. But distance learning is only effective when there is a good blend of content, presentation style, and ability to learn from the information or situations presented. Courses that are suitable for distance learning should meet the criteria discussed in the following sections.

CRITERIA FOR EFFECTIVE DISTANCE LEARNING COURSES

Almost any course can be taught through distance learning, but not every course can be taught well in a distance learning environment. Each course should be considered individually as to its suitability to be offered through distance learning, and then the real work begins.

After a course is selected as a candidate for inclusion in a distance learning program, it must be analyzed to determine which type(s) of distance learning are appropriate. Only then can suitable instructors for this course's content, and the technologies involved in distributing information to learners, be selected and provided with the resources they need to develop effective materials for the course.

Even when a course has been developed and presented, the work continues. A distance learning course may seldom, if ever, be presented the same way twice because subject matter, learners' needs and expectations, and technology keep changing. The cycle continues with the evaluation of the course's strengths and weaknesses and the ongoing improvement of content, methods, and technologies to ensure that the distance learning course is the best it can be.

Some areas to analyze as you determine the suitability of a course for distance learning include the following: the availability of an appreciative audience, course content suitable for widely diverse audiences, whether the information must be seen to be understood, the amount and type of interaction required by learners and educators/trainers, the availability of the technology the course requires, and the way to ensure high-quality education or training.

Appreciative Audience

Distance learning is especially useful for disenfranchised audiences, people who normally would not have the opportunity to take this course, but who would benefit from it. People who are forced to take a course will not be learners. That's why it's important to have an appreciative audience, people who want to take the course, who see some benefit from it, and who would not otherwise be able to take it at this time, for this cost, in a convenient location, and so forth.

If you're designing a distance learning course, you should ask these questions about your audience:

■ Who wants or needs to take this course?
■ Where else can they take this course?
■ When else can they take this course?
■ How does this course meet a currently unmet need for this type of instruction?
■ How can the targeted audience be made aware that this course is being offered?
■ How is this course equal or superior to any other similar course offering?

These questions help you to analyze not only your target audience(s) (which will be useful in everything from course planning to design to implementation to marketing), but also your competition for these learners. Analyzing your target population of learners helps you understand the educational or training niche you're trying to fill, and how your courses or programs compare with other vendors of similar distance learning offerings. Your answers illustrate your strengths and weaknesses and help you pinpoint approaches toward distance learning.

Course Content Suitable for a Wide Audience

Not all courses are designed for mass instruction; some can be taught to one person or hundreds of people at the same time. For example, skill development is best completed individually, with some type of guidance. Whether the skill is setting up a home page or dissecting the model of a frog, each person has to practice that skill and get feedback on it truly to develop the skill and knowledge base to master that subject. Watching someone else do the task might be part of the instruction, but at some point the individual must perform the task, receive feedback for improvement, then practice the task again. Teaching a group to do the task and expecting mastery from large-group instruction is not very productive.

However, the background information needed to understand what to do, how to do it, when to do it, and why you're doing it that way could easily be the topic of a group lesson. Content about a topic can be presented as a lecture, discussion, demonstration, and/or simulation through a hypermedia Web site, a taped or live broadcast, or a desktop videoconference. A single learner or many learners at different locations could learn about the subject at the same time.

Practice activities or exercises are required so that the learner develops a skill and can perform a task accurately and safely. Although some tasks require groups to work together, most job-related activities involve individual effort. With the background information in mind, individuals can apply their knowledge to the skill and receive feedback on their performance.

An online tutorial, for example, can allow a learner to move at his or her pace through a series of activities. The programming can include different feedback mechanisms, from responses to the learner's answers to an online quiz, to pop-up help sections, to automatic correction of incorrect selections during a simulation. Although many people might access the program at the same time, across different locations, the learning takes place individually, as each learner makes different choices and proceeds at a different pace. Tutorial and other practice-based learning activities might be offered through a tutorial stored in a Web site, on disk, or paper-based instructional materials.

As you develop the content for a course, you should determine if a particular lesson, or even a whole course, is based on memorizable facts to develop a knowledge base or on the development of skills and completion of tasks. You should also determine how wide an audience can use this material at the same time. For example, is the information at the level for adult learners, or is it suitable for all ages? Does the material require a great deal of previous knowledge about the topic or experience with the task, or is the subject general enough to appeal to people with little prior knowledge or skill? Determining how wide, or how narrow, the audience is can help you determine if a particular course, or even part of a course, is suitable for a certain type of distance learning.

As you analyze the course content you may want to offer in a distance learning course, you can ask these questions:

■ How much of the course content is based on memorizable facts or a core body of information?
■ How much of the course content should rely on activities, such as practicing skills, observing a task, demonstrating a correct procedure, and applying information learned in the course?
■ Should learners work alone to gather information and complete activities?
■ Should learners work in groups to gather information and complete activities?
■ When are group activities (e.g., discussions, presentations) used within the course?
■ When are individual activities (e.g., reading, completing a simulation) used within the course?
■ Are different lessons structured for different types of course activities?
■ What is the primary method of instructing learners in this course?

These questions provide a starting point so that you can clarify how much of any course will rely on activities or use of databased information, on individual and group interaction, and on reusable or rapidly changing subject matter.

Course Content Suitable for Viewing

Some courses contain information that has to be seen. It's one thing to have someone describe how to pilot a plane, but it's quite different to understand how to be a pilot. Distance learning can provide simulations that create a virtual environment in which the learner can "experience" the subject. With the use of virtual reality modeling language (VRML), or even Java applets, more virtual, multidimensional environments are becoming commercially available on the Web. Even simpler Web-, floppy disk-, or CD-based simulations can help learners see, hear, and interact with information. Sound effects, animation, and video and audio clips, for example, can electronically enhance learning.

Demonstrations and special events presentations also should be seen. Broadcasts from one location, such as the eye of a hurricane or the floor of the

U.S. Senate, give an insider's view of a subject. Satellite uplinks and downlinks and teleconferencing—as well as desktop videoconferences—illustrate subject matter live, as an event takes place. Even taped demonstrations and events can enhance the learning process by showing, rather than simply describing.

If your course's topics often should be seen, in addition to being discussed, explained, and described through personal narration, lecture, and print materials, for example, you probably will need to include different types of audiovisual materials in your distance learning program. If the majority of materials should be seen and heard, you should emphasize live or taped broadcast in your choice of educational technologies.

Teleconferencing, desktop videoconferencing, and Web-based multimedia, for example, are effective when they allow learners to see, hear, and do. Effective distance learning courses involve visual media and require interaction among individual learners, the educator/trainer, and the information. When you plan a distance learning course, try to anticipate how you can make the instruction more visual and involving. Ask these types of questions:

- What should be seen in an observation?
- When is a demonstration necessary?
- What should be discussed "in person" during a lesson?
- What types of graphics are appropriate to show important topics?
- When do learners need to see each other?
- When do learners need to see the educator/trainer?
- How can more interactivity be designed into the course?
- How can more visual information be presented in the course?

Determining the number and types of visuals, and learners' interaction in using them, can help you structure course activities and determine the types of equipment best suited for presenting the information.

Appropriate Amount of Educator/Trainer-Learner Interaction

Before the first distance learning course is offered, the amount and type of interaction between learners and the educators/trainers outside of class should also be determined. Some types of correspondence courses providing information to build a knowledge base—for example, a literature or a history course—might require little interaction on a daily basis. Skill-development courses, such as a writing course, require more feedback and more frequent interaction, especially when learners work on and complete assignments.

When you're planning the course, anticipate the amount of time "out of class" that educators/trainers and learners must spend together. Then determine how and when this interaction should take place. You might ask these types of questions to help you establish some parameters for interaction:

- How often will learners and educators/trainers see each other for discussion, questions, and instruction?
- How much of the coursework can be completed by learners themselves?
- How much of the coursework depends on guidance from the educator/trainer?
- When will learners need to meet with other learners or with educators/trainers?
- When will learners need individual communication with the educator/trainer?
- How much communication will take place each week?
- How much communication will take place in the course?
- How accessible should educators/trainers be to learners?
- How much face-to-face communication is necessary? desirable?
- What process should learners follow to communicate with educators/trainers (i.e., What is the appropriate protocol?)?
- How quickly must educators/trainers respond to learners?
- What types of interaction are appropriate for the distance among participants?
- What types of interaction are appropriate for the type of course?
- What types of interaction are appropriate for the type of technology being used in the course?

Technically Appropriate Information and Tools

Before a course can be offered, the company or institution needs the appropriate types of technology to conduct the desired type of distance learning offerings. Some equipment might need to be purchased, leased, shared, or rented, for example. Not every distance learning provider can offer every type of learning method and do a good job of updating the technology, maintaining the systems, and generally keeping all types of learning programs going equally effectively. Some specialization is required.

If you're planning courses, ask these questions as you plan the direction in which you're headed as a distance learning provider:

- What is the most appropriate type of distance learning (e.g., satellite transmission, mailing of prerecorded videotapes, e-mail, Web site) for the courses to be offered?
- What type of distance learning technology is best suited for the type of courses we currently offer? courses we plan to offer in the future?
- What type of distance learning technology will make us stand out from our competitors?
- What types of equipment are currently needed to offer a single course? multiple courses?

- How are the technological needs likely to change during the next six months? year? three years?
- How quickly can we update our equipment to meet changing technical demands?
- What is the cost to provide one course? several courses?
- How can this cost reasonably be accounted for (e.g., through course fees, grant moneys, collaboration with other providers, assistance from businesses)?
- How can this technology be expanded as additional types of distance learning courses are proposed?
- How can we collaborate with other institutions, organizations, or businesses for our benefit and the benefit of more learners?

The equipment and technology support the best type of instruction for your target population of learners. By answering the first several series of questions listed in the preceding sections, you're more likely to know exactly what types of equipment or technology will be best suited for your distance learning program. Also, you'll begin to anticipate the number of partners you'll need to share their expertise, funds, or equipment so that you can make the distance learning plan a reality.

Guarantee of High Quality

One of the concerns about distance learning is the guarantee of quality. With so many private and public providers of noncredit, for-credit, and accreditation-preparation courses from which to choose, consumers often have a difficult time deciding which courses are worthwhile for them and how one course compares to another. If you're offering a distance learning course, make sure that the courses are evaluated by other educators/trainers and by the learners who have taken the course. Use the results of the evaluation to improve the quality of the course content, method of providing education over a distance, and quality of instruction.

Publicizing the results of the course and using testimonials in your advertisements help encourage feedback. You can also make potential learners aware of the ongoing evaluation process. In addition, you need to make announcements of the course attractive and innovative. This is especially true if you're advertising courses as well as offering them on the Web. Web users like glossy, high-tech, easily usable, and innovative designs, and your course information should look attractive, well-designed for an electronic medium, *and* appropriately "educational."

If you're planning to take a distance learning course and have a choice of vendors for the course you need, check with the institution or company offering the course to see how it has been evaluated. Institutions often are accredited by educational associations; learn if your potential vendor has been accredited. Ask others, even through a post to a mailing list, newsgroup, or bulletin board, if they have had positive experiences with this vendor or within the course. Shop around to see what types of distance learning courses are available to you. In short, do your own homework before you decide to take a course.

THE EDUCATORS/TRAINERS

Although the technical considerations are important, the instruction itself is what determines the success of a distance learning course. The course content and preparation can be flawless and the method of receiving and sending information to learners technically feasible and accessible, but if the people conducting the course are not comfortable with or well suited to distance learning courses, the course will not be successful.

What do educators or trainers need to work successfully with distance learning? They should have four qualities: ability to learn new technology, a performance personality, flexibility, and time to create new materials and methods.

Ability to Learn New Technology

"Distance learning" encompasses many tools and runs the gamut from low-tech to high-tech applications. The technology and uses for it continue to evolve, and the applications in business and academia keep pushing learners' and educators' expectations for more effective forms of education. That's why educators and trainers must be willing to learn how to use new tools, combine tools in different ways, and adapt their educational strategies and materials to incorporate these tools.

Educators do not need to understand all the ins and outs, whys and wherefores of computers, broadcasting, engineering, and electronics. They don't need to be technicians. But they do need a basic understanding of how they're sending and receiving information from learners, so that they can create effective materials for the course. They also need a rudimentary understanding of how the tools work together, so that if something breaks down or goes wrong, they know what to do or whom to call.

What educators do need is a sense of fun and an enjoyment of learning how to work with new tools. That simple joy of learning something new and the expectation that their job will change (two attitudes good educators should have in abundance anyway) are all that's necessary to understand how the technical aspects play into a good distance learning course.

A Performance Personality

Not all distance learning technologies require educators to be "on," or even to be seen, by the learners taking their course. However, many distance learning technologies do require an educator's lessons or sessions to be videotaped, audiotaped, broadcast, or otherwise transmitted and stored. They require educators to be seen by learners and to "perform" for them. Some educators may teach a session before a classroom full of learners in one location and also be linked via satellite or computer to similar classrooms in remote locations. The connection may allow one-way or two-way visual and/or audio communication.

To be successful, an educator in this situation must do more than lecture or lead a discussion; he or she must also involve and interact with people seen only on a television monitor or heard over phone lines. Even if the educator and learners can see each other through this technology, it's up to the educator to create a sense of community among all the participants, making sure everyone can see, hear, and participate—responding to the needs of potentially hundreds of learners during one session. When educators or trainers broadcast information, preferably through two-way voice and visual communication links, they should practice using a few techniques to enhance the effectiveness of their presentation style. If you're an educator or a trainer whose presentation will be broadcast, practice the following.

Maintain Eye Contact with the Audience/Camera

When addressing a learner, whether in the same room or thousands of miles away, look directly toward that person. When addressing a group, scan the faces of people in the same room, as well as direct remarks to the camera. Always maintain eye contact with a person or people, even if it's through the camera. Never turn your back to the group or to the camera. Make sure you can be seen when you're conducting a lecture or leading a discussion.

Check the Camera's Position

The camera's ability to capture your movement as you facilitate the lesson is important, so that you're always visible and large enough on the screen that your movements are easily seen. You may have learners with special needs, so it's doubly important to make sure that you can be seen and heard within a classroom and across a transmission. Any hand gestures and facial expressions, as well as demonstrations and experiments, should be clearly seen.

Enunciate your words and speak at a slow, but conversational pace. Some distance learning systems may have a slight audio delay; a steady, but not rapid speaking rate is easy to understand.

Check the Audio

Make sure that your words can be easily heard. Practice using the microphone or walking around the room where microphones are stationed to ensure that you always can be heard. Many microphones in teleconferencing classrooms are designed to pick up and magnify sounds within a certain range. Always make sure that you can be heard when you're presenting information or answering questions, but that you don't inadvertently make distracting conversation or sounds when you're within range of sensitive microphones. When you present information to learners, speak clearly and loud enough to be heard through the microphone, with a natural, conversational inflection.

In addition, make sure that each learner can be heard, both in the room with you and across the network. If learners' desks or work stations aren't equipped with microphones, make sure that you repeat the comment or question so that learners in a remote location understand what's being said in the educator's/trainer's location or make sure that a microphone is made available to learners before they address the group.

When you show overlays, computer screens, handouts, or other visual aids that are viewed when you are not visible on screen, make sure that your audio descriptions match what is being shown. In other words, read, explain, or clarify what you're showing in the visual aid. Learners who may be unable to hear you, for example, need to know that what they see on the screen is what is being described.

If you work primarily with learners who use closed-captioning, check to make sure that all sites have the technology to use captioning. Some distance learning providers (such as Gallaudet University) offer captioning as part of their teleconferencing services.

Design Materials for Easy Showing on Camera or Computer Screen

The camera, whether in a larger teleconferencing room or connected to an individual personal computer for a desktop videoconference, should pick up and enlarge to the monitor's size any visuals you use during a presentation. Some teleconferencing classrooms allow two to four sites to be viewed on a monitor at one time, so the information you present may be drastically reduced on the monitor if your location is shown on a half to a quarter of the monitor's screen. If you're switching to a single view, so that all learners in all sites can see materials on the monitor, but not the other sites, explain when and why you're changing the monitor's viewpoint, then return to a more interactive setting when you've finished showing the materials you need to highlight.

If you're going to refer to handouts or numerous pages, for example, you may need to send copies to learners before the presentation. That way they can become familiar with the information you refer to or highlight. They also can follow their copy of smaller print or elaborate diagrams more easily than they might see the same materials on the monitor. If the presentation is going to be videotaped or audiotaped for later distribution to other learners, make sure that the materials you refer to are clearly identified and that copies will be made available to people who view only the tape.

Before a transmission, run a test broadcast to ensure that all materials may be seen during a broadcast. For example, information on a chalkboard or markerboard may "wash out" under lights or may not be easily contrasted with other backgrounds. Check to make sure that overheads, including information from LCD displays, can be easily viewed.

Keep the Energy High

Boring presentations are never desirable, but in a videoconference, taped program, or other distance learning broadcast, dull, stilted presentational styles seem even deadlier. Just because you're using state-of-the-art technology doesn't mean that you'll automatically have a high-quality presentation. You must constantly monitor the *performance* and ensure that you consistently meet your learners' needs.

You can keep up your energy level by talking with, not to, learners and by practicing your presentation ahead of time so that your style is smooth. You should be comfortable with the materials and the organization of topics for a session.

By being prepared, you're more naturally relaxed and you can more easily respond to learners' questions and comments. More of your personality comes across and helps build a link between learners working in the same room with you and the learners who see the presentation at another location or even at a later time.

A performance personality is especially important for educators or trainers working with broadcast media, including presentations that are videotaped. However, audiotaping, one-way audio transmissions, and even voice mail also require a performance personality. When learners can only hear you, but will not see you, your voice's projection, modulation, inflection, clarity, pace, and tone have to convey not only the content, but also the spirit of the presentation. You need a more descriptive style, and a pleasing voice, to present information only vocally.

Again, practice and playback of taped sessions can help you make your voice even better suited to distance learning relying on audio. Keep in mind that taped lessons, whether audio or video/audio, probably will be replayed several times. A good performance is worth repeating, but an annoying, grating, tired, blaring, or whispery soundtrack is difficult to hear once, much less several times. Make sure that your performance is worthy of multiple replays.

Even through e-mail, you should be outgoing, friendly, and professional in your performance. When learners rely on your written, sometimes informal messages as a primary means of communication in the course, your personality must be conveyed through your word choice, use of punctuation, chunking of the important ideas in the message, and the frequency of your messages. The same is true of any correspondence with learners, including letters and memoranda, as well as feedback on assignments and evaluations.

Flexibility

Good distance learning educators and trainers are flexible. They realize that sometimes the technology will not operate as they expected and that the technical capabilities probably will change during a course or before the course is offered again.

Flexibility in this situation also equals confidence. Educators should know the subject matter, feel comfortable with the technology, and also know how to vary their lesson plans, materials, and course-related activities to meet the needs of different learners or changing situations. They must update their materials frequently and keep checking the applicability and availability of resources used in their courses. This is particularly true of educators and trainers who work with Web sites, whose content, location, and even existence can change dramatically almost daily.

Flexibility should equal responsiveness. As more distance learning courses are offered, the marketplace becomes more competitive. Educators and trainers have to keep updating materials and looking for trends and changes within the subject matter. They must develop more involving, interesting ways to present the information and have learners participate in the course. Their presentational skills must be practiced and improved so that they offer the highest quality instruction possible. The technological expectations, and demands, of learners need to be met, which means that new materials and formats will have to be developed to take advantage of new tools or combinations of tools used to present information across a distance.

Time to Develop New Materials and Methods

The success of a distance learning program often relies on educators' and trainers' ability to work with the tools needed to transmit and receive information, develop materials suitable not only for the course content but also for the type(s) of distance learning employed, and test teaching or training methods to ensure that all learners' needs and learning preferences are being met. A great deal of time is needed to develop, present, update, evaluate, and plan changes for the next sessions of each distance learning course. Unfortunately, some administrators or executives fail to understand the need for or provide the resources, including time, that are necessary to develop an effective distance learning course. It may fall to the educators and trainers to advocate and explain the ongoing need for course development.

Much effort must go into the initial planning and development of distance learning materials and setting up the mechanics of sending and receiving information between learners and educators/trainers. But follow-up evaluations and ongoing planning to improve materials and methods are also crucial for a distance learning course's, or program's, success.

Each course must be evaluated. Its content, materials, and presentation styles and formats should be critiqued. Educators'/trainers' methods and presentational effectiveness should be evaluated, as should the technical aspects of the program, including cost, availability of resources, types of distance learning used in the course, and technical requirements for learners. The effectiveness, including an analysis of the costs and benefits to the educators/

trainers, learners, and institution offering the program, must be considered each time the course is offered.

It's not enough to be able to offer a distance learning course. The course must be worthwhile for all involved; it must show why distance learning, following a model of one educator/trainer per X number of learners is more effective than many educators/trainers for the same number of learners.

LEARNERS

How do you know if distance learning is a good way for you to increase your knowledge and skills? Some people learn better in a setting with other people than they do alone; some learners prefer working directly with an educator or a trainer, instead of working primarily on their own. Although distance learning can offer many benefits to learners, it is not a panacea for all educational or training needs. To help you decide if distance learning in general is a good alternative for you, ask the following questions.

Why Do You Want to Take a Distance Learning Course?

If you're required to take a course, and it's offered by your company, you have little choice in whether you'll be enrolled. However, you should also determine what, other than job security, you want to get out of the course.

If you're taking a course for personal reasons, determine why you want to take this particular course, what it will offer you in the short-term and the long-term. Taking a course just for the sake of something to do isn't a good reason; you'll need to be highly motivated to complete the course to your satisfaction.

What Motivates You?

If you motivate yourself, because you have a clear understanding of what you want to get out of the course and the benefits you'll receive upon its completion, you're a good candidate for distance learning. The most successful distance learners are self-motivated; they want to learn and they make sure they participate fully in the course.

If you need a nudge to motivate you to study, gather materials, complete assignments, participate in discussions, and so forth, you still might benefit from a distance learning course, but you'll have to get help in becoming motivated to complete the required course activities.

You might want to take the course with a friend or colleague, so that you have your own support network. You might also want to communicate with other learners taking the course, even if your communication is limited to e-mail, for example. Just knowing that you have support, and other learners also rely on you, can help motivate you to do your best.

Do You Prefer to Work Ahead or Do You Often Procrastinate?

One of the benefits of distance learning is the ability to learn at your own pace. Most courses provide a general framework for learning, so you can speed up or slow down as your schedule or personal needs dictate. However, if you procrastinate seriously enough that you might never complete the course requirements, you should develop a support network of people to motivate you to continue working toward the course's completion.

Some distance learning courses are more highly structured. They require participation in videoconferences at certain times or there may be a short turnaround time when materials are made available to you or expected to be submitted. Depending upon your learning pace and schedule, you might find a structured course meets your needs. Check with the vendor to learn how much flexibility you'll have in completing the course requirements.

How Many Other Responsibilities Do You Currently Have?

Distance learning courses take time and energy, and you have to complete much of the work on your own. If you're taking a noncredit course just for fun, you might not mind as much if you sometimes don't put 100 percent effort into the coursework. But if you need to master a subject as part of your ongoing education and career preparation, you need to give yourself adequate time to take the course and complete the work to your satisfaction. Before you take a course, make sure that you can devote as much, if not more, time to learning as you would if you took a course on-site.

Can You Take the Course in Another Setting or at Another Time?

Is distance learning the only option for you? If you might do better in a traditional course on-site or when you have more time to devote to learning, you probably should postpone taking a distance learning course.

If you are the type of learner who thrives on independence and is self-motivated, you probably will be equally or more successful in a distance learning course than in a traditional course, because you often can tailor the course to meet your personal needs.

How Well Do You Work in a Virtual Environment?

Isolation is a problem for some distance learners, who like to be with real people, not images on a computer screen or television monitor, much less those faceless entities represented by e-mail messages or voice mail. Distance learning has the capability of bringing learners together to share in a course, even though they're geographically isolated. Many courses are designed to promote, rather than inhibit, interaction among learners and educators/trainers.

Distance learning by itself doesn't imply an individual learning alone, unaided by peers or educators, any more than sitting in a traditional classroom assures that each person will talk with other students or the instructor. Depending upon your need for personal attention and interpersonal communication, you can select the appropriate type of distance learning course for you, to maximize or minimize the amount of communication you have with others.

CHECKLIST FOR EVALUATING POTENTIAL COURSES

If you're an adult learner planning to take a distance learning course, carefully check the program to be sure that it will meet your needs. The amount of interaction with educators, course requirements, the number and type of courses available through distance learning, the cost, and the quality of instruction are just some topics you'll need to investigate.

Many learners only want to take courses to brush up on skill areas, pursue an interest, or develop a new hobby. If that's your level of involvement with distance learning, you have more options for courses. Some online courses are free or are offered for a nominal fee. These courses are not offered for credit, but simply to help people learn.

Even if you take a highly structured course, you probably have fewer constraints on the amount of work expected from you and the way the work will be evaluated. Of all learners, you may have more opportunities to shop around for suitable courses; a variety of private vendors, individuals, academic institutions, companies, and nonprofit organizations can provide you with instruction.

On the other hand, you may be interested in a complete degree program. If so, you have more to investigate before you begin a course of study. For example, you'll need to find out if you can take all the required courses through distance learning or if you'll have to take some courses on-site.

Even if you can complete the degree through distance learning, you still may have to go on campus at some point. Some institutions require you to take exams on campus or at least go to a location where someone can proctor exams. You may have to go through an orientation or consult an advisor in person. In addition, you might receive a degree by taking courses from several institutions that have established cooperative programs or you might begin a degree program with distance learning courses, then switch to on-campus courses before you complete your degree work.

As more academic institutions develop distance learning programs, you'll be able to find more degree programs that can be tailored to your needs. Currently, however, you may need to check the specifics of what is expected of you and how much of your education can be completed through distance learning before you begin a particular program.

Employees who need specific training or additional coursework for a current or future job may need to take distance learning courses or seminars periodically. Although educational institutions may provide suitable courses, other providers also offer worthwhile training materials and activities. More private vendors offer distance training; in-house training programs increasingly give the option for videoconferencing and online training for their employees. Even certification programs or seminars to help employees pass exams, such as those for certified public accountants, for example, are commonplace.

Younger learners also may complete a good part of their education through distance learning. Accelerated courses, for example, provide children or teenagers with the opportunity to take additional courses that may not be offered in their schools; foreign language, music, and college-level courses are some types of classes suitable for distance learning. By taking additional courses, learners may receive college-level credit that can later be used toward a degree program or the knowledge and skills may be used for general education and self-improvement.

Learners who've had difficulty mastering a subject can find additional tutoring and assistance through other types of distance learning programs. By working at their own level and pace, learners can progress with materials that may have been difficult to understand in a traditional classroom setting or at the pace of other learners.

Children and teenagers who, for one reason or another, attend classes at home can use distance learning courses to enhance their education or to meet the educational requirements imposed by the school district or state. By participating in several types of distance learning activities, these learners can create a well-rounded program equal or superior to the type of program found in the traditional classroom.

If you're a learner of any age, motivated by personal interest or career-related need, you can use the list of questions in Figure 5.1 to help you evaluate the distance learning program or course you're considering. If you're an educator or a trainer, you should use this checklist to see if you're a good match for the type of course to be offered or developed.

Whether you're an educator, a trainer, or a learner, this checklist can help you determine if your needs fit with the type of course being considered or offered. Educators and trainers, too, need to see if the institution's or company's ideas about distance education match their own ideas about what is needed to develop a successful distance learning course.

Course Content

- What will be covered in the course?
- How will information be provided?
- How long will the course last?
- How long do learners have to complete course work?
- What type of evaluation is provided?
- What type of course is this (e.g. for credit, non-credit, toward a degree, toward a certification)?
- How transferable is the course credit?
- Who is the educator/trainer?
- What are the educator's/trainer's credentials?
- How does this course compare with on-site courses?
- How do learners interact with each other?
- How do learners interact with educator/trainer?
- How frequent is interaction among learners and educator/trainer?
- What are the course requirements?
- What types of distance learning are involved?
- How much of the course can be completed only through distance learning activities?
- How have other people evaluated this course?
- How does this course meet learners' needs (e.g. toward certification, toward degree completion, for personal interest, for skill development)?
- How does the type of interaction or teaching method match with my preferred method of learning?

Degree Programs

- How many courses can be taken through distance learning?
- How many courses must be taken on site?
- How are administrative duties (e.g. registration, payment, scheduling, advising) completed?
- How long do I have to complete the program?
- What are the requirements?
- How does this program compare with other degree programs offered through distance learning?
- How does this program compare to the degree program offered on site?
- What are the credentials of this institution/organization?
- What types of distance learning are involved in this program?
- Who are the educators?
- What are the educators' credentials?
- How have other people evaluated this program?
- How many courses can be taken at one time?
- When are courses offered?

(continued)

Figure 5.1 Checklist for evaluating distance learning courses.

- Which courses are offered if each course is not always available?
- How often are materials updated?

Time Frame

- How long does the course last?
- How long are materials made available?
- What is the time limit for completing activities?
- What type of follow up is provided after the course?
- How quickly can the course be completed?
- How often is the course offered?
- How flexible is the course (e.g. requirements to participate in a videoconferencing sessions held only on certain dates and times, 24-hour access to materials online)?

Cost

- What is the cost of a single course or seminar?
- What is the cost of an entire program?
- What are the costs for materials?
- What are the costs of instruction?
- How is the cost structure determined (e.g. flat fee per learner, a discount for multiple learners at same location)?

Technical Requirements

- What type(s) of equipment are learners required to provide or use?
- What types of materials, including software, are learners required to provide or use?
- Where can the course be taken?
- How will learners be connected with the sources of information?
- How are learners expected to participate in the course?
- How can course materials be accessed?
- Who is responsible for bringing together learners and educators?
- What type of distance learning set up will be used?
- How will the course be set up to meet learners' special needs (e.g. for signing or lip reading during a broadcast, mobility during a videoconference, larger print size for printed materials)?

Figure 5.1 Checklist for evaluating distance learning courses, continued

SUMMARY

The possibilities for designing materials, presenting them in different combinations, and developing programs offered at different times, in different ways, for very different learners makes distance learning exciting. The key is in determining how best to present information to meet a certain audience's needs for education and training, then designing courses to meet those needs.

E-Mail, Faxmail, and Voice Mail as Distance Learning Tools

Several communication tools, including e-mail, faxmail, and voice mail, help bridge the communication gap in distance learning courses. Although each tool can be used as the primary means of disseminating information in a distance learning course, each is better suited to supplementing other instructional tools. Sending messages electronically is an important component of any distance learning course; use of e-mail, faxmail, and/or voice mail creates a more personal educational or training atmosphere. It makes communication possible at any time, and allows the one-to-one communication not always possible in other distance learning technologies (e.g., through Web materials, via broadcast).

Electronic mail (e-mail) is one of the simplest, yet most effective communication tools; of the three tools discussed in this chapter, it's the only one around which an entire distance learning course can be based. Similar to the way familiar correspondence courses using surface mail operate, e-mailed course materials and correspondence with educators can be sent to individuals who enroll in a course. But e-mail offers a faster method of communication and also serves as a link to more than just one person at a time. These two factors make it more desirable than surface mail for correspondence courses.

Faxmail is a newer tool that combines the best of e-mail and faxed communication. Although it's not in common use now, some universities (e.g., University of Phoenix) have incorporated faxmail into their distance learning technologies. Future courses may be built around this communication medium.

Voice mail has even been used as a primary method of sending and receiving information in some distance learning courses, but telephone calls, much less voice mail messages, are seldom ideal for the complexities of running most distance learning courses. Voice mail, however, is a good supplement, because it allows a more personal communication. Although e-mail messages may be more elaborate and allow documents to be attached to the messages, voice mail lets learners and educators/trainers hear each other. The nuances of spoken language come across more clearly in voice mail messages, unlike e-mail or faxmail.

These three tools can enhance other forms of distance learning; educators/trainers should consider how one or all can be incorporated into their distance learning programs.

NETWORKS AND E-MAIL

E-mail is a flexible tool, because it can be used in-house to connect people via intranets or it can send messages across the Internet. E-mail can be sent to users though a local-area network (LAN), such as a network linking all company employees or students within a university. A network limited among users within a geographic area, such as a town, may even be considered a LAN, and the learners within a geographic region can participate in distance learning courses with local institutions or businesses.

An intranet is an internal or in-house network designed for use within a company or an institution. In-house correspondence and announcements of upcoming distance learning courses may be sent through the intranet. Most companies are creating intranets to link employees' workstations electronically and enhance in-house communication. Training is only one area to benefit from intranets. Not only can e-mail be used to send messages to all employees about upcoming training opportunities, but also individual messages can be directed to employees taking a course. Taking an in-house, e-mail-based course can be an efficient way to complete a company's training requirements, because employees can send and respond to e-mail whenever they have a break in the work day. They don't have to leave their workstation to attend a training session or travel to another location for days at a time. Intranets can make in-house training more efficient for trainers and learners, and more cost effective for supervisors.

The most popular network, the Internet, goes beyond the limitations of a LAN, as users can converse with anyone who is connected to this largest of all wide-area networks (WANs). E-mail sent through the Internet might be directed from one user to another, but it also might involve messages to and from mailing lists and bulletin boards. Many Web sites include hypertext links to a company's or an individual's e-mail; these mailto: links and e-mail hypertext links allow users to send e-mail while they browse a Web site. E-mail along the Internet can enhance distance learning programs as well as serve as a primary means of communication among learners, educators/trainers, and the institution or company offering the course.

Although e-mail systems can be quite advanced, allowing users to attach text and graphics or serving as a secondary tool during videoconferences, even the simplest, plain-text systems offer educational advantages. Because e-mail can be sent from one person directly to another, or to a group simultaneously, it creates a network of users who can discuss their ideas, share information, and evaluate documents, for example.

E-MAIL CORRESPONDENCE WITHIN COURSES

Some educators/trainers rely on e-mail as a primary means of transmitting course information. Distance learning courses can be structured around e-mail as the only method of disseminating information. More often, however, e-mail supplements other types of instruction. In addition to simple e-mail messages, mailing lists, discussion groups, and multiple-user domains (or dimensions), known as MUDs, also facilitate learning.

E-mail can be used in conjunction with desktop videoconferences during a conference session as well as sent separately outside conference times. During a videoconference or in a MUD, several people may *converse* by keying in information that the group can see and respond to at the same time. However, e-mail is often used because it's perceived as a more personal, immediate, and private form of communication, similar to a letter, memorandum, or voice-mail message.

Educators and trainers use e-mail more flexibly than any other electronic distance learning technology. Most computer users are familiar with e-mail and it is inexpensive and more widely available than other electronic distance learning tools. These reasons make e-mail an increasingly common part of education in general and distance learning in particular.

E-mail is becoming increasingly important in a traditional classroom or even within an in-house training program. Other instructional methods might be very traditional. The educator or trainer may provide in-person instruction to a group within a traditional lab, classroom, or boardroom. Learners usually work with traditional paper-based materials, like books, articles, and other primary documents, as well as electronic media, such as Web-based information, multimedia presentations, and hands-on demonstrations.

But e-mail adds another dimension to the way that educators and learners interact. It provides more opportunities for "conversation" outside the traditional classroom and it encourages learning to take place any time, any place. Because e-mail can be sent at any time, it's an ideal way for learners and educators who don't work typical 9-to-5 days.

Employees may not have time to concentrate on the information they gained in a seminar or a training session until several hours after they get home or can take a break on the job. They may think they understood everything—until they try to complete a job task and need to clarify some information. As they think about what they've learned, they may have ideas to share with the trainer and the group or they may want to ask more questions so they can learn even more about a topic. These situations probably don't occur when the educator and learner can meet face-to-face, and the learner may not be able to wait until the next *official* session to ask a question, make a comment, or suggest a solution. E-mail helps learners capture the moment when they need to "talk" to the educator, but he or she is unavailable personally.

In the same way, educators may receive several messages from learners who sent messages at 3:00 A.M., or who periodically had questions throughout the day. Late at night, early in the morning, on a brief break, or at a regularly scheduled *correspondence* time, educators can sit down to read through messages, prioritize them, and respond to learners, individually or as a group. A phone call, an in-person visit, or discussions before, during, or just after a training session or class meeting might not be convenient ways for an educator to provide learners with the information, or the personal attention, they may need. E-mail lets educators take as little or as long as they need to meet learners' needs, but it allows this communication to take place at the educator's convenience.

Although convenience of writing and responding to e-mail all at one time and the possibility of sending e-mail at any time can certainly be benefits, e-mail also has some other advantages. It can encourage more communication among participants in a course. For example, it encourages many learners to ask questions, request clarification, receive additional assistance, and present progress reports. Some people are simply shy in a group setting; they don't like to ask questions, or they may feel intimidated by other learners or even the subject matter. Somehow a question sent via e-mail doesn't seem as potentially "stupid" as a learner may feel it might sound in person.

Because e-mail tends to be sent quickly and spontaneously, and the messages usually are short and direct, learners send more messages—whenever they need to communicate with the educator or trainer. Educators, too, are encouraged to write more often. They may not want to single out one person for additional guidance or correction, but with a personal e-mail message, they can spend more time, and give more direction, to people who need their assistance. That, in turn, encourages learners to request more assistance, because no one else in the group has to know that they wanted, or needed, additional help.

E-mail also allows more interpersonal dialogue between learners or learners and educators. Discussions within a course are usually limited by the amount of work that needs to be completed in a session and the time constraints of a single session. E-mail expands the time for discussion, because participants can take the discussion off-line and write directly to each other, as often or as little as needed to finish the conversation.

E-mail is a practical way to transfer more formal information, too. For example, it's easy to send notices about upcoming quizzes or evaluations to the group or to individuals. Reminder notices, descriptions of assignments, and basic course information like schedules, reading lists, and objectives can be mailed, and assignments, drafts of documents, progress reports, and other course-based materials learners are required to complete can be returned to educators electronically. Each person who receives the information can then decide to store the message for future reference, download the information to disk or a printer, or simply delete it after reading the message.

E-mail as the primary means of communication in a distance learning course works similarly to e-mail used as only one method of transmitting and sharing information. Educators work with e-mail in the following ways as the foundation of a distance learning course.

Communication with Students Individually

Individual responses to learners' questions and comments can be sent from the educator/trainer to the learner, without other learners "listening in" on the conversation. These messages are best suited to personal communication, such as evaluations of the learner's performance or additional tutoring.

Frequent use of e-mail helps educators/trainers and learners build a personal relationship with each other which, in turn, encourages more frequent communication. Learners who feel comfortable using e-mail like the fact that they can disclose personal information or simply information they don't want other learners to know; they can ask questions they may not feel comfortable asking in a classroom or during a training session; they can discuss concerns and share ideas in greater detail than time might allow in a training or classroom session or during the breaks before or after the session.

Most e-mail systems automatically record when an e-mail message was sent, when it was received, when it was saved, and when or if the recipient responded to the message. Referring to saved messages, or even tracking whether you responded to a message, are easy tasks. Using e-mail can thus help educators/trainers keep track of how much time they're spending with each learner, what each message was about, and how they responded to the messages. This type of tracking can also help administrators when they compile records of educator/trainer-learner interaction and the effectiveness of using e-mail instead of or in addition to other communication tools.

Communication with Students as a Group

Group messages are an efficient way to share course assignments, announcements, and core materials. Longer texts and graphics can be attached to the message so that learners can download, save, or read the information once.

E-mail can reach many people at the same time and can save paper resources. A course outline, for example, can be used and stored electronically, then it's up to the individual learner who received the outline through an e-mail message whether to download the information on paper.

Communication with the Organization or Institution Originating the Course

Administrative tasks, such as course registration and payment, and general information about the course, schedule, and institution/organization can be completed via e-mail before learners ever participate in a course. Notices of upcoming courses, reminders about upcoming events, and announcements of changes in procedures are common types of administrative e-mail messages.

Communication with Outside Resources

E-mail messages are often sent to experts in a particular field, specialists within an industry, or even the general public through discussion groups, newsgroups, and mailing lists, for example. Using e-mail sent to individuals or a list can be one way for learners to gather more information to supplement the materials and information they receive as part of the course.

Seldom is learners' work limited to e-mail messages only, but e-mail provides a way regularly to contact other participants in the course. A typical e-mail-based course might work like the following scenario.

The institution or organization offering the course places announcements in electronic journals, at its Web site, through mailing lists and bulletin boards, and in print media, as well, to announce the course and generate interest in it. When a potential participant learns of the course, there may be several ways in which to sign up, everything from an in-person registration to mailed registration to electronic application and payment. Registration and other administrative tasks are completed before the learner begins taking the course.

If the course is a regularly scheduled offering, such as a university's quarter or semester course, usually there are firm time limits for the beginning and the ending dates. Between these dates learners may have a great deal of flexibility in completing assignments or they may be required to participate in as highly structured activities as they would if they took the course on-site.

If the course is offered as a noncredit course or by a private vendor, frequently learners have as much time as they need (within some minor limitation, such as up to a year) to complete the course. In-house training programs may be more highly structured, to fit with the company's needs for a trained workforce within a specified time frame.

Within the course, the educator or trainer establishes guidelines for e-mail. Course announcements, assignments, and core materials, such as study outlines and objectives, may be sent directly to each student on a designated day. Evaluations, such as comments on assignments or test results, might be provided at a later time in the week. Learners who have received the materials and are working through a lesson have the opportunity to write to the educator or trainer, and possibly other students, to discuss the materials, ask questions, and get feedback about the lesson.

Follow-up with educators or trainers can also take place after the coursework is completed. Some institutions offer e-mail services up to one year after learners take a course, in case they have questions, concerns, or simply want to keep in touch.

This type of course is best suited for learners who are highly motivated and work well on their own. Although e-mail can be a very personal way to communicate—in fact, many writers disclose more information when they write messages—it also is one-sided. The learner submits a message, then waits for a response. Even if the response is sent quickly, the reader receives the information in a vacuum, without the familiar cues of body language, tone, and inflection to help convey the message. If the reader then wants to respond, the communication again is a one-sided comment on the previous message, with perhaps new information provided or requested.

E-mail is convenient, but sometimes learners prefer the face-to-face communication found in a classroom or training center. If the writer fails to craft the message carefully, the words can come across as flat, dry, angry, bored, and so forth—even though the writer didn't intend this interpretation. If the writer responds hurriedly or fails to proofread the message, the message's organization, word choice, and grammar might not convey exactly what the writer intended. E-mail's effectiveness often relies on the quality of the writing. Even so, e-mail is often more efficient than correspondence courses conducted by surface mail and it encourages more interaction between the learner and educator or trainer.

SETTING UP AN E-MAIL COURSE

Whether learners and educators/trainers participate in a distance learning course exclusively or partially via e-mail, the first step in setting up a course is to make sure everyone can communicate with this technology. Learners and educators usually exchange e-mail addresses, just as they might exchange phone or fax numbers, so they can easily communicate with each other. People who have more than one e-mail address should specify which address should be used for correspondence about the course; there's no point in sending information to a mailbox that won't be opened for several days or one that receives perhaps hundreds of notices a day from a mailing list. Creating an e-mail directory for participants in a course and distributing the list is important to encourage people to send messages.

Sometimes users need to communicate with people they haven't met "personally" on the Internet and they have to track down an Internet address. A good place to locate information about people who have an e-mail address somewhere in the United States is the Internet White Pages, a Web-based directory that locates individuals by name. (Many browsers, such as Netscape, include a menu item, button, or hypertext link to take users directly to the White Pages. The Internet White Pages link through Netscape is currently found at http://home.netscape.com/home/internet-white-pages.html.) Depending upon the format of the browser or the user's selections from White Pages searches, the listing may provide an individual's name, street address, phone number, and/or e-mail address. The directory may be expanded to all countries in North America, but currently it lists U.S. users.

Another way to locate addresses for e-mail correspondence with individuals or companies is to check the Web pages of individuals, companies, or organizations that interest you. Often there's a *mailto* link on a Web page that not only provides immediate access to e-mail, but also lists the e-mail address when the link is highlighted. The following pointers can help educators or trainers use e-mail more effectively in their courses.

Set Up Guidelines for Using E-mail

Learners should know when it will be appropriate to send e-mail, as well as how you expect to work with them electronically. Setting up a schedule when information will be posted to the group or made available to individuals is a good idea; it sets up the expectation that materials will be available on a certain date and provides some structure for the course. State how often learners are required to respond to assignments or how they are expected to use e-mail within the course. Provide examples or instructions for writing appropriate e-mail messages.

Determine the Length of a Typical E-mail Reading/Response Session

Some educators complain that their work would never be finished if they didn't set limits on the amount of time they work electronically in a single day. You might decide to spend one hour at the end of the workday to answer e-mail and post new information. Otherwise, you might find that you spend too much time answering a few messages.

Learners should know when you typically read your e-mail. If they like to send messages at 4 A.M. and need a response by 8 A.M., they need to know if you generally read your mail early in the morning, whenever you have a few minutes, only every other day, and so on.

Also, remind learners of your time zone. This is especially important when learners are separated across different time zones, which is very likely for courses offered nationally or internationally. Make people aware of your geographic location, especially if you regularly schedule time for working with e-mail. Although e-mail can be sent and retrieved at any time, learners may expect an immediate response. Knowing when you tend to read your e-mail can save learners frustration in wondering if their message has been received and when you might respond.

Announce Your Unavailability

If you know you won't have access to your mail for a day or longer, let people know. They may wonder if the message was received or if your response was lost. Announcing times when you, or your e-mail system, will be unavailable also saves you from reading hundreds of backed-up messages when you get a chance to catch up on your mail.

Run a Technical Test Early in the Course

Before you assume that the course will run smoothly from a technical standpoint, conduct a test session to ensure that all participants can send and receive information in a useful format.

Develop Suitable E-mail Materials

Long documents, especially those with several chunks of information, may not be suitable as an e-mail message. They might be usable as an attachment, but keep in mind that learners, like educators, prefer short, direct messages that take little time to read. Long, scrollable documents full of long sentences or paragraphs are not very readable.

Graphics should be chosen carefully. If you don't provide or specify the type of e-mail software, or the type of hardware required to work with the chosen system, make sure that the graphics you send can be read. Simple graphics are preferable to elaborate graphics that require more memory.

Although e-mail encourages interaction, and more instead of less communication should be encouraged, avoid inundating learners with dozens of messages at a time. Clearly label each message so that learners understand that it's for the course; then they can prioritize the message by its timeliness and topic.

A FEW E-MAIL BASICS

For e-mail to be an effective educational tool, both educators and learners need to know how to use it wisely and politely. Although e-mail use is generally a positive experience, it can be ineffective, or downright painful, if some simple rules of composition and etiquette aren't followed:

1. Keep the message short. A short message is much easier to read and respond to than a long, scrollable message.

2. Get to the point. Know what you need to explain or ask before you start to write the message. Clearly state the purpose of your message and use a direct style.

3. Be polite. Brevity doesn't mean abruptness; you have the space to be polite. Request information and explain why you need it or how it will be used. Indicate if you're responding to someone else's message. Thank the person who'll receive the message for the information you're requesting.

4. Write a coherent, grammatically correct message. E-mail should be less formal than a letter, memorandum, or other document, but it still should follow the conventions of standard English. Write complete sentences. Use punctuation and use it correctly. Structure the message so it flows logically from beginning to middle to end and indicates the relationship of ideas. Choose your words precisely and accurately. Check the spelling.

5. Avoid the cutesies. If you develop a standard signature, header, or footer, make it look professional. Avoid "cutesy" graphics or quotations. Save the smiley faces, frowny faces, and other graphics for personal messages to your family and friends.

6. Know where you're sending the message. If you intend to send a message to a mailing list or newsgroup, for example, check the address to ensure that the message will be sent to the entire group. If you're sending a message only to an individual, double check the address for accuracy. If you're using a *forward* or a *reply* function, check the address to ensure that your message will be sent to the person or group you really want to read the message. If you take a moment to double check the address where you're sending the message, you don't inadvertently send the message somewhere else, creating a situation that's confusing or embarrassing at best.

7. Make sure that the receiver knows how to send you a return message. Write a unique, specific subject line. Include your return address or other identifying information so that the receiver can tell at a glance who sent the message and where a response can be directed.

8. Give people time to respond. Although e-mail encourages quick response times, remember that sometimes servers go down, people go away and don't have access to their e-mail for hours or days, or your message may require some research or consideration before a response can be sent. Send your messages in a timely manner so that you have a little time to wait for a response. If you don't receive a response within a few days, at most, send the message again.

9. Know the protocol for the group, if you're sending to more than one person simultaneously. *Lurking*, or silently reading messages sent to a newsgroup, discussion group, or mailing list, is fine as you learn how the group operates, what it's unwritten rules of conduct are, and how people typically structure and respond to messages. When you become familiar with the group, you should actively participate in it. It's always a good idea to read any notices posted from the list server, as well as learning the group's dynamics, before you post a first message to the group. If you learn the group's protocol first, you can generally avoid being *flamed* by group members.

10. Give some specific cues as to your attitude, priority of your message, and so forth. A specific subject line, accurate word choice, and a few minutes of care in writing, rereading, and revising your message can help ensure that your message conveys exactly what you want. Because readers can't see you when they read your printed message, they have to fill in the gaps about the context of your message. Providing word cues to indicate your mood, tone, and meaning help keep readers from misinterpreting your message.

A FEW EXAMPLES OF E-MAIL USE

K-12 students especially enjoy e-mail; teachers can use e-mail pen pals to help younger students learn about other countries and other regions of their own country. E-mail can strengthen writing skills and improve computer skills at the same time. Gathering career information from mentors and tutors via e-mail can supplement other school-to-work initiatives. In these and many other ways, e-mail can be an effective educational networking and correspondence tool.

One educational network for K-12 students is described in Figure 6.1. The eMail Classroom Exchange can be used to link younger learners with learners in other schools world wide. Information about the home school can be exchanged with learners from other schools and the database of participants continues to grow as new schools join the network.

Higher education and adult training courses can also be e-mail-based. One example is the online arts courses offered by the Virtual Art School (see Figure 6.2). A portion of the Web site's description of the courses explains how e-mail is used to send graphic and textual information to learners, receive information from learners, and communicate with a personal tutor. The complete course is conducted *virtually*, and the primary communication medium is e-mail. Learners can download software to help them work with the materials, but all necessary course materials are provided electronically.

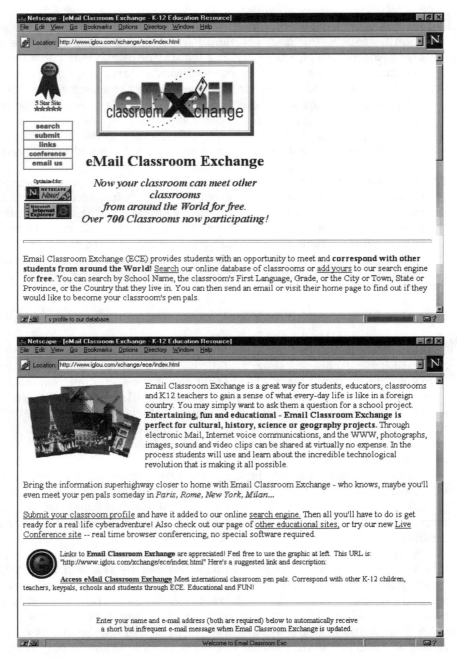

Figure 6.1 Classroom E-mail.

http://www.iglou.com/xchange/ece/index.html
© eMail Classroom Exchange 1996

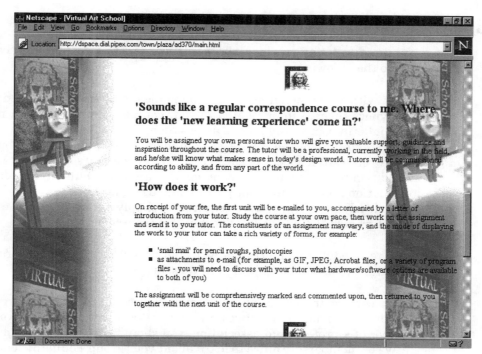

Figure 6.2 Virtual Art School.

http://dspace.dial.pipex.com/town/plaza/ad370/main.html
© Virtual Art School 1996

BULLETIN BOARDS

Bulletin boards, by themselves, are not suitable for presenting content in a distance learning course, but they can provide supplementary information. A university's or an organization's electronic bulletin board can be the recognized site for posting announcements, changes in courses, announcements of new courses, registration deadlines and procedures, calendars, and information about other special events.

Many professional societies and associations maintain bulletin boards not only for members, but also for people with similar interests or potential interests. Educators may want to get a list of professional associations appropriate for their course's subject and help learners gain access to the associations' bulletin boards. The notices might lead learners to other sources of information and educational or training experiences that can supplement the instruction given in the course. And additional work with other electronic sources is also useful for learners who hope to understand more about increasing their knowledge through electronic sources of information.

USING BULLETIN BOARDS IN A DISTANCE LEARNING COURSE

If you're an educator or a trainer who wants learners to access bulletin boards, you can do the following:

1. Check with professional societies, companies, and organizations dealing with topics covered in or related to your course's content to learn if they have bulletin boards and how to access them.
2. At the beginning of the course, post guidelines for accessing the bulletin boards you want learners to check throughout the course.
3. In addition to the technical instructions for accessing bulletin boards, post information about protocol for posting and using notices.
4. State clearly how learners are required or simply encouraged to use information from bulletin boards as part of their course activities.

If you're an educator or a trainer who offers a distance learning course, you may also want to use bulletin boards in these ways:

1. Check with your institution or organization to learn about appropriate bulletin boards for your notices and how to post information. If you're a member of a professional association, you should check with the administrative or membership office to learn about your group's bulletin board and how it can be accessed. You may need to start a bulletin board for learners taking your course, with the approval and guidance of administrators or managers at your institution or company. You also may want to set up a distance learning bulletin board within your company or institution to keep everyone informed about your courses and upcoming educational or training sessions.
2. Develop notices that will stand out from all the others. Write a catchy title or phrase. Keep the description brief, but provide everything potential learners will need to become interested in the course and register for it. Use graphics, color, and hypertext links to attract favorable attention and to connect learners with sources of additional information.
3. Update notices frequently. Readers tire of old notices or electronic information that looks the same visit after visit. Take the time to craft the notices so that they inspire potential learners to find out more about your distance learning course. Delete outdated information.

MAILING LISTS

Like bulletin boards, mailing lists are not appropriate for transmitting the bulk of information for a distance learning course, but they are another good source of supplementary information. Mailing lists provide a forum for discussion groups.

Anyone can join one or several mailing lists, and subscribers can post messages as often as they like. Mailing lists can be found for almost every interest area imaginable. For example, Table 6.1 indicates the diversity of mailing lists.

To subscribe to a mailing list, address a message to the *listserv*, according to the address you've located for the mailing list to which you want to subscribe. Usually, instructions are provided, but in general a new subscriber types the *listserv*'s address in the e-mail message's *To* line and skips the *Subject* line. In the body of the message, the following should be keyed in:

```
subscribe [your e-mail address]
```

Here is an example:

```
subscribe lporter@bgnet.bgsu.edu
```

Within 24 hours, if the subscription has been noted and "approved" by the *listserv*, the new subscriber receives information about the mailing list. Instructions for *unsubscribing*, or getting off the list, as well as for posting notices, responding to individuals and to the list, and following the list's protocol, are provided. Sometimes the *listserv* sends the FAQ for the list, which new users

Table 6.1 Representative General Mailing Lists

Main Menu Listings include the following categories:	*Within each category are several newsgroups. For example, the misc.* listing includes hundreds of newsgroups, including these representative listings:*
alt.*	misc.activism.*
bionet."	misc.answers
bit.*	misc.books.technical
biz.*	misc.business.*
comp.*	misc.consumers.*
courts.*	misc.creativity
general.*	misc.education.*
k12.*	misc.entrepreneurs.*
misc.*	misc.fitness.*
news.*	misc.forsale.*
rec.*	misc.handicap
sci.*	misc.headlines.*
soc.*	misc.health.*
talk.*	

are encouraged to save for future reference. This introductory message should be saved, at least; it might be handy to print a copy.

Active mailing lists generate dozens, if not hundreds, of messages each day, so subscribers should be warned that messages can pile up very quickly! People who don't access their e-mail often, or who subscribe to several mailing lists, probably will find their mailbox overflowing within a day or two. Because mailing lists are so active, they're a good source for discussing topics, asking questions, sending advice, sharing experiences, and simply networking with people who share the same interest. Learners can therefore build a network of international contacts quickly and they can learn a great deal by asking their online colleagues for guidance or assistance. Mailing lists are an excellent way to foster mentoring relationships.

USING MAILING LISTS IN A DISTANCE LEARNING COURSE

Because subscribers of mailing lists dealing with work-related topics (in contrast to hobby-oriented or fun mailing lists) tend to be professionals who joined the list to share business-related concerns, protocol for mailing lists about professions should be followed exactly. Very practically, learners who send messages to their colleagues, or potential employers and colleagues, should carefully write and respond to posts to the list; their messages will be more carefully scrutinized than those sent to hobby-related lists.

Many professionals are encouraged to follow threads of discussion about topics they need to understand for their job; they may become impatient if the list becomes clogged with irrelevant or poorly written posts. These readers simply don't have the time to read through, much less respond to, posts from *newbies* who fail to follow the list's protocol. Educators/trainers should therefore make sure that learners understand the purpose of each mailing list and the protocol for the lists, whether very informal or highly professional, before they begin posting messages to a list.

If you're an educator or a trainer who wants to supplement course materials with discussions on a mailing list, you should do the following:

1. Locate the addresses of mailing lists about your course's content.
2. Subscribe to and monitor the lists you want learners to join. Become familiar with the audience and common topics covered by the list.
3. Download and distribute the introductory notice from the *listserv* to learners who will be subscribing.
4. Ensure that learners are familiar with writing effective e-mail messages.
5. Provide learners with the addresses of lists in which they may want, or will be required, to participate.
6. State clearly how learners will use information gathered from mailing lists in the current course.

7. Send a message to the list, explaining how the people participating in your course will be using the list. Encourage the current members of the list to welcome the newbies.

NEWSGROUPS

Newsgroups are often called discussion groups, as are mailing lists. Discussion groups also can be created within a LAN, such as a group of learners who want to discuss a topic just within their group. This group may set up a specific time in which to conduct a discussion with numerous participants. A newsgroup or a mailing list, on the other hand, is a wide-open forum for anyone with access to the Internet to add comments to an ongoing discussion, provide news, start a new thread of conversation, and so on.

Newsgroups, like mailing lists, are listed by interest area. If a course involves travel, for example, participants may want to post general questions to other people outside the course so that they can learn more about travel to a particular area. Messages are usually grouped by theme, so that the original message and responses to it can be easily located.

Each message's title will be displayed on a menu list of hypertext links directly below the originally posted topic. To view the ongoing thread of a particular discussion, readers only need to move from one link to the next in the hierarchy to follow the comments. If some messages in the hierarchy don't seem interesting, they can be skipped; the posts can be read in any order and readers can see all, a few, or none of the posts, as they like. The following messages in Figures 6.3 and 6.4 illustrate such an original message and one reply.

Subject:	Need a Distance Learning Course
Date:	Sun. 20 Oct 1996 04:33:35-0700
From:	brfraser@xxxxx.com
Organization:	XXXXX Corporation
Newsgroups:	misc.education.adult

I'm looking for a distance learning course about physics. I have an undergraduate degree in business and general science, so I'm interested in either an undergraduate or a graduate level course. This should be a credit course, and I'd prefer to take the course through the Internet.

Does anyone know of an upcoming course that meets my requirements?

Figure 6.3 E-mail request for information.

Subject:	Re: Need a Distance Learning Course
Date:	Sun. 20 Oct 1996 06:40:50-0700
From:	sjbecket@XXXXX.XXX.edu
Organization:	XXXXX University
Newsgroups:	misc.education.adult

XXXXX University offers several introductory physics courses through distance learning programs. The course I'll be teaching next term is offered on site and through the Web. If you'd like more information, visit our Web site at http://www.xxxxx.edu/disted/physics. You can write me directly off line for more info about my course.

Figure 6.4 Newsgroup response to request.

Most browsers have a separate button, menu item, or hypertext link to locate an updated list of all newsgroups. From this general listing, users can move through other layers of links which refer to more specific lists of topics. For example, a list of newsgroups marked "rec.*" may include several listings for newsgroups about recreation, including such diverse topics as skydiving, video, biking, and travel. A click on the specific hypertext link referring to a recreation topic, like travel, brings up the most recent posts for that newsgroup. Previous posts can be retrieved through another hypertext link. Clicking on a particular post brings up the specific message, which can be read, printed, saved to a file, or responded to. Users who want to reply to the posted message can immediately send a message, which will be added as the next post in the continuing discussion of the topic. The newsgroup continues *discussing* the item of interest until the thread dies out, usually within a day or two.

Newsgroups are a good way to generate comments and feedback about a particular topic. They can be useful to learners and educators who want to expand the number of perspectives offered by the current group of course participants. However, like individual e-mail messages or those posted to discussion groups or mailing lists, the information from a newsgroup is as likely to be inaccurate, misleading, inappropriate, or useless as it is to be helpful, insightful, polite, and accurate.

In short, information gleaned from newsgroups should be scrutinized just as carefully as information from any other source. Simply because someone posted a reply doesn't mean that the information is more useful or accurate than information from other sources. However, newsgroups do generate lots of comments and a hot topic can provide lots of open-ended discussion for several days. They can be an interesting source of information to be used with courses. (See Appendix B for a list of newsgroups dealing with distance learning.)

MULTIPLE-USER DOMAINS/DIMENSIONS (MUDS)

A multiple-user domain, also known as a multiple-user dimension (MUD), facilitates conversation in real time among several participants. Although many people still think of MUDs as places where users can role-play or create an elaborate game setting, MUDs are increasingly used in educational settings. They allow learners to take on a persona, if they like, to role-play work-related situations, for example. They also give participants a place in which to *chat* with others about a topic.

MUDs can be very simple, involving text-only conversations that have to be keyed in. However, with the advent of more advanced hypermedia applications, MUDs may allow participants to talk to each other. The latest technology allows users to scan in images, such as a head shot, that can be attached to a movable on-screen "body." This virtual person can be manipulated around a virtual coffee shop, library, or other setting to interact with other virtual people. As the technology becomes more sophisticated and more commonly used, MUDs can provide a virtual environment for more formal collaboration, simulations, demonstrations, and role playing.

USING A MUD IN A DISTANCE LEARNING COURSE

If you're an educator or a trainer interested in using a MUD for people enrolled in your course, you might try the following:

1. **Determine the best time for a group meeting.** If learners are scattered across different time zones or are limited in their online access, you may have to set up several times for the meeting.
2. **Establish rules for using the MUD, so that everyone can participate equally.** If you're developing a role-play, state the rules for adopting roles and acting out a scenario. Make sure that some outgoing personalities don't take over the role-play; monitor the MUD to ensure that everyone is participating.
3. **Publicize the MUD well in advance of its use.** Make sure that all learners know how to access the site and what to do, as well as when the MUD will be active.
4. **State how the MUD will be used in the course and how learners will use the information and experiences gained from their participation as part of the course.** The course syllabus, as well as assignments and reminders

before the MUD, are good places to describe the MUD and how it should be used. You may want to set up a FAQ if you're also providing information at a Web site.

5. Facilitate the MUD and oversee its use. As real-time online interaction becomes more accessible to all potential users, MUDs will provide more educational and training opportunities. As learners interact in virtual environments, the types of simulations and skill practice they can encounter are "virtually" limitless.

FAXMAIL IN A DISTANCE LEARNING COURSE

An "in-between" technology that in some ways resembles e-mail, fax, and voice mail is faxmail. This fax and voice mail system allows learners and educators/trainers to send and receive messages anytime. The "voice mail for faxes" is delivered to an electronic address, from which the recipient can retrieve the information via a fax machine or fax modem. This system allows learners to receive and send information even when they aren't near a computer to pick up their e-mail messages. All learners need to do is find a fax machine so they can retrieve the information about their course.

Sometimes long documents may be difficult to attach to e-mail messages. Faxmail helps solve the problem of long attachments or documents with lots of graphics.

This type of communication can be the primary means of transmitting information among educators/trainers and learners, as the University of Phoenix's Center for Distance Education uses for distance learning courses. Faxmail can also be used as a way to supplement other types of communication, including e-mail or voice mail.

VOICE MAIL IN A DISTANCE LEARNING COURSE

Voice mail allows the personal touch of voice communication, with all its nuances; this tool lets learners and educators/trainers develop a better sense of the people behind the course. Because most phone systems are designed to record voice mail messages at any time, learners and educators/trainers can communicate with each other at any time, from any place with available telephones. Like faxmail, voice mail can be picked up at any time and no computer technology is required to access the message. These strengths can make voice mail more useful to learners who currently lack access to e-mail.

Nevertheless, voice mail offers some obvious disadvantages, too. The length of the message may be limited to three or fewer minutes, which may not be enough time to leave the complete message. If the person leaving the message is skilled in leaving a voice mail message, the recording can be an effective communication tool. If the person meanders around the reason for the message, lacks focus, or has distracting vocal mannerisms, the message may be difficult to understand.

To make the most of voice mail communication, follow these guidelines when you leave a message:

1. Know what you want to say. You may need to jot down the key points or questions for your message before you dial. If you are requesting information or need to ask a question, be specific in identifying exactly what you need. If you're leaving information that's been requested, write it down so that you can clearly and easily give the pertinent information.
2. Identify yourself. State your name, phone number, and so forth, so that your listener knows immediately who you are and where you're from.
3. Keep the message brief. If you have several points to make, you may need to leave more than one message. If you do, make sure that each message has its own purpose and main point. Be direct; state your message clearly. Limit the amount of information in one message so that you don't have to rush through the information.
4. Speak clearly and loudly enough to be recorded. Enunciate. Speak in a normal tone, with conversational inflection. Be pleasant.
5. If you don't receive a response (and one was required) within two days at most (depending upon the urgency of the message), make a follow-up call.

When you play your voice mail messages, follow these guidelines:

1. Write down the caller's name, phone number, and purpose of the message.
2. Listen to the rest of the message.
3. Save the message.
4. Replay the message to check the information and pay attention to vocal cues indicating the caller's mood.
5. Respond to the message after you've played all messages.
6. Keep a log of the messages you send and receive for each person during the course.

CHECKLIST FOR E-MAIL, FAXMAIL, AND VOICE MAIL COMMUNICATION IN DISTANCE LEARNING COURSES

E-mail can be used as a primary means of transmitting course information, similar to correspondence courses offered through surface mail. But e-mail, faxmail, and voice mail also can become important supplementary components in distance learning courses offered through other technologies. If you're planning to use any or all of these tools in your course, you should ask the following questions as part of your checklist to help determine how these devices can be used most effectively:

- Should e-mail use be required or simply encouraged?
- Should faxmail use be required or simply encouraged?
- Should voice mail use be required or simply encouraged?
- Will all these tools be used equally or will learners be encouraged to use one tool more than others?
- What are the e-mail technical requirements for participants of the course?
- What are the faxmail technical requirements for participants of the course?
- How can the course be simply structured so that most information can be completed with online texts and simple graphics that can be sent via e-mail or faxmail?
- How can e-mail, faxmail, and/or voice mail supplement other types of instruction (e.g., distribution of materials by surface mail, videoconferences, use of Web sites to store information)?
- How often will information be sent to learners?
- How quickly will feedback be provided?
- How often will feedback be provided?
- How often will learners be expected to respond via e-mail, faxmail, or voice mail?
- In addition to regular e-mail, what types of electronic communication are required for the course (e.g., subscription to mailing lists)?
- In addition to regular e-mail, what types of electronic communication are encouraged or suggested for the course?
- How much instruction will learners need to use the e-mail, faxmail, or voice mail system(s)?
- How familiar are users with the protocol of writing and responding to e-mail, faxmail, and/or voice mail messages?
- What are the guidelines you've established for conducting the class via e-mail, faxmail, or voice mail?

SUMMARY

E-mail, voice mail, and faxmail are simple tools, not nearly as technically advanced as other online distance learning technologies, but alone or collectively they can be highly effective in providing materials and communicating with learners. Many learners will be familiar with e-mail and voice mail, although they may have little experience with other forms of electronic information. E-mail may be more easily accessible than other electronic tools, too, although learners without constant access to computers may not want to rely only on e-mail for course communication. At times, faxmail or voice mail, which can be accessed without computers, may be preferable to e-mail or other distance learning tools.

When you're planning a distance learning course, you should try to include e-mail as at least one communication method to link learners, educators/trainers, and experts who can provide other sources of information. Voice mail and faxmail can be good supplementary tools to work with e-mail or other distance learning technologies.

The World Wide Web in Education and Training

The World Wide Web (WWW, Web) has become one of the most popular methods of disseminating distance learning programs. In fact, if learners and educators/trainers don't need face-to-face communication during the course, it is one of the best methods of providing information for learners.

Information stored on a Web site can include hypermedia (such as video clips, animation, sound effects, music, voiceovers, photographs, drawings, and documents), hypertext (documents and static [nonmoving] graphics), and un-linked text or graphics. The prefix *hyper* simply means that the information has been designed to link that chunk of information with a related chunk of information. The benefit of the Web is the use of hypertext and hypermedia to link plain documents or multimedia information.

More learners have access at home or in the office to the Web, as well as other parts of the Internet. Although the basic coursework might be completed by using information and resources linked through the Web, many educators/trainers who use the Web as an educational tool also assume that learners have access to e-mail, mailing lists, bulletin boards, and other Internet services. Therefore, other Internet-related activities are often an expected part of a Web-based course.

WEB-BASED INSTRUCTIONAL ACTIVITIES

For educators/trainers, a benefit of the Web is that the types of information that can be used in a course are almost limitless. Because the information is stored electronically, learners with access to the site can download or use online the information as long as it is stored there. That makes it easy for learners to work at their own pace and to visit the site as frequently as they like, whenever they have time. Some information can be stored at the site indefinitely, but other information can and should be updated frequently. Electronic storage makes it easier for educators/trainers to provide the information learners need throughout the course, as well as assignments, examinations, and samples that may be useful to have at the site only for a limited time.

Educators/trainers usually provide background information, such as a course syllabus, on the Web, but cyberspace is also a good place for sample documents and simulations. Multimedia demonstrations and samples are two types of primary materials that educators/trainers may use to present basic information about the course's subject matter.

In addition to reading, seeing, hearing, and interacting with Web-based information, an instructional site can also help learners communicate with their instructor. Depending upon the type of hypertext links set up within the site, learners also may be able to send e-mail messages directly to the educator/ trainer, institution, or business through a mailto: link. Learners therefore don't have to wait until they enter their e-mail systems to discuss information they found on the Web site; they can ask questions, send comments, and request information while they work on the Web.

Because the course's Web site might link learners with related sites for additional information or activities, research and reinforcement activities can be easily developed in conjunction with the original Web site. Educators/trainers may link some sites they want learners to visit, as well as merely list other resources that learners may want to locate on their own.

CHUNKING INFORMATION

Educational information designed for the Web should be more than documents uploaded and linked electronically. Course content should be designed specifically to be used with an interactive, electronic medium that is capable of accommodating different types of audiovisual information.

When people read a hardcopy document, they generally read from the top to the bottom of the page. In U.S.-based culture, they read from the left to the right side of a line. Although they may skip from section to section, read the last chapter before the first, or use an index to locate information they want to read first, most people employ a linear approach to reading a document, reading from the front cover to the back.

However, users approach electronic, hyperlinked information very differently. They seldom read paragraph after paragraph and scroll through screen after screen of text and/or graphics. Instead, they prefer to scan a screen to find the bits of information that are most important to them. If the information takes too long to load, if the first screen lacks the information they want, or if the screen design doesn't capture their attention and make them want to investigate the site further, they simply move to another site.

This scanning process may take fewer than five seconds, but Web users are notoriously impatient. They like to find information quickly; they want the links to work; and if they're frequent Web users, they know what's trendy as well as functional in page and screen design. When you design information for the Web, you need to make the site both attractive and usable, and you need to break down information into usable pieces that people can find quickly.

A basic principle in designing information for the Web is *chunking*. A chunk, or the smallest piece of information that makes sense by itself, is a manageable amount of information. It might be an icon or a symbol, a paragraph, a menu, a photograph—whatever has independent meaning without needing a further context.

Each chunk of information then must be arranged on a screen in whatever order will be most useful for learners. The course designer must decide which chunks should fit on the home page, or first viewing screen, and which chunks should be located elsewhere but linked to chunks on the home page.

This partitioning of information into manageable units and linking the chunks to form meaningful units is the structure of the Web. Educators and trainers who design information for a Web course must break their material into chunks, link the chunks to form a comprehensive and easily usable web of information, and ensure that the chunks provide information in the appropriate textual or visual formats for the type of information being conveyed.

When learners work with course materials on the Web, they must be able to do the following:

- Easily move among chunks, both within a single Web site and among Web sites
- Browse through the information, by scrolling or through links (including buttons, menus, hypertext links, and icons)
- See the relationship of chunks and not get lost in cyberspace (for example, by using a directory, table of contents, list of links)
- Upload and/or download information
- Understand where information is located and how to work with the information (i.e., a transparent interface)

The ease with which learners use information stored on the Web isn't entirely in the hands of course designers, however. Different browsers (for example, Netscape, Mosaic) make working with the Web easier or more difficult. Some browsers accommodate text-only, whereas others can load text and static or moving graphics. Some browsers have the capability of handling highly interactive graphics and all types of sound (e.g., music, voiceovers, sound effects), but the user's computer may not have the software, cards, or memory to present the information on screen. Even if the computer can handle the amount and type of information and the browser supports the types of information that can be downloaded from the Web site, the computer's processing speed or memory allocation may make downloading some information a very lengthy process. That's why many users give up during a long wait, preferring to go to another site and see less technically sophisticated but faster loading information.

If learners are working in a location that's been wired to the *backbone* of a computer network, they don't need a modem to make an Internet connection; also, the information-loading times may be much faster than if they use a modem from a remote location. Learners who work at home or in an office away from a network may need a modem that can receive and transmit the type of information required in the course.

Course designers may need to tell learners exactly what type of browser, hardware, or software will be needed to use all the information stored in the site or at sites learners will be required to visit during the course. Educators/trainers should explain, sometimes in great detail, how learners can connect their computer with the Internet and locate the course's Web site.

Educators/trainers may not have the control they'd like over learners' computer systems and Web capabilities, but they can do a great deal to ensure a Web site's usability. By carefully designing materials for the Web that the majority of learners can find and load quickly and easily and by updating the site regularly, they can help ensure that learners will have the amount and types of information they need to complete the course.

The following sections from the home page of the University of Missouri's Center for Independent Study illustrate the principles of chunking. Figure 7.1 shows the breakdown of primary chunks of information; this section is located at the top of the home page.

Below this introductory set of chunks, links (see Figure 7.2) indicate (from left to right, in order of importance) places where learners may logically want to go next. Each link is a separate chunk of information, arranged in a specified order. A list of additional links, further down the page, provides potential learners with the option of finding more general information about the University (Figure 7.3). At the bottom of the page, learners see other important information that stands alone and is not linked hypertext.

Each chunk of information can stand alone, either as a link to other, related chunks of information, or as a separate piece of information that has meaning on its own. The page is arranged so that learners can first understand the hierarchy of information to be presented at the site, then can choose from a series of links. If learners choose to keep scanning the page instead of moving to another site, they can select links to learn more about the University in gen-

University of Missouri
Center for Independent Study

General Information
University Courses
High School Courses
Continuing Education Courses

Figure 7.1   Chunks from the University of Missouri Web site.

http://indepstudy.ext.missouri.edu/
© University of Missouri 1996

General Information / University Courses / High School Courses / Continuing Education Courses

Figure 7.2   Chunks (Links) from the University of Missouri Web site.

http://indepstudy.ext.missouri.edu/
© University of Missouri 1996

Some other sites of interest:
University of Missouri Showme Home Page
University of Missouri School of Journalism Home Page
University of Missouri Extension
Edupage
Harvard Graduate School of Education
U.S. Department of Education On-Line Resources

Figure 7.3   Chunks (list of additional links) from the University of Missouri Web site.

http://indepstudy.ext.missouri.edu/
© University of Missouri 1996

eral, or, if they continue to scan the page, can find other (nonelectronic) ways to receive more information about the University or the program in which they're interested. The page is easy to read, functional, and chunked for easy access to different types of information.

BASIC QUESTIONS FOR DEVELOPING A WEB-BASED COURSE

By now, you should have determined if a Web site is the appropriate form of distance learning for the course you plan to present and the learners who need the information. You may require little direct contact with learners or the amount and type of communication can easily be handled through telephone calls, voice mail messages, e-mail messages, surface mail, or even the occasional teleconference or desktop videoconference. You may require learners to interact with each other and professionals outside the course through participation in mailing lists, discussion groups or newsgroups, and multiple-user domains/dimensions, for example. However, you've decided that the majority of course content can be presented in a Web site.

Learners can therefore visit the site whenever they choose, use as many or as few links as they deem necessary, work with the information in the order of their choosing, and go back over information as little or as many times as they need to master the subject. The information will be designed to meet the needs of many different learners, so that some information will be more visual (e.g., static or nonmoving graphics like photographs and drawings or moving graphics like video clips), aural (e.g., sound clips, music, special effects), or textual (e.g., sample documents, descriptions, definitions).

You've determined that learners will need to interact with the information and you've planned how much or how little interaction will be required. For example, you might create an interactive quiz section in which learners can read a question, choose an answer, and have that answer locked in. You might then receive the completed quiz from the learner, so you can comment on it more personally, through e-mail perhaps, or you might allow immediate electronic feedback about the learner's response to each question. In short, you've analyzed the need for a Web-based course and you're confident that this type of distance learning is appropriate.

Now you need to work as part of a team consisting of technicians, who will help set up, maintain, and update the site (as well as work with the server and other computer resources); educators or trainers, who will develop the course materials and work with learners; and administrators or executives, who usually oversee the projects in general and allocate funding and resources. As you plan the course, you should agree to the answers to the following administrative and course-design questions.

Administrative Questions

Administrative questions help you determine who should have access to the information, if security measures should be in place and if so which ones, and who should perform each course design and maintenance activity.

Who Needs Access to Everything on the Web Site for This Course?

Learners who are currently taking the course and the educators/trainers leading the course obviously need access to all the information. However, they may be the only persons who need complete access to the site. Some links may need to be designed as *subscription* links, so that only learners who have paid for the course can have access to assignments, examinations, notices and announcements, and important content materials (e.g., sample documents, simulations). If learners are paying a fee for the course, you need to make sure that security measures are in place so that only the paying customers receive all the information.

If you're offering a free course for general interest, then anyone who wants to view the site, whether he or she is taking the course, can have access to all information. In fact, you want to encourage more people to visit the site and use the information. If you're also offering a paid version of the course, with more information or more activities, you'll probably want to maintain two sites, with a link from the free information to instructions for taking the fee-based course. Even if you're not offering two versions of the materials, you might want to provide a free sample course, but then link that site to information about the fee-based (perhaps for-credit) courses that your business or institution also offers. Learners who enjoy the free course and find the style and amount of content appropriate for their needs may then be interested in taking additional courses that relate more to career than personal interests.

In addition to the learners who will take any type of course from you, full site access may be required by your colleagues. For example, you may need to provide access for administrators, executives, technicians, and other people who will be working with the course, even peripherally. These people may want to check the site periodically to ensure its maintenance or they may want to "show off" the information during meetings, at conferences, and for potential customers. Also, because academic institutions offering distance learning courses periodically are evaluated for accreditation or individual instructors' courses are monitored to ensure the quality of instruction, supervisory personnel may want to monitor the site and distance learning activities.

Anyone else who doesn't need full access to the site may be locked out from using some or all links. You may need to write a subscription screen, explaining where interested persons can find more information about your distance learning courses and how learners can gain access to the site. The technical personnel in your company or institution who help you set up the Web site should be able to help you design the appropriate security measures for your materials.

Who Needs Access Only to Some Materials on This Web Site?

If you want prospective learners to view some sample materials or see representative information, such as a course syllabus and objectives, you may want to make some information available to anyone who visits the institution's or business's Web site. However, the course content for all lessons, as well as other materials used by learners currently taking the course, might be secured from the general public.

You may need to limit access to some materials for learners currently enrolled in the program, also. For example, although all the exams may be prepared online, you may want to deny access to upcoming exams until a certain date or until learners have completed a certain number of course activities. As the site changes throughout the course, you should let learners know exactly what is available at all times and what is available only for limited time periods. It's usually a good idea to warn learners if they won't have access to some links that they previously could use, if new links have a restricted access, or if new links are replacing old links.

Sometimes the technical personnel need to make a site unavailable for several hours or days while the computer network, hardware, and/or software are being maintained, installed, or upgraded. If your site will be down for awhile, you should warn learners of the impending unavailability of information. Don't leave learners frustrated when they no longer can access a site and may wonder what's going on.

If you plan to allow open access to some links but limit access to others, you should carefully design the Web site so that the materials available to everyone might be linked to the same page—for example, a home page or a *samples* site.

How Will Access Be Limited?

The technical staff can suggest ways to limit access to your particular site, according to the guidelines set by the server, your service provider, or your business or institution. Some common ways to limit information include use of a password or identification code set by or given to learners when they take the course. Passwords and codes should be changed at the end of a course. You can also create a subscription link that requires users to register with your institution or business and/or pay a fee to gain access to information.

No matter how you try to secure the information, you should realize that any information on the Web can be read and retrieved by people other than those who pay for the course. No information sent electronically is completely secure. Security devices like passwords may give the impression of completely controlled access, but the site can be viewed, and any information learners send to you or receive from you, can be viewed by other people, if they want to see the information.

Most adults taking a course understand this, but you may want to remind learners if they'll be requested to give personal information or may want to disclose confidential business or personal information. Each person is responsible for the electronic messages he or she sends. Although most people respect the confidentiality of all types of electronic messages, technically the information can be viewed by people other than those intended to see it.

Who Will Update the Information on the Web Site?

The educators/trainers who lead the course should determine when, how much, and what kinds of materials are updated, because they structure the course content. They also may be in charge of updating the information for the Web site.

More technical types of updates, such as the structure and links within the site or launching new information with the server, might be the responsibility of technicians or computer service staff who maintain the whole computer network for the institution or business. The site's designers (probably the educators/trainers) should be familiar enough with HTML and the company's or institution's policies regarding the Internet to update the content and basic design. Nevertheless, more extensive design changes or system-related upgrades and changes usually are completed by the technical personnel in charge of the company's or institution's networks. Sometimes technicians and educators/trainers have a joint responsibility for updating information; they work together to provide new information and redesign the site at regular intervals, depending upon what needs to be done.

Your institution or business may have guidelines or job assignments that delineate the responsibility for updating information. The times and ways of updating information should be clearly established, however, because the site will require numerous updates, not only in content, but also in design.

Who Will Monitor and Maintain the Web Site?

Improving the site's effectiveness and maintaining its technical accuracy are important tasks. Again, these jobs may fall to educators/trainers and/or technicians.

The site should be checked frequently to ensure that all links, whether internal or external, are current and working. Outdated links should be deleted or changed and new links may need to be added to reflect new Web sites or additional resources that have become available.

People who regularly visit the same Web site often get bored with the site's appearance if it stays the same for long periods of time. Therefore, the site's design should be modified to ensure its usability and attractiveness. Although you don't want to be just a follower (or a victim) of trends, your design probably will reflect trends in the use of color, music, sound, graphics, and interactive tools. Frequent Web users like to see that you know what's current with Internet technologies and designs; however, you should judiciously follow online trends to ensure that your site's design remains attractive, functional, and best suited to meeting your particular audience's needs. Whoever is responsible for maintaining the Web site should also have the responsibility of browsing the Web to learn what's new in site design and to see what currently is making Web users' work easier.

Who Will Maintain an Archive, Mirror Site, or Backup Disk of Information That Has Been Used at This Web Site?

Educators/trainers who develop materials for the course should keep backup copies of their files and the Web sites they launch. Probably the people who design and lead the course should maintain backup disks that can be placed back on the Web if the original site is damaged or needs to be removed for awhile before the course is offered again.

Some institutions or businesses also maintain an online archive of documents, for example, so that if the *glossy* site with complete graphics and texts is not available, backup documents, usually in text-only format, can be accessed at another location. The technical staff may be involved with maintaining mirror sites.

How Long Will the Course's Web Site Be Available?

If the course will be available to learners at all times, course materials only need to be updated regularly, but the site can remain on the Web indefinitely. If, however, the course is only offered periodically, you may want to make the site available for a certain number of weeks, then delete the site for awhile, before relaunching it when the course is offered again. In either case, learners should be aware of the course's availability and the amount of time they'll have to complete coursework.

Course-design Questions

Every time a course will be offered on the Web, the designers (probably the educators/trainers who will be leading the course) should answer the following list of questions. The Web site's design should be useful and attractive, which means that the screens' "look" should be updated regularly. Because learners' needs change and some subject areas revolve around new or changing information, the online course materials should be modified to keep the course current, interesting, and accurate. The following course-design questions should help you develop a new online course or update a previously offered one.

What Types of Materials Will Be Included on This Web Site?

Most course designers provide background information about the course, provide links to assignments and sample documents, and provide graphics and/or sound to supplement the information contained in texts. In some courses, simulations, interactive quizzes and tests, and e-mail correspondence are appropriate. You need to decide which types of materials can best present the subject matter and meet the diverse learning styles of your audience.

How Should the Materials Be Linked?

You might work only with internal links, so that one hypertext link leads to information located within your Web site. For example, you might have a link from a table of contents to each lesson's core text; from a document to further illustrations, examples, or definitions; or from a test item to the reference materials on which the test item is based.

Although these internal links probably will be numerous and will help learners move from basic information about the course to more specific lesson- or activity-related items, external links to other sites are also useful in most courses. External links might refer learners to other Web sites affiliated with your business or institution, such as a campus registrar, a course catalog, library resources, or in-house departments. Other external links might help learners find information about topics related to the course. Links to the Web sites of professional associations, nonprofit organizations, community resources, libraries, and online databases or documents are also common.

Not only do you need to plan how many internal and external links are appropriate, but you should also carefully design the type of link that will make the connection. Hypertext links may involve a word or phrase that links learners with related chunks of information. It's helpful to learners if the textual link changes color once they have used that link, although the link can be reused many times. This color reference helps learners remember which links they've used. If you don't determine the sequence in which links should or must be used in the course, learners can choose to use the information in any order they like. Designing links to change color helps learners chart their progress through the materials.

You might decide to supplement hypertext links within the Web site with hypermedia links, so that learners click on an icon or a graphic to follow the link to related chunks of information. Each graphic should be an intuitive link, so that learners know at a glance that the graphics can be used as clickable links, as well as underlined text items. Usually, you'll want more than one link to lead to the same information; having a graphic and a textual link to the same chunk is a good idea.

Additionally, some navigational links might be duplicated on a pull-down, pull-over, or pop-up menu or on buttons placed along a margin or within a graphic. The most important links, such as those to the home page or to key concepts or main areas of the Web site, are often repeated in different forms and places on a screen.

Other links, like a mailto: link, allow learners to send information, instead of leaping to a new chunk they passively read or view. If it's important for learners to send their questions or comments to you while they're working with the Web site, you should use a mailto: link. If you want people browsing the home page to request registration information or otherwise contact you to express their interest in your course, you should include a mailto: link at least on the home page, although it's a good idea to have a mailto: link at the bottom of each linked screen within the Web site. Most often the mailto: link is placed close to a copyright notice and/or a company's or an institution's identifying information.

If you're designing information that will be used with learners in public settings, or in other environments where learners may not have access to a mouse or a keyboard, you might need to make the links operate by a touch to the screen, instead of a keystroke or a point-and-click of a mouse. Kiosks in public settings, such as community information centers, malls, libraries, or even lobbies of businesses, for example, can provide information about your business or institution. Providing information about training or educational opportunities can be a good marketing tool, so that people who might not know about your distance learning courses can begin to associate your company's or institution's name with distance learning opportunities. Information on a kiosk usually is called up on-screen when someone touches a button or icon, but the structure and types of information you want to include on a general information kiosk are the same as those for your screen design of a Web site.

However you link information, whether on a Web site or through an intranet via kiosk, the interface should be transparent, so that learners intuitively know what a link looks like and how it can be used to connect chunks. At least two navigational tools (e.g., text, graphic) should be used to link the most important chunks of information.

How Often Should the Materials Be Updated?

Some subjects change very little; for example, fundamentals of many academic subjects, from biology to history to discourse, can be presented in the same way in course after course. As approaches to teaching the subject matter change, the course needs to be updated; as new information becomes available, it should be added to the existing body of knowledge about that subject.

If your subject matter changes very little, you may be able to refer learners to the same core documents for a long time. However, to keep the course fresh and to meet the needs of different learners over time (as well as the changing expectations for a Web site and the demands of technology), you still should alter the materials periodically. You might redesign the information, add new samples, include more graphics, make online activities more interactive, and so on—to keep the course fresh.

On the other hand, some subject matter changes dramatically within a short time, such as that dealing with research and theory. If new advances in technology and science, for example, advance professionals' knowledge of the subject, you may need to update your materials daily, weekly, or at least before the course is offered again.

No matter how quickly or slowly the subject matter changes, learners who work with a Web site always like variety. They usually browse among many Web sites throughout a day or week, and they're aware of trends and technical advances in Web sites and site designs. To keep your course interesting and innovative, you need to update the "look" of the site, even if the basic information you need to present changes little. You should check not only other popular Web sites in general, but also sites providing information about the course's subject matter, to see how information about your subject matter is being presented at other sites.

If your course will be offered indefinitely and is unstructured, so that learners can begin to use the information at any time and have few or no restrictions on the length of time to complete the course, you may plan to update materials at specific intervals, such as every week on Friday. If the information will change on a regular schedule, you need to let learners know when new information will be available.

Updating information must become a regular activity in presenting a course on the Web. The frequency with which you update information depends on the subject matter, the speed with which technology advances, learners' specific needs, and learners' expectations for the site. As a course designer, very practically, the number of times you update the information may depend on your schedule.

How Will Learners Work with the Information on This Web Site?

Depending upon your previous analysis of learners who are currently taking and who may take your course someday, you have a good idea about the ways your target audiences prefer or are required to receive information and meet course requirements. You now need to determine how learners will work with the information as they take the course. Will they read documents? Will they view examples? Will the examples require graphics? Will the graphics be non-moving or moving? Will they interact with examples and manipulate them? Will they take interactive quizzes and tests? Will they send e-mail directly to you from the Web site, perhaps as they have questions or comments? These and similar questions help you determine what type of browser, computer system, and type of interaction learners will be required to use to complete course activities.

The more interactive you can make the site, the easier learners will understand the course content. Even a text, which can be read passively, can be linked to more interactive assignments or activities to follow the reading. Interactive review questions with programmed responses, mailto: comments, and research or practice activities related to the text learners have just read are a few ways to increase learner interaction with the subject matter. Although reading text is still an important way to gather information—and some documents certainly will be part of every course—many learners prefer to gather information in other ways. They may want to view a video, for example, which provides information in a different format. However, "viewing a video" is also a passive activity, even though it may require more visual involvement than reading. At the conclusion of the video segment, you should link activities that require learners to respond to what they've seen. Make learners do something—write an e-mail message, complete an assignment, discuss the information within a MUD, participate in a videoconference to ask questions or summarize what they've learned, or complete a simulation to apply their knowledge. When you design a Web site, you must include several ways to make learners interact with the information.

When you find ways for learners to respond to the information, such as writing an answer, asking questions, making decisions, or completing a task, you reinforce their learning. Learners who take an online first aid course, for example, might learn a great deal from reading about correct procedures and even seeing graphic examples. However, an even more effective follow-up activity to this basic presentation might involve a simulation, in which a learner must decide on a type of treatment, then act out giving that treatment.

The system might be designed to illustrate the probable results of the learner's decisions and provide feedback about the learner's effectiveness in solving the medical problem. Of course, not all courses require this type of interaction. However, you must make the site as interactive and innovative as possible to ensure that learners gain not only knowledge, but experience.

What Other Types of Communication with Learners Will Be Necessary?

The Web site is the primary location for information about and for the course. However, because the Web is part of the Internet, most learners also have access to other Internet services. In addition to requiring learners to work with the Web, you might ask them to send e-mail messages, subscribe to mailing lists, or participate in discussion groups, newsgroups, or MUDs. Outside the Internet, other methods of required communication might include surface mail, phone or voice mail, videoconferencing, or teleconferencing. For example, although you regularly communicate with learners through e-mail and online discussions, some documents may need to be mailed to you for a final evaluation. Even if the primary method of gathering information is through the Web site, learners may be required to participate in a teleconference once during the course.

If you require or recommend communication beyond use of the Web site, you should explain the amount and types of required communication as part of the basic course description on the Web. Many learners like to use a Web-based course because of its convenience and relative anonymity. Therefore, if you decide to require additional, more structured methods of communication, you should make the requirements as easy to complete as possible.

Welcome to the Center for Credit Programs in the Division of Continuing Education! We are anxious to tell you about the opportunities waiting for you at the University of Iowa. Whether you are working toward a degree or taking classes for your own enjoyment, there are a variety of options to meet your needs. We're making continuing education meaningful and convenient.

TO CONTACT UI CREDIT PROGRAMS and REQUEST INFORMATION

Figure 7.4   University of Iowa's request for information links.

http://www.uiowa.edu/~ccp
© University of Iowa 1996

The results of course-design and administrative questions are evident in the following excerpts from Web pages from the University of Iowa and the California College (Online) for Health Sciences. The screens (and individual chunks) were designed to provide answers to learners' most common questions about the course and the way they'll interact with it. Also, you can see the result of some answers to administrative questions and practical issues, such as registration and payment.

Figure 7.4 illustrates one link (of several within the Web site) that potential learners can follow to request more information from the University of Iowa. If learners need still more information about the practicalities of taking courses, they can follow some of the University's other administrative links (see Figure 7.5).

Using a FAQ list is a good way to help learners know more about the time frame in which they can take classes, payment policies, tuition reimbursement, credit options, and so on. California College for Health Sciences uses a FAQ to answer learners' basic questions about courses and procedures; a sample question and answer are shown in Figure 7.6. The College's transfer policy is described online, as shown in Figure 7.7. Each administrative policy or procedure is described similarly at the Web site.

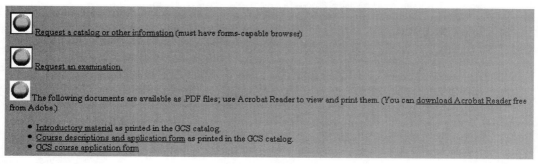

Figure 7.5   University of Iowa's links to other administrative information.

http://www.uiowa.edu/~ccp
© University of Iowa 1996

Q. *When do classes start?*

A. Whenever you want them to! With distance learning, you can start your studies any tome. There are no rigid semesters or quarters to contend with. In fact, with CCHS distance learning there are no attendance requirements at all. And the Colleges resources - including student services and instructor support - are all available to you every regular business day. You can contact CCHS Monday through Friday, except major holidays, from 7:00 a.m. to 5:00 p.m., Pacific Standard Time.

◆Just click here to fill out a Request for Application form.

Figure 7.6 California College for Health Science's FAQ sample.

http://www.cchs.edu/faq.html
© California College for Health Science, 1996

Q. *Can I transfer credits earned at CCHS to other schools and colleges?*

A. Yes! Thanks to our recommendations by the American Council on Education, it is easier to transfer your credits. Here are just a few of the major universities that have recognized American Council on Education credit recommendations:

- Indiana University
- University of California, Berkeley
- Johns Hopkins University
- Ohio State University
- University of Texas, Dallas
- University of Tennessee, Knoxville
- Florida State University, Tallahassee

Most of California College's courses have been favorably reviewed by ACE and our graduates are already transferring credits to the college of their choice. Whether you choose to continue your education at CCHS or to attend as campus near your work or home, your credits are valuable and transferable.

◆Click here to learn more about transferring your college credits.

Figure 7.7 California College for Health Science's transfer policy.

http://www.cchs.edu/faq.html
© California College for Health Science, 1996

Since there are no semester deadlines, you may register at any time and take up to nine months to complete a course.

More than 160 courses are available, covering a variety of interest areas, chiefly in the liberal arts. A study guide replaces typical classroom meetings. Within the guide, you'll find commentary by the instructor, reading and mail-in assignments, study suggestions, instructions for completing the course, and information on taking exams in your area.

Figure 7.8 University of Iowa's information about distance learning courses.

http://www.uiowa.edu/~ccp
© University of Iowa 1996

If you live in the Iowa City area, you must take your examination on The University of Iowa campus at the GCS testing center, room 36 International Center, downstairs from our main office at room 116. You do not need to complete the examination request form, but you must schedule your exam at least 24 hours in advance by contacting the GCS office.

GCS office hours are 8 a.m. to 7 p.m. (Monday through Thursday) and 8 a.m. to 5 p.m. (Friday). Call 319-335-2575 or 800-272-6430. Exam times are listed below. They are subject to some variation and are reduced during holidays, semester breaks, and summer session.

Bring two forms of identification to the testing center, one of which includes a photograph (such as a driver's license).

Figure 7.9 University of Iowa's examination information.

http://www.uiowa.edu/~ccp
© University of Iowa 1996

The University of Iowa provides potential learners with more information about their distance learning courses, so that learners understand exactly how the courses operate and what requirements they have to meet. Figure 7.8 provides information about the University's distance learning courses. Figure 7.9 provides information about the University's examination policy for learners living within driving distance of the University. (Other chunks at the Web site provide additional information for learners living outside these boundaries.) All learners should understand the distance learning procedures for this university's courses simply by reading the chunks of information provided at the Web site. The site clearly describes what is expected of learners and educators.

TYPES OF INFORMATION NEEDED IN YOUR WEB SITE

The entire Web site should have a variety of information about your company or institution and its distance learning programs. Within the Web site, you should include identifying information and details about each course or program, which usually includes the following:

- Name of the institution or business offering the course
- Title of the program of which this course is a part
- Course title, number, and a brief description
- Names and e-mail or Web addresses of the educator(s)/trainer(s) leading the course
- List of required and/or suggested materials needed to complete the course

- Brief description of course requirements
- Syllabus or a brief description of the time frame for completing the course
- FAQ about the course, institution, or business

Instructions for working with the site and finding other information about the institution or business should also be provided. You might need to instruct learners how to do the following activities related to a single distance learning course or several courses:

- Register for this course
- Communicate with educators/trainers
- Communicate with other learners
- Receive or locate course-related information
- Send materials for evaluation or discussion
- Take tests or quizzes
- Complete assignments
- Use the links associated with the site
- Locate the core materials (e.g., online documents, simulations)
- Locate referential materials
- Complete and submit exercises, activities, and exams

DESIGNING A HOME PAGE FOR YOUR COURSE

Because the home page represents you and your company or institution, it should be the most attractive, most precise representation possible. People browsing the Web may spend only a few seconds looking at this home page, but it should be memorable. Current trends in home page design include the use of more bulleted lists, which usually are links not only of textual items, but also to related chunks on other screens. Graphic and textual icons to the same information are important, so a single background graphic with clickable icons, buttons, or pictures is a good choice for the home page. An effective home page should take up only one screen, so that learners (using whatever type of monitor) can see all the information on this page at one time.

Although each Web page/screen should be carefully designed, the information learners immediately see when they view your home page should be interesting, easy to read, and involving. Keep in mind, too, that unless you use graphic images to capture a particular font (like a script style or an Old West design), you can't determine the font or typeface learners will see when they read your information. Hypertext markup language (HTML) allows you to place graphic images and wrap text, for example, but the font and typeface will default to the preferences the learner has set for his or her browser. Some learners' browsers may not allow them to see graphics but only read text. Therefore, when you design any information for the Web, keep the design simple, well chunked, and easy to read, no matter which font or typeface may be used.

In general, a good design for a Web page is one that is easy to scan. Many viewers spend only a few seconds at a Web site before they move somewhere else. Therefore, you must attract their attention and provide them with the most important information they need to know. You should identify yourself (your course or your institution or business) and your purpose, but provide that information in a visually interesting way.

Let people do, as well as see: Keep the site interactive. The site should be easily accessible, no matter what type of browser learners use or how technically experienced or inexperienced they may be. For example, you might have a wonderful home page design, with plenty of colorful graphics and intriguing wallpaper, but if the site takes 10 minutes to load, most viewers will be bored and leave the site before they can see the completed design. If you've provided many links, but the links don't work, learners will also become discouraged and frustrated.

Because the Web is international, keep in mind the use of color, design, and nuances of language as you plan your site. The site should be attractive, with compatible and contrasting colors. However, if you rely on color symbolism as part of your message, for example, remember that colors may symbolize different concepts in different cultures. Although in the United States, learners might associate green with money and being "in the red" as a bad business practice, learners from other nations may not readily perceive the same associations. If you use humor in the site, keep in mind that jokes and plays on words translate differently across languages and cultures. In addition, popular cultural references differ around the world; what might be an obvious reference to you might be incomprehensible to learners. Finally, if your course will be offered to an international audience, you may need to present information in multiple languages.

Although the information that should be found within the Web site, as described in the previous section, is important for the entire site, you have to decide how much information should be placed on each screen. In general, you should design the home page, then the linked screens/pages that make up the complete site. As you design the Web site, you might follow a plan of allowing users to move from the most general information on the home page to more specific linked screens, which in turn can be layered to lead to even more specific screens. This general-to-specific pattern is most effective when you design a Web site; it keeps you from trying to place too much information on the home page or in one location. You might include the following information on the home page:

- Name of the institution or business offering the course
- Other identifying information about the institution or business (e.g., address, phone number, fax number, mailto: e-mail link for communicating directly with the institution)
- Mission statement or *brief* description of the company's or institution's purpose, type of services or products, and subject areas of emphasis

■ Brief description of and link to fuller descriptions of distance learning courses (or merely a link to the distance learning Web site, if the home page belongs to a large institution)

A graphic, such as a corporate logo or a photograph of the institution, along with a pleasing arrangement of the information, should make an effective first impression. The limited number of chunks and links provides potential customers with enough information to know who you are and what you can offer, but it doesn't clutter the home page.

The density of the home page should be less than the density of information on other linked screens. *Density* refers to the amount of information on the screen and the technical sophistication of the design and interaction. For example, a low-density screen, such as a home page, should include the most important chunks and links. It might involve text and graphics, but it doesn't require lots of bells and whistles. If your company or institution specializes in high-tech products or services, you might include information that flips, crawls, blinks, and so forth, or that involves animation, video, or sound, for example. However, most institutions and companies should have a very simple, very clean, but very easy-to-use home page design. At the opposite end of the scale, a high-density screen offers more chunks of information, may include longer blocks of text, and may require more time for learners to work with the information. Scrollable screens of text, multiple graphics, or video clips, for example, create a higher density of information.

DESIGNING OTHER WEB PAGES FOR THE SITE

Users who see your home page, then select a link to more detailed information about courses are ready for a higher density of information. However, you should keep the number of chunks and the amount of technical sophistication for each screen manageable. Don't overload your viewers with volumes of information or many competing visual images. You can keep the design simple, but still include a higher level of detail.

You might need to design layered screens of information. If the home page is the top layer, the links from that page to more detailed screens of information create a second layer. Within each detailed screen of information, users may need even more details or more in-depth coverage of a topic. Links from the second layer to a third, fourth, or greater layer of information allow users to find increasingly detailed screens of information. Layering information in a Web site prevents information overload among viewers and it makes your job of designing the amount of information on each screen much easier.

In addition to the appropriately detailed (and usually denser) information found on subsequent layers of screens, you might have standard identifying information on each screen. Your company's or institution's name, a mailto: link, and copyright notices, for example, are commonly found on every screen of information. You should also include a link up to one higher layer of screens, as well as a link to the home page. The linked screens for your distance learning site might include the following information:

- Title of the program of which this course is a part
- Course title, number, and a brief description of each distance learning course currently offered
- Names and e-mail or Web addresses of the educator(s)/trainer(s) leading the course
- List of required and/or suggested materials needed to complete the course
- Brief description of course requirements
- FAQ about the course, institution, or business

A lower layer of information, linked to the course title, for example, might include the following:

- Syllabus or a brief description of the time frame for completing the course
- Instructions for participating in the course (e.g., registering, communicating with instructors, taking exams, completing assignments)
- Links to the core materials (e.g., online documents, simulations)
- Links to referential materials

If your institution or company offers several courses, you might have a separate linked area of the Web site for each course. If you offer only a few courses, course descriptions might be listed on the same screen.

CREATING A VISUALLY INTERESTING SCREEN

Whether you're designing a home page or a linked Web page, each screen should stand alone, as well as support the design for the entire site. Limit the number of pages that have scrollable screens, so that users can see as much information as possible while they're looking at one screen. Keep in mind that your screens should reflect good electronic information design principles, which often differ from good hardcopy design principles. Try to avoid a *block* arrangement of information, much as you would design pages of a book or a newsletter. Instead, incorporate three-dimensional graphics to keep your page from looking two-dimensional, or break up the placement of chunks to avoid a linear, square look to the screen.

Although there are many good examples of simple, clean, but less blocky Web designs, the home page for Kodak (see Figure 7.10) illustrates principles

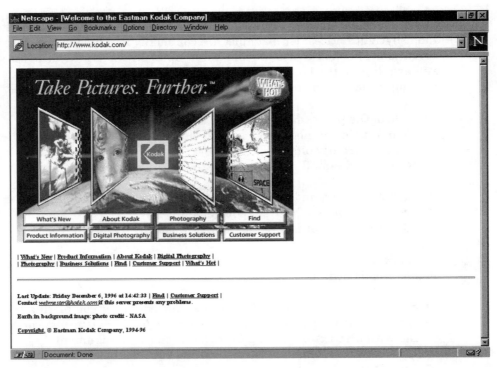

Figure 7.10 Kodak's home page.

http://www.kodak.com
© Eastman Kodak Company 1994–1996

of good home page design. The topic isn't about distance learning, but the principles of setting up a good home page can be used by educators/trainers in their home pages. The graphics create depth; several textual and visual links lead to in-depth information on other screens; basic identifying information about the company appears on the bottom of the home page (and linked screens). By learning what works in corporate and individuals' home pages and Web site designs, you can incorporate the best designs into your home page and Web site about distance learning.

SAMPLE DISTANCE LEARNING SITES

Although the way information is displayed varies according to the designer's plan for the course, the institution's or business's other Web sites, and the need for continually updating the site to make it more attractive and usable, several good examples of Web site design can be found among the many institutions and businesses offering distance learning courses. (See Appendix E for Web addresses relating to distance learning and institutions or businesses offering distance learning courses.)

The following examples of home pages showcase a few approaches to presenting information about a course. The links indicate additional information that can be found through internal and external links to other Web pages and sites.

Figure 7.11, the ICONS home page from the University of Maryland, incorporates several colors, from the light blue and green in the globe to a brighter design for the ICONS logo. The basic design is very simple and there are few chunks of information. The most important information to be provided in more detail on linked screens is itemized in the series of links at the bottom of the screen. The entire design fits easily on even a small screen.

One of the linked pages at this site, describing simulations used in the high school educational program, contains much more in-depth information. Several paragraphs detail the simulations and explain the program. This linked screen has a much higher density of information and was designed for users who want much more information about the simulations.

Two other higher-density pages describe the simulations in greater detail; they also have links to other layers of even more specialized information, such as a glossary. Although scrollable text may not always be appropriate for all distance learning pages, in some situations—such as a high school simulation requiring a great deal of explanation as preliminary background—text can be useful, as long as the information is chunked into manageable paragraphs.

The home page of the University of Southern Queensland's Distance Education Centre (Figure 7.12) is colorful, with a light yellow background and purple sidebar, to create a unique, but visually pleasing color combination. The links on the home page are the most important chunks of information; most links are internal, but some (e.g., to the International Council for Distance Education) are external. Again, the home page fits neatly on one small screen. One of the linked screens lists degree programs available via distance learning; this information has a higher density, but the lists are easily scanned.

The University of Waterloo's Distance and Continuing Education home page provides a chunk of description about this division of the University (Figure 7.13); the program's home page is linked to the University's home page. As such, the Distance and Continuing Education home page provides more information than a general, or first-level, home page. Nevertheless, the Distance and Continuing Education home page limits the number of chunks and provides a scannable, easy-to-use design. Important links on this home page include cute, brightly colored icons and standard text to take users to more detailed information about distance learning and continuing education, among other related sites. A text link at the bottom of the screen directs potential learners to the registrar's office for more information about courses and regis-

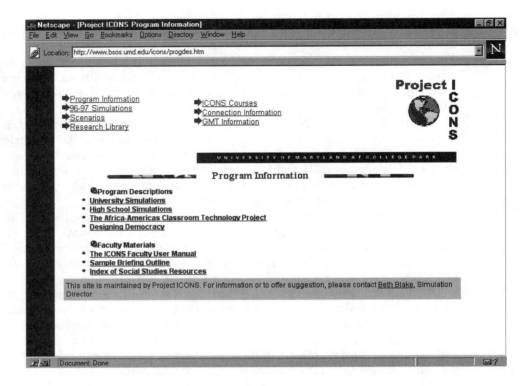

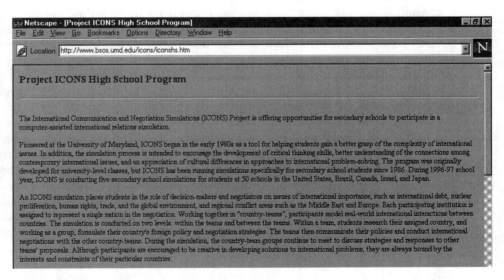

Figure 7.11 University of Maryland, Project ICONS.

http://www.bsos.umd.edu/icons/prodes.htm
© University of Maryland 1996

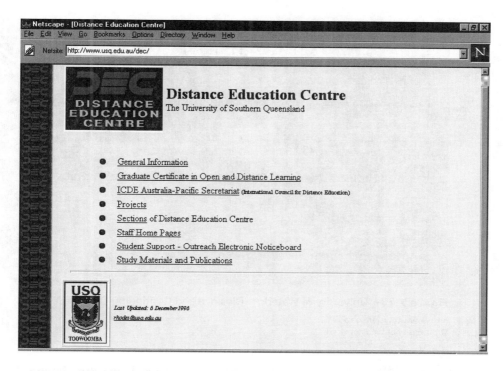

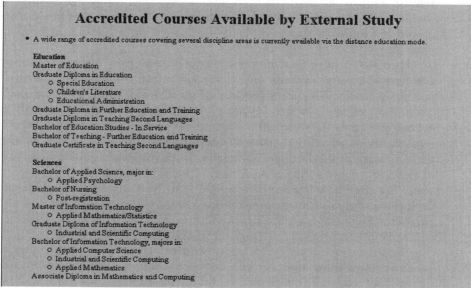

Figure 7.12 Distance Education Centre, University of Southern Queensland.

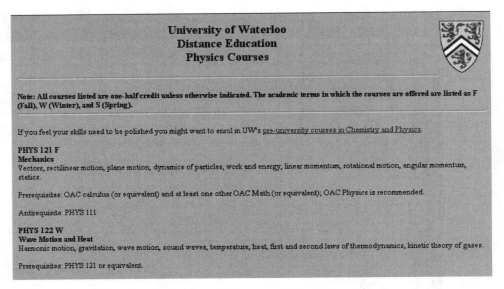

Figure 7.13 University of Waterloo, Distance and Continuing Education.

http://www.uwaterloo.ca
© University of Waterloo 1996

tration. One of the many layered linked screens through the distance learning series of links provides course descriptions. A few samples of physics course descriptions indicate the basic course information that should be included in your Web site.

Humber College On-line's home page (see Figure 7.14) is too long to fit on most conventional screens, but the information is highly functional. The top section provides a visual overview of the College and gives users a sense of what the College is and represents; it also helps students who will know the school primarily as a virtual college to develop a clearer sense of the real College. A series of links, both icons and text, lead users to the same layer of screens with more detailed information. An interesting feature at the bottom of the home page is the series of navigational icons and their descriptors; these icons are used consistently throughout the Web site. By clearly providing descriptions of these navigational links and indicating how they should be used, the home page helps novice users to locate all the information they need within the Web site, without getting lost in the site.

As shown by these home pages and linked screens within the Web site, there is more than one correct or effective way to present basic information about your course, institution or business, and/or program. Your Web site should reflect your course's and institution's or company's uniqueness.

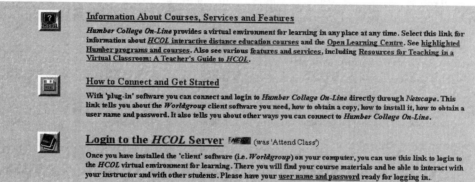

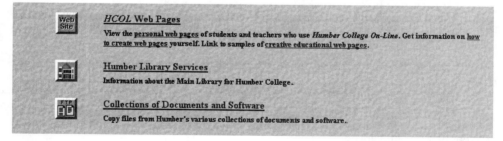

Figure 7.14 Humber College.

http://hcol.humberc.on.ca/
© Humber College 1996

QUESTIONS ABOUT WEB SITE DESIGN

To help you get started in designing a Web site, use the following series of questions every time you design a site and each screen/page that is linked within it. Figure 7.15 can be used as a general checklist to help you plan your design.

Purpose of the Site

- Why will people visit this site?
- When will people visit this site?
- What do they need to know first?

Purpose of the Page/Screen

- Why will people visit this page?
- When will people visit this page?
- What do they need to know at this time?

Content

- How much information will be provided about the subject matter?
- How much information will be navigational?
- How much information will be instructive?
- How much information must be on the home page?
- How much information must be available on the site?
- Should the information be accessible only as text?
- Should the information be accessible only as graphics?
- If both graphics and text are used, what should be graphics, and what should be in prose?
- How should the information be organized for clarity of meaning?

Frequency of Update

- How quickly will the information be outdated?
- How much information will become outdated?
- How much information will remain constant?
- How often should the information be updated?
- How easy is it to update this information?

Links

- To what addresses should this information be linked?
- How will people find this site?
- How much information should be linked within this site (e.g., how many internal links are needed)?
- How much information should be linked outside this site (e.g., how many external links are needed)?
- What types of links are appropriate?
- How many types of links (e.g. hypertext, menu item, icon) should be available for the same information?
- How can links be made "intuitive," so that learners immediately understand how to use them?
- Do the links work?
- How often should the links be checked to ensure their continuing accuracy?

Design

- What should be the overall impression of the first screen (e.g. trendy, scientific, businesslike)?
- How much information must appear on the screen at one time? (Remember that you have no control over the learners' browser and the preferences set, therefore, the amount of information on a single screen may vary depending on the defaults that the learners set.)

Figure 7.15 Design questions about your Web site.

- Which types of information should be provided?
- How can individual chunks of information be arranged for effective organization and for pleasing appearance?
- What effect should be created?
- How many different types of media will be used in the design?
- Which colors will accent the design?
- What sounds should be used?
- Which pictures will best illustrate the message?
- What music should be used?
- Is the overall design functional and attractive?
- Is the overall design well suited to an interactive electronic medium?
- How often should the design be updated?

Figure 7.15   Design questions about your Web site, continued.

Table 7.1 is a quick reference of do's and don't's about the most common design problems novice Web designers face as they plan their first home pages. By looking at several Web sites, you can probably add your own do's and don't's of designs.

A good way to study Web sites' designs is to browse the Web regularly. Keep track of the sites that are particularly appealing and designs that are appropriate for the type of course you're providing. Look at the "best" and "worst of the Web" lists and see what makes certain sites popular and other sites laughable. Look at the HTML source codes of the sites that interest you most; see which color combinations and types of links seem most effective. Then you can incorporate the best designs into your Web site.

You also should practice working with HTML. By using one of the many commercial or shareware HTML editors or code generators, you can design a Web page without having to know much about HTML. Of course, you can always type in HTML codes in a plain text document, if you don't have access to HTML software. Although software is making it easier to create Web sites, the more you know about HTML and other software, such as Java, for example, the easier it is to create more innovative designs and learn from viewing the HTML source documents of the sites you find most effective.

Once you've designed your basic home page and a few related screens, look at the design critically with one or more browsers, and encourage feedback from your peers. Create a few of these trial designs before you launch your Web site, just to make sure the links and design work the way you want them to work and that you have the best design possible when you first introduce your course.

The best measure of your Web pages' success is your learners' evaluation. Throughout the course, ask learners to evaluate the site's usability and design. Let learners know that you sincerely want to make the site better and discuss ways to make the information more effective.

Table 7.1 Design Do's and Don'ts for Web Pages

Do's	Don'ts
Identify yourself, your company, your institution, etc., so that users know who you are and where they are.	Use bright background colors (e.g., fluorescent pink, orange, red, chartreuse).
State, show, or clearly imply the purpose of your screens.	"Play" with Java or other programming to include lots of flashing, scrolling, blinking, or otherwise distracting images.
Use easy-on-the-eye colors as backgrounds. Blue and green (if not glaringly bright shades) are good choices.	Use highly patterned wallpaper or backgrounds.
Choose colors that provide a good contrast to text and graphics colors, so that backgrounds stay in the background and important text and graphics can be easily read.	Wash out the text or graphics with backgrounds or wallpaper.
	Use a counter unless it's necessary.
	Use an Under Construction sign.
Choose colors that are compatible next to each other.	Link your site to sites most users know of (e.g., Yahoo, AltaVista).
Avoid "busy" backgrounds, such as wallpaper with designs that pull the eye away from the text or graphics or that create distracting patterns (e.g., paisley, plaid, zigzag).	Link your site to outdated sites (i.e., users keep finding No Site at This URL messages when they select your links).
	Develop dead-end links with no way except back to move from the site.
Use upper- and lowercase letters for text.	Use uppercase letters only in the text.
Chunk information.	Use the spelling checker and/or grammar checker to ensure that your site is linguistically accurate and appropriate.
Ensure that the size of graphic means the graphic can be loaded easily and quickly using the most common browsers.	Add photographs of you and your family, pets, friends, or unprofessional or inappropriate graphics for this site.
Check links frequently, especially if you've used links to other people's Web sites, to ensure that the links work and the information available via the link is still accurate and available.	Use long blocks of text or graphics so that users have to scroll through several screens to understand the main points.

SUMMARY

Designing a Web site should be an ongoing challenge and adventure. As technology changes, you can offer more interactive devices at your site and modify the learning environment continually to enhance learners' educational and training experiences.

Teleconferencing and Desktop Videoconferencing

Teleconferencing and desktop videoconferencing may not be the most popular forms of distance learning yet, but they're becoming increasingly common. As more software becomes available to assist educators/trainers and learners in "conferencing" face-to-face via computers and telephonic technology, this option should become more popular. Although any course may involve desktop videoconferencing or teleconferencing, some courses especially well suited to teleconferencing and videoconferencing are those requiring learners to see demonstrations, participate in discussions, listen to lectures, view presentations, or otherwise work within groups. When face-to-face communication with the educator/trainer or other learners is required, teleconferencing and desktop videoconferencing are most effective.

Teleconferences and videoconferences may be the entire method of transmitting information for a distance learning course; many universities and colleges offer term-length courses through this type of technology. Some institutions offer a schedule of teleconferences, similar to their schedule of on-site classes. Learners are expected to participate in the teleconferences, which may take place once or several times a week, just as traditional students are expected to attend classes regularly. Those learners who need the motivation of a set schedule and benefit from direct interaction with other learners, as well as educators/trainers, will benefit more from these forms of interactive learning than will self-starters who prefer working alone.

Because teleconferencing and videoconferencing mimic some elements of traditional classroom education or training, traditional learners may feel more comfortable with this form of distance learning. It reminds them of what education "used to be" which, for many learners, translates into "supposed to be." Although distance learning programs can provide them with the educational or training opportunities they may not have had in the past, with greater convenience, other forms of distance learning may seem strange. For these learners, teleconferencing or videoconferencing can provide the best of both worlds: distance learning and a familiar classroom environment.

Teleconferencing and videoconferencing appeal to more senses, too. Educators/trainers should work with printed documents, demonstrations, workshops, lectures, multimedia presentations—in short, all formats of information. In this way, all learners' preferences and needs can be met better.

Even if your distance learning course's subject matter, or the needs of your learners, dictate that teleconferencing or videoconferencing is not the one best way to present information, you still might consider using these teaching or training technologies in special circumstances. Occasional teleconferences and videoconferences can enhance other instructional methods.

For example, special sessions from a conference or a meeting can enhance learners' grasp of a subject or allow them to see what's going on at a professional gathering. One-time events, such as demonstrations and workshops hosted by a business, an agency, or an association can be viewed by learners. Learners who may not have the time or money to attend a professional meeting or conference may be able to see one or more presentations or discuss concerns with other professionals through a teleconference or videoconference, even though they can't physically attend the sessions.

A videoconference or teleconference can be used for a discussion or forum among learners. A session can bring together groups of learners to share materials gathered earlier in the course or to discuss projects they may have completed individually. The use of teleconferences and videoconferences, even sporadically, can enhance the educational potential of many courses.

A BRIEF OVERVIEW OF TELECONFERENCING AND DESKTOP VIDEOCONFERENCING TERMINOLOGY

Before you commit to purchasing an expensive conferencing system, or decide to put up with a lower quality system because of the cost of more advanced technology, talk with the technical experts at your institution or company. The following overview should give you a starting point from which to ask these experts which types of connections are best for the type of distance learning course or program you're planning, the types of distance learning you want to offer in the future, and existing technology at your site. You should also consider what types of equipment your learners have or to which they have access, and how quickly the technology is expected to change. If you want to learn more terminology and develop a fuller understanding of teleconferencing, you may want to read publications and consult with representatives from telecommunications companies (including, for example, AT&T, Sprint, and others); understanding more about telephony can help you understand more about teleconferencing, especially using compressed video.

When analog video is digitized, computers can manipulate the data. Digitizing makes each frame of video become a two-dimensional array of pixels. When an educator/trainer is shown on camera, the transmitted image made up of pixels is read by the receiving site's equipment and projected onto the monitor. Full-motion video allows the educator's/trainer's movements to be shown smoothly. Some teleconferencing systems don't use full-motion video. Instead, when an image is transmitted, some parts of the image that haven't moved or changed since the last time the image was transmitted aren't updated. The parts of the image that have moved (e.g., the speaker blinked or gestured) are updated; those pixels are sent to the receiving site to update the image. Depending upon the speed of transmission and the carrying capacity of the channel used to transmit the data, the resulting image on a monitor may be delayed or jerky. The more video that can be transmitted along a channel, the better the image.

Audio takes up a consistent amount of transmission space on the channel—a constant bandwidth. That's why audio is never compromised. If you increase the carrying capacity of a channel, you're increasing its video-carrying capability, not its audio-carrying capability.

The carrying capacity of a communication line or channel is its bandwidth. *Bandwidth*, in very general, nontechnical terms, is the amount of information that can flow through the line at one time. Bandwidth is measured in bits per second (bps). When thousands of bits per second are described, the measurement is given in kilobits per second (kbps).

The amount of bandwidth available for your use determines how much information can be sent at one time. Video communication requires a great deal of bandwidth; audio communication requires less bandwidth. For example, if you double the bandwidth, you're doubling the video-carrying capacity, but the audio capacity remains the same. The communication lines can transmit both audio and video. Integrated services digital network (ISDN) is one network that offers higher bandwidth than traditional phone lines; Ethernet is another.

Ethernet and ISDN represent two different types of communications channels: circuit-switched and packet-switched. ISDN is circuit-switched; Ethernet is packet-switched. When you use a circuit-switched communication channel, you (the user) theoretically can maintain the connection as long as you like. When you're connected through this channel, it provides the necessary bandwidth and no other user can use that bandwidth.

In contrast, packet-switched communication channels share bandwidth among all the users in a system. When a packet-switched channel is being accessed by many users, it takes longer to send and receive information than it does when the channel has only a few users. When you work with desktop videoconferencing, you ideally want a continuous stream of information, which means that a circuit-switched channel is better. Currently, ISDN is the circuit-switched communication channel you can use.

ISDN recently became available for homes, classrooms, and smaller businesses, although the technology has existed for several years. It uses phone communications for transmission. ISDN frequently uses two communication lines, called bearer (or B) channels.

Each B channel can simultaneously transmit 64,000 bits of information (64 kbps) per second. You may also use a data (or D) channel, which can transmit 16,000 bits of information (16 kbps) per second. ISDN signals are digital signals; therefore, you'll need an adapter and perhaps other devices to make the connection work.

A T-carrier service provides T1 and T3 circuits. A transmission that originally was formatted to carry digitized voice communication can allow several circuits over one line. T1 is a dedicated digital circuit that allows 24 64-kpbs channels. T1 transmission can be made over copper wire, coaxial cable, fiber optic cable, or satellite.

T3 lines can carry more information than T-1 lines. A T-3 line equals the capacity of 28 T-1 lines. T-1 and T-3 lines allow more multimedia information to be sent along the line; they can carry voice, video, and data transmissions.

You may also work with fractional T-1 lines, reducing the amount of information that can be carried at one time, but also reducing your cost. The cost of using fractional T-1 and T-3 lines, for example, varies among regions and telecommunications companies. You should check in your area to learn the current rate. (For example, in some midwestern U.S. communities, 1/4 (fractional) T-1 use costs about $20 per hour. The costs increase as the amount of carrying capacity increases.)

Basic rate interface (BRI) and primary rate interface (PRI) are two basic types of ISDN service. If your course requires less carrying capacity, you can use BRI. Basic rate interface is made up of two 64-kbps B channels and one 16-kbps D channel. If your course requires a greater capacity for information transmission, you can use PRI. Although the capacity varies with the service, usually PRI consists of 23 B channels and 1 65-kbps D channel. To work with BRI or PRI services, you will need special equipment that your service provider can help you determine.

Another important concept is frame rate, or the number of frames of video information that can be transmitted within a given number of seconds. The higher the number of frames-per-second, the better the viewers' perception of the video's quality. Full-motion video (which means you see smooth video, not a series of jerky images) is 30 frames-per-second. The rate at which the information flows through an ISDN channel roughly translates into a frame rate of one new frame being transmitted every four seconds. So, although ISDN can provide better information flow, the system is far from flawless.

That's why Ethernet may be a good choice. Although it is a packet-switched channel, when few users are sending information at the same time, an Ethernet connection can transmit almost three frames per second, which provides you a smoother moving picture. ISDN and Ethernet are both in use for videoconferencing, although if you read much of the distance learning literature, ISDN seems to be more common in practice.

Compressing the video enhances viewers' perception of the video's quality. A *codec* (compression-decompression) is a device to convert video signals into digital signals for transmission. It then converts incoming signals from digital signals into video signals. Most codec units you can purchase come with a camera or multiple cameras.

Although most learners quickly adjust to seeing lagging video, you have to determine how important and cost-effective it is to increase the video quality for a teleconference. You may decide that the video quality can be less than perfect and still be acceptable. You can also work with educators/trainers to make sure their presentation style allows easier transmission of visual data. For example, instructors who like to pace, or who move a great deal in front of a moving demonstration or simulation, are increasing the number of pixels that need to be "updated" so that the image can be seen. The amount of visual information being sent along a limited channel may bog down the system and make the video difficult to view. It's generally a good idea for instructors to limit unnecessary movement or gestures and use body language, including gestures, to emphasize important points or to point out information on slides, transparencies, and so forth. Unnecessary movement should be avoided, both for a better presentation style and more efficient broadcasting.

BASIC EQUIPMENT NEEDS FOR A TELECONFERENCE AND A DESKTOP VIDEOCONFERENCE

When you design a teleconferencing room, you'll need a codec unit if you're working with compressed video. If the unit doesn't come with cameras, you'll need to purchase cameras. (However, most codec units come with a camera or multiple cameras.) You may want two to four cameras to capture the course adequately.

You'll also need a copy stand, similar to an overhead projector with a video camera. (One popular brandname is an Elmo; you'll often come across this term when you look at Web-based descriptions of distance learning programs involving teleconferencing.) The copy stand can show three-dimensional graphics, such as slides. The educator/trainer can write materials that can be seen on the monitor and in remote locations. You may also want to have a blackboard or a whiteboard on which educators/trainers can write.

Microphones are necessary for educators/trainers and learners; they can be arranged in several ways to meet the course's and educators'/trainers' needs. Some desks and tables may be equipped with built-in microphones that become active whenever a learner speaks. The educator's/trainer's workspace may also have a built-in microphone. Removable microphones may be a good option if the room will be rearranged for different courses.

Because the technology changes rapidly, you'll never be able to keep up with state-of-the-art equipment. Every few years (if not sooner), you'll have to update your equipment. However, you can get the most use out of your equipment if you compare brands and types that can be enhanced with software updates and those that require hard-wired (equipment, hardware) updates. Purchasing equipment that allows you to upgrade the technology by updating software may be a good option for your program. Nevertheless, at some point, you'll have to invest in newer technology in order to provide effective teleconferencing services. You'll want to discuss compression/decompression devices (codec units), types of updates, and brands of equipment, for example, with your technical experts to see which types of hardware and software are most cost-effective and usable for your distance learning programs.

If you plan to use desktop videoconferencing in your distance learning program, you can use a range of technology, from simple (including shareware or inexpensive) software and hardware to more technically advanced equipment. At the least, every participant will need a computer capable of handling video and audio and the software needed to run a video conference. Each computer also must have a camera and a microphone so that each participant can be seen and heard.

If you'll be doing a lot of videoconferencing in your programs and require visuals that are more fluid, in color, and with little or no communication lag time, you may want to investigate the use of ISDN telephone lines. These lines can give you more bandwidth, or information-carrying capacity, than the typical modem linked to a telephone line. You may also want a codec board to compress the outgoing video signal and decompress the incoming video signal.

Check with the technical staff at your business or institution to see what type of hardware and software is best for the videoconferencing uses you're planning. You may also want to compare the various videoconferencing computer kits on the market, as well as the less expensive software (such as CU-SeeMe software that can be downloaded from a Cornell University Web site).

TELECONFERENCING IN A DISTANCE LEARNING COURSE

Teleconferencing refers to long-distance courses in which the educator/trainer presents information that is uplinked and downlinked, sometimes via satellite, among remote locations. It is a "live" presentation; educators/trainers can respond in real time to learners, who may be in classrooms, conference centers, or businesses—anywhere that the technology is available to send and receive the teleconference.

Teleconferencing may be called by different names, such as interactive video education or interactive television, depending upon the mode of transmitting the broadcast. Teleconferences may include two-way audio and one-way video communication, two-way video and one-way audio communication, or, what's preferred, two-way audio and video communication.

An individual educator/trainer can make a presentation that is seen and responded to by individual learners or groups of learners in distant sites, as well as at the origination site. For example, an educator/trainer may be teaching a group at one location. The group in a remote location can see and/or hear the class working with the educator/trainer, and the group working in the same room with the educator/trainer can see and/or hear learners in a remote location or locations.

Other teleconferences involve smaller groups of learners. For example, a teleconference can involve only an educator/trainer and one or two learners in remote locations, much like a business teleconference. However, using teleconferencing for very small groups may not be cost-effective.

Some courses may meet on a regular schedule, much the way a closed-circuit TV course or an on-campus or in-house program is offered. Every week, or several times a week, learners can gather in specially equipped sites to participate in the teleconference. Having an established schedule of classes may be beneficial to learners who require more structure in their distance learning education, whereas other learners may find this more traditional classroom structure doesn't fit well with their schedules. The effectiveness, and thus the success, of teleconferencing depends on the way this method of distance learning meets individual learners' needs.

Other courses may involve periodic or special event teleconferences to supplement other methods of instruction and sources of information. A special event may be taped, and the tapes later viewed by participants who missed the live session, archived in a video library, or sold to learners. However, before any type of special event is taped, you must seek copyright permission for using or reproducing the tapes outside the original presentation, pay licensing fees to download and record the session, or otherwise take care of the legal and business issues surrounding recording teleconferences for future use or profit.

Sample Distance Learning Services and Programs

The Distance Learning Network's Web site describes its teleconferencing services, as shown in Figure 8.1. This network provides continuing education programs for health care professionals, busy people who need to update their skills and information to keep up with changes in technology and science, but who may not have the time to travel to an educational institution or partici-

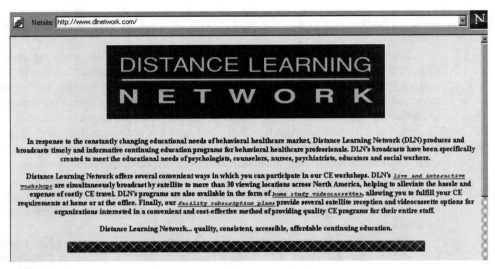

Figure 8.1 Distance Learning Network.

http://www.dlnetwork.com/
© Distance Learning Network 1996

pate in a term-length course. Interactive, satellite-based courses can help meet the continuing education needs of this group of specialists. Also, note that the Distance Learning Network's workshops are made available on videotape, so that learners can view the session at their convenience. This type of broadcast can enhance not only traditional educational programs, from kindergarten through higher education, but also it can make specialized continuing education and training available to professionals who aren't looking for a degree program.

As Figure 8.2 illustrates, participation in the Distance Learning Network's program requires registration before the broadcast. A toll-free telephone number, as well as an online registration form, make it easy for learners to sign up for and receive information about the broadcasts.

Butler Community College's Web site describes its available distance learning and satellite programs (see Figure 8.3) with an itemized list of benefits for groups who want to participate in distance learning courses. This institution boasts 2,700 host locations, making it easy for many learners to participate in courses without traveling far to a site that can receive the teleconference.

Teleconferencing is used by many educational institutions. Gallaudet University provides satellite-broadcast interactive programs from its campus to national or international sites. Participants in the teleconference can see and hear people broadcasting from the Gallaudet campus site and interact with the speakers/presenters through telephone and fax. A special benefit of Gal-

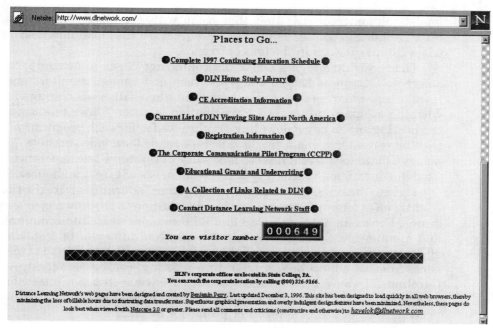

Figure 8.2 Distance Learning Network's registration information.

http://www.dlnetwork.com/
© Distance Learning Network 1996

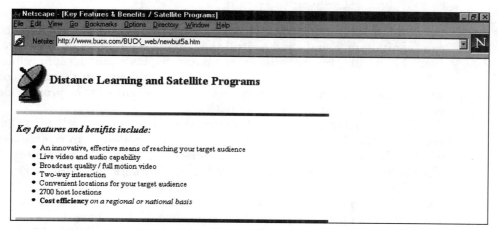

Figure 8.3 Butler Communications, Inc.'s distance learning and satellite programs.

http://www.bucx.com/BUCX_web/newbut5a.htm
© Bulter Communications, Inc. 1996

laudet teleconferences is that they come with open captions and American Sign Language signing, as well as voiceovers, so that deaf and hearing audiences can participate in the teleconference.

The receiving site of a Gallaudet conference needs to be equipped with a steerable C-band or Ku-band satellite dish and enough monitors and phone lines to allow learners to see the broadcast, then call or send a fax to interact with the speakers/presenters. Participation in one of these sessions requires the hosting site to pay a downlink or a license fee for each program, which can then be viewed live and a single videotape made for a video archive. The technology allows for a great deal of flexibility in the ways teleconferences can be used in education and training to meet the needs of target audiences.

Private businesses, consortia, and other educational institutions frequently offer teleconferencing services in addition to their own courses or programs. For example, South Carolina ETV combines satellite communications and a statewide closed-circuit television system to create teleconferences. It offers services to businesses and the community, so that any type of teleconference, from an educational session to a meeting, can be broadcast. As South Carolina ETV's Web site indicates (http:// www.scetv.org/), teleconferencing can be an effective tool for training and professional development, as well as a practical way of bringing together people for meetings.

Typical Teleconferencing Scenarios

Teleconferencing can involve compressed video within an interactive classroom set up to be used primarily for teleconferences. The classroom used for teleconferencing is usually dedicated to this type of instruction; it has been equipped with special consoles, in-table microphones or moveable microphones that allow the room set-up to change with the type of course, and television monitors. Educators/trainers typically work from a console, from which they can manipulate visuals and control the camera's emphasis on their presentation. Documents, transparencies, computer displays, photographs, slides, and other graphics can be displayed for a viewing audience in the classroom and the remote site(s). Educators/trainers can project samples or provide close-up demonstrations and workshop activities.

The instructors also present information on screen, as well as in the classroom, and television cameras show the viewing audiences in remote locations what is being presented at the site where the broadcast originates. Microphones located at the console, as well as on learners' tables or workstations, allow learners and educators/trainers to talk with each other within the classroom, as well as discuss coursework with learners in a remote location. Many rooms are set up so that the video can be switched to show the person who is speaking; in this way, the educator/trainer knows who is speaking and can communicate directly with that learner.

Learners in a remote location can see what's happening in the site originating the transmission, but the educators/trainers and learners at the origination site also can see and/or hear the participants in remote sites. When two-way audio and video communication is established, the classroom or training site really becomes multiple sites, because learners and educators/trainers interact face to face, whether they are physically in the same room or separated geographically. If two-way audio and video communication isn't possible, two-way video and one-way audio (from the educators/trainers to the remote site) at least allows participants in remote locations to see what's taking place at the transmission site. As described in the Gallaudet University example, some teleconferences allow learners to send messages to the educator/trainer by phone or fax, instead of directly through the broadcast. The capabilities for interaction depend on the technology used. However, the distance learning course is much more effective when everyone at each location can hear and see, and therefore fully participate, in the teleconference.

Teleconferencing can involve a satellite uplink and downlink to provide full-motion presentations and a better image. The cost of the technology required for this type of distance learning may be prohibitive for some programs, because the receiving location must be equipped with downlink equipment, and the transmitting location must have a studio or appropriate remote location or an interactive classroom from which to broadcast, complete with uplink and downlink equipment. The equipment to complete satellite transmissions provides a better quality visual, but the cost is higher than that of compressed video.

In addition to using the technology to create the teleconference, educators/trainers who work with teleconferences need a *presentation personality*, as described in Chapter 5. Even if they're using the latest technology, the quality of the course depends on the educator's/trainer's effectiveness in presenting information to learners. Teaching or training via teleconference in many ways is similar to classroom or on-site presentations, and effective educators/trainers know how to work with their audience and present information in several different formats. In this way, they better meet the needs of learners with different learning preferences. They also keep the course presentations lively and interesting.

WHEN IS TELECONFERENCING BENEFICIAL?

Teleconferencing is not a perfect educational or training tool, but it can offer several benefits to educators/trainers and learners. There is a limit to the number of sites that can be linked in a teleconference, either because of the number of sites with the available technology or the number of participants that one or a few educators/trainers can work with effectively at one time.

Depending upon the technology used, for example, compressed video connections can link from two to four sites, which can be displayed on a monitor. Even if the technology allows more connections, viewing learners in remote locations on a half to a quarter of the monitor's screen is about the limit for effective communication. At times, only one site may be viewed on the screen, so that a demonstration or materials being shown by the educator/trainer can be more clearly seen by learners in every site. Despite the limitations to effective viewing and communication, one educator/trainer still can serve more learners, in widely separated geographic areas, via teleconferencing and create a "real" classroom by "virtually" being in several places at once.

Teleconferencing can bring education and training to learners who otherwise wouldn't have access to the course or program. These learners would be left out if they didn't participate in a teleconference-based course, because the instruction isn't available in a close location and travel costs or inconveniences can keep learners from going where the instruction is offered. Convenience and additional educational and training opportunities are important points in teleconferencing's favor.

Another benefit for the vendor offering courses through teleconferencing is a broader revenue base. Learners who just wouldn't take courses because they aren't available in their travelable region can take distance learning courses; the vendor who offers programs people need to this previously untapped market can generate more revenue. Making more educational and training opportunities available in a format that's highly desirable for learners is a good way of marketing a distance learning program and increasing income.

An important communication benefit of teleconferencing within a course is the increased contact between educators/trainers and learners. The technology allows real-time interaction, which may be especially effective for some types of instruction (e.g., demonstrations, workshops, discussions) or subject matter. Teleconferences create the illusion of a real classroom, because learners far distant from the educator/trainer still can see and/or hear the instructor and other learners.

In addition, teleconferences can be video- or audiotaped for later reference or use. The tapes may be sold, as well as loaned to learners. People who miss out on a teleconference or who want to review a class session may borrow or buy the tapes. In addition, people who are interested in teaching or taking a course using teleconferences can view or listen to the tapes to learn more about the way a teleconference works in a distance education program. These benefits may make teleconferences a good supplement to your distance learning program or convince you to use teleconferencing as the primary means of instruction in a distance learning course.

Teleconferencing is not ideal in all distance learning situations, but it is effective within specific uses. More than many other distance learning technologies, teleconferencing brings learners and educators/trainers face-to-face;

it creates a sense of community and allows more personal interaction among participants. It can offer the best parts of classroom or in-house instruction with the benefits of learning at a distance.

DESKTOP VIDEOCONFERENCING IN A DISTANCE LEARNING COURSE

Desktop videoconferencing (or just videoconferencing) is similar to teleconferencing. An educator/trainer can be seen and/or heard by a single learner or groups of learners for real-time interaction. However, instead of relying on another form of telecommunications to transmit and receive the presentation, the course session is conducted online through personal computers that may be connected by modems to telephone lines. Desk videoconferencing involves individuals who can be seen by a camera linked to their personal computer; in effect, the "conference" is created through a LAN consisting of the videoconference's participants. Learners and educators/trainers can discuss information, ask and respond to questions, and share documents and other materials in real time, but they can conduct the desktop videoconference from any personal computer equipped with the technology (e.g., a camera, conferencing software).

When educators/trainers conduct a videoconference, they can see and hear the participants through Internet technology. In addition, through a video window on their computer screen, they may share documents or even send e-mail messages. Unlike a teleconference, in which learners usually don't send documents to the educator/trainer, during a desktop videoconference, learners may share documents stored on their computer or attach documents to e-mail messages. Because the conference links individual personal computers, the session may be more interactive for individual learners, who can choose to share information directly or ask questions about materials stored on their unit.

If videoconferencing is part of your distance learning program, you should clearly explain to potential participants what kind of equipment, including hardware and software specifications, they need to be able to participate in a videoconference. Some learners may need to purchase software or upgrade their computers, for example, so that they can take a videoconference-based course. Some employers may decide to purchase equipment so that more employees can be trained via videoconferencing. You should let potential participants know long before the first videoconference what is required of them and how to set up the system to enable a videoconference.

Developing protocols for the videoconferencing, like protocols for using e-mail or other Internet communication, is important to make sure everyone follows the appropriate netiquette. Sometimes during a videoconference there is a lag in communication time between the moment a person finishes speaking and the moment that the communication "arrives" on screen. If you work with videoconferencing and experience a communication lag, you might want to establish a procedure to indicate when one participant finishes talking and another person can begin. Although overlapping conversations are possible among multiple participants in a videoconference, they often can be difficult to follow.

Videoconferencing allows participants to work together in real time, but it doesn't create the same classroom feeling as a teleconference does. Learners and educators/trainers still primarily work alone at a personal computer; although the videoconference may involve several people, each person still is isolated at his or her computer. However, videoconferencing offers a benefit over teleconferencing: Participants don't have to meet at a prearranged teleconference site to be able to see and hear the course; they only need access to their computer set-up, which may be at home, in the office, or at another work site. Videoconferencing through the Internet may be more flexible than teleconferencing for many learners.

BENEFITS OF DESKTOP VIDEOCONFERENCING

Desktop videoconferencing allows individuals to "call" other learners and educators/trainers from their home, office, or work-site computer. The communication can be much more personal and interactive than voice mail, faxmail, or e-mail, and it provides the benefit of letting participants see, as well as talk with, each other.

Videoconferencing allows a more personal touch to electronic communication than, for example, e-mail or the use of Web sites. When participants first use videoconferencing, they can express themselves more often and spend more time working with fewer people, because videoconferences generally accommodate fewer people than teleconferences. Individuals may receive more attention from educators/trainers and may feel more relaxed because they're conducting the conference from their home or office computer.

However, some learners may feel self-conscious using a videoconference, if they're not used to being on view when they normally work at a computer. Nuances of language and expression come across during a videoconference and any "quirky" facial expressions or distracting mannerisms can detract from a participant's communication effectiveness. Since each participant can be seen and heard, learners and educators/trainers should make a special effort to communicate effectively, whether they're keying in information, talking with other participants, or listening. However, this face-to-face communication is primarily a strength of videoconferencing, simply because participants can see and hear each other.

The convenience of videoconferencing from a home or office computer usually makes up for the lack of perfection in the video or audio quality. Learners can schedule videoconferences with a smaller number of people and can therefore adjust conference times to accommodate learners' time zones and schedules. Also, because videoconferencing doesn't require reserving a room equipped for broadcasts, videoconferences may be scheduled more quickly, as the need to share information in-person arises. More videoconferences (than teleconferences, for example) may be able to be scheduled.

ADDITIONAL TELECONFERENCING AND VIDEOCONFERENCING BENEFITS FOR EDUCATORS, TRAINERS, INSTITUTIONS, AND COMPANIES

Teleconferencing or videoconferencing can assist educators and trainers, too. Educators/trainers who are away from their regular classroom or training site can still present their regularly scheduled courses while they're away. With a videoconference or teleconference, the educator/trainer can be anywhere and still meet with learners regularly.

Educators/trainers whose institutions or companies lack the resources (in time and/or money) to send them to remote locations can still *virtually travel.* Teleconferencing and videoconferencing bring people together without the hassles and costs of travel. However, to be fair, you should balance the cost of equipment against the cost of travel before you determine if teleconferencing or videoconferencing are ultimately cost-effective for your institution or company.

In addition, a teleconference or a videoconference can be used to introduce potential learners to an institution's or a business's programs or site. An "open house" can be offered so that learners can see and/or hear discussions, ask questions, and "meet" the people with whom they'll work. Later courses may or may not involve regularly scheduled teleconferences or videoconferences, but the initial "welcome" and information-gathering sessions can be held face-to-face through the technology.

Being creative in your use of teleconferences and videoconferences can help you promote your distance learning programs and show people unfamiliar with the technology how it can be used to enhance education and training. Using teleconferences and videoconferences as part of your institution's or company's promotional activities allows the community to see your level of technical sophistication, which can enhance you and your institution's/company's professional reputation. It also makes people aware of the variety of services you can provide. Finally, it can help you partner with other businesses, especially those in the telecommunications industry.

When other professionals know of your interest in teleconferencing and videoconferencing and can see your current and planned future capabilities, you're more likely to generate interest from potential partners. These partners may work with you to provide additional technology or expertise to help you plan the next wave of distance learning courses. They also can be valuable resources when you write the next grant proposal or seek sources of future funding for your projects. In many ways, showcasing your company's or institution's teleconferencing or videoconferencing capabilities can be helpful now and in the long run.

As distance learning technologies become more common, the use of different telecommunications tools can enhance current course presentations or expand the number and types of courses that are offered. You don't have to be a technical specialist to work with teleconferences or videoconferences. If you have a basic vocabulary (see the Glossary for additional terms) and an understanding of what you want to accomplish through a teleconference or videoconference, you can work with the technical experts at your company or institution to develop an effective single session or an entire course.

SUMMARY

Although teleconferencing and videoconferencing bridge the "distance" gap in distance learning, they still resemble many aspects of traditional classroom or on-site education or training courses. What is good about face-to-face instruction can be what is good about teleconferencing or videoconferencing. However, if the educators/trainers lack a good broadcast personality or design information that is difficult to see on screen, or if they don't work well with the technology, the benefits of this type of presentation are lost. To make the best use of teleconferences or videoconferences, educators/trainers must carefully design materials to be seen and used by all learners, but they must also respond individually and to groups of learners in a real-time setting.

Advertising Your Distance Learning Program

9

When you've developed a distance learning course or program, you want others to know about it. Even if you're only planning a course or changes to a program, you might want to alert professionals and prospective students to your plans, so that they can keep up with changes in your Web site or look for upcoming announcements. Depending upon the medium or media used in the distance learning program, you can use a variety of media to advertise your courses or announce upcoming programs.

Just as the development of your distance learning program should be carefully planned, so should advertisements. And just as you may want to bring together a team, including professionals who specialize in design or technology, to develop a Web site, set up a teleconference, or otherwise plan an effective distance learning program, so you may need to bring together a team of advertising and marketing professionals who will help you plan the most effective advertisement campaign. The need for outside assistance depends on your experience with marketing and your expertise in targeting the audience(s) for your product.

Terms like *marketing* and *advertising* may sound crass when applied to education or training. Some educational professionals resist using these terms. After all, education and training should be noble aims, not a marketable product. However, because information has become a commodity, and education and training a lifelong need, the market for gathering information and developing new skills has become more competitive. As telecommunications technology becomes accessible to more homes and businesses, our lives seem to become more crowded with activities and responsibilities. Consequently, learners' expectations for their education and training are heightened. Thus, marketing and advertising are crucial to a distance learning program's success.

Advertisements are especially important with distance learning courses, although all educators and trainers may need to promote even local or in-house programs. After all, you want to reach learners across the barriers of time and space. Therefore, you need to make this potential market aware that you offer high-quality distance learning courses. You need to advertise your programs using several possible media across the miles, nationally and/or internationally. Marketing your programs is another ongoing task and challenge.

FORMS OF ADVERTISEMENTS

When you decide to advertise your program, you probably will take a multi-pronged approach, using different media at different times to reach different parts of your target market. Therefore, you may need to design several varied advertisements and announcements to promote your program. A basic decision should involve the types of media appropriate for advertising your program. You may work with one or a combination of these media: print, broadcast (e.g., radio, television), and online (e.g., Internet, Web sites, mailing lists).

Another consideration should be the availability of various forms of media in the area you wish to market your distance learning programs. Some markets may have limited television or radio broadcast sources, and viable alternatives, such as local access cable television, may need to be utilized. Some market areas, where print media is extremely limited, may require you to focus more on broadcast outlets. In every instance, it is best to consider the availability of media before launching a promotional campaign.

When you designed your course(s), you determined the potential audience(s) who might be interested in taking the course(s). Use this audience analysis to determine where your market might be, which media may be most effective in reaching them, and how often and when these ads should be directed to them. This audience analysis can help you decide which medium or media are appropriate for each part of your target market. After you decide which media are appropriate, you (or you and professional marketing representatives or advertising agents) can begin to plan a strategy for developing and presenting advertisements.

PRINT ADVERTISEMENTS

If your market does not have easy access to online information, or is not computer literate, but still needs to take a distance learning course, you can reach them with print advertisements. Likewise, if your distance learning course involves more print than broadcast or electronic technologies (e.g., surface mail of printed materials), print advertisements are a good way to let people know about the course.

If your audience regularly uses broadcast or electronic media, but you want to reach them when they're not viewing or listening to broadcasts or browsing the Internet (e.g., when they're traveling by plane, sitting in a waiting room, relaxing at home), then you can use print advertisements as part of your marketing strategy.

Print ads can be placed in larger publications, such as newsletters, newspapers, magazines, and journals. They may be complete entities, such as brochures, flyers, and booklets. Because print ads are portable, potential learners can take the ads (or the documents in which the ads were placed) with them for future reference. Therefore, a major benefit is that print ads can be read when other media are unavailable. Often, print ads are much less expensive in total cost (but not necessarily in cost/per person who sees the ad).

For example, you might place an advertisement about the distance learning course in your institution's or company's in-house newsletter or magazine, so that employees and current students know that training and educational programs are available in other formats. You might include a Web address in a full-page ad in local or regional newspapers to advertise an upcoming term's courses, both on-site and via distance learning. Those people who are used to seeing upcoming courses advertised then know that distance learning options are available, and those who have Web access can check the home page to learn more.

If you're an independent vendor, or if your business consists of developing distance learning programs (including on-site workshops and teleconferences), you probably will need more print advertisements than a half- or full-page ad in periodicals. Most consultants or vendors develop a brochure, booklet, or at least a mailer/flyer to describe their business, courses, and services.

You may need to purchase the mailing lists from professional associations whose members may be interested in your courses' subject areas or target a bulk mailing to persons within a particular region. Your advertisement must clearly identify who you are and what types of distance learning you offer. Attract the reader's attention immediately and make your ad stand out from other mail, including the daily junk mail that may be tossed without a second glance. Glossy print pieces, especially multiple-page brochures and mailers, may be expensive to produce and mail. If you use these print pieces, you should carefully target the people who will receive them to ensure that you reach your potential learners, but don't break your advertising budget.

As part of your marketing strategy, target previous customers (people who have taken at least one course from your institution or business in the past two years) for a mass mailing before you announce a new slate of courses. The mailing may consist of a brochure that outlines upcoming courses for the next term, quarter, or six months, for example. Within the print information should be references to your institution's or business's e-mail and Web site addresses.

You may also decide to develop a brochure that can be given to prospective learners, sent with other items in a mailing, or handed out at trade fairs and conferences. This brochure may have more permanent types of information that don't become outdated quickly, such as general course and program descriptions, registration information, and background about your institution or company.

If you're involved with in-house training programs, for example, you may generate more interest in the distance learning courses by developing a corporate newsletter with regular features on training and in-house distance learning opportunities. The publication probably should be in print, so that it can be mailed to other people outside the company who might be interested in learning more about distance learning, but an electronic newsletter may also be a good venture to promote your programs.

BROADCAST ADVERTISEMENTS

Broadcast advertisements may be placed with local or national radio or television stations. However, most vendors of distance learning programs won't need to target a national television or radio audience. Even though you're working with a distance learning program, it might be more economical and effective to target a particular broadcast area for your ads. For example, blanket a state or a region where you think there are more potential learners. Within that smaller geographic area, place ads with most or all radio and TV stations before the next time that you offer a course or begin a term. Your ads can be very specific at these times.

In addition, if you're a vendor who offers distance learning courses and programs throughout the year, consider developing more general spots to advertise your company or institution. Place these ads throughout the year to let your market learn more about your programs and the services offered.

Broadcast spots vary in cost by the number of ads, their placement in the broadcast schedule (e.g., at different times of the day or night, whether in a prime viewing or listening time, on certain days), and the length of the spot. In addition, your cost will vary depending upon the station's popularity (e.g., usually as measured in ratings and demographics by the type of audience the station and its programming attracts). You might be able to save costs by buying a specific number of airings or purchasing a package of airings, in which you can vary the number, placement, and length of spots for a set price.

In addition to buying the air time, you probably will want the station to produce an advertising spot or you may hire an advertising company to create one for you. That means an additional cost for production, including the talent, music, effects, props, sets, and studio or location, not to mention mixing, dubbing, editing, and other production techniques. However, this type of ad may reach more people and be reused more than some print ads.

If you're interested in reaching a wide audience, but one that has specialized interests, your company or institution might sponsor a program regionally. For example, if you will be offering a new series of courses about marine biology, you might sponsor a locally shown PBS program about marine studies, undersea exploration, or another related topic. You may be given several spots for your sponsorship of the program and possibly some promotion when the program is also advertised. Sponsorship can be expensive, but it can be effective if you need to reach an audience with specific interests.

ONLINE ADVERTISEMENTS

Some print-type ads appear as banners above frequently visited Web sites, like the home page of a browser or a popular address, such as the *search* page for AltaVista, Excite, Magellan, Yahoo, or another search engine. The ad might be very simple, looking much like a two-dimensional print ad, or it may involve programming so that the ad has animation, counters, or a special effect (such as "flashing" or "blinking"). The cost of an online ad in a very public forum often depends upon the ad's complexity, size, and the length of its stay at the site. This type of advertising may cost several thousand dollars, but it can reach thousands, if not millions of people, during a single day.

If you need this type of coverage, the cost per person reached may be economical. However, few distance learning vendors need this type of coverage, at least now. Distance learning vendors who truly have an international market all year may use this form of advertising more than companies or institutions that offer limited distance learning programs. Although general Internet advertising hasn't been frequently used to promote distance learning programs in the past, it should become a more popular advertising venue in the future.

Online advertisements can be simpler and less costly if they are placed in your program's or your institution's or company's Web site. For example, if you already offer Web-based distance learning courses, you can easily promote upcoming courses for the next term or next series to learners currently taking courses. Adding information about upcoming courses—like announcements—alerts learners to additional courses they may want to take.

If you wish to expand your advertisements to a slightly wider audience, make similar announcements about upcoming courses to newsgroups, via mailing lists, and on electronic bulletin boards. Also, make sure your site is linked to other Web sites that are visited frequently. For example, ensure that your site is referenced by several different search engines, so that when potential learners want to learn about a particular course or even search for general information about distance learning, your site will be listed.

The following figures illustrate one site offering links to educators who offer courses online. By filling out an online form, educators can add a description of their course to the database. When potential learners want to access information about courses dealing with a specific subject matter, they can search among

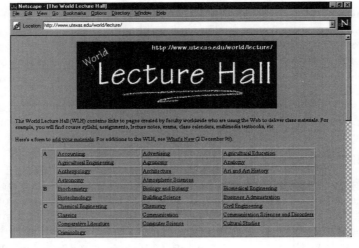

Figure 9.1 The World Lecture Hall.

http://www.utexas.edu/world/lecture
© University of Texas 1996

the current descriptions of online courses for that topic, no matter where the course originates. The home page in Figure 9.1 describes the database.

Within the database, as well as in the "updates" link, educators have listed course descriptions, such as new information in the update file, as shown in Figure 9.2.

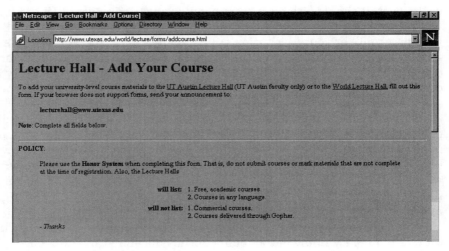

Figure 9.2 World Lecture Hall course policy.

http://www.utexas.edu/world/lecture
© University of Texas 1996

Figures 9.3 and 9.4 show segments of the online form educators fill out and submit electronically when they want to add their course description to the database. By carefully writing the description, as well as choosing the links representing the course and its location in the database, educators can make

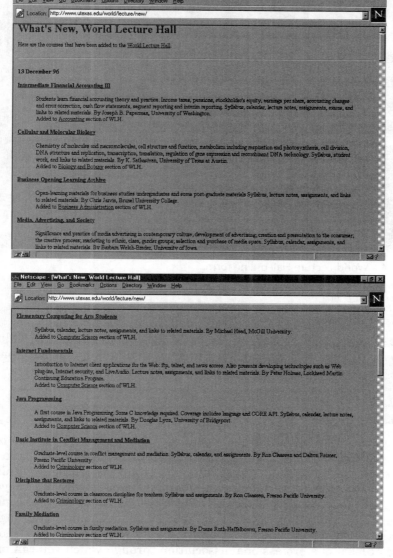

Figure 9.3 World Lecture Hall online form—descriptions.

http://www.utexas.edu/world/lecture
© University of Texas 1996

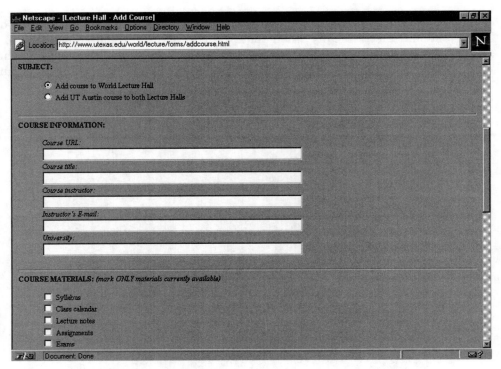

Figure 9.4 World Lecture Hall online form.

http://www.utexas.edu/world/lecture
© University of Texas 1996

sure prospective learners have an accurate idea about the course. Educators can also make their course description unique, so that it stands out from other entries.

OTHER FORMS OF PROMOTION

Promotion can take many forms, depending upon your region, type of business, type of distance learning program, and academic emphases. If you offer a wide variety of courses and target different groups of learners within your market, you have several different professional groups with which you can associate and different events through which you can promote your courses. If you offer a few courses or have a very specific educational or training focus, your promotional efforts may be more narrowly focused, but you should be aware of at least one professional association through which you can promote your program. In addition, community events give you an opportunity to show others what your business or institution has to offer via distance learning.

Conferences, Trade Fairs, Career Fairs, and Open Houses

Educators in academia have other ways of promoting their distance learning courses or programs. Because most educators are encouraged, if not required, to attend meetings and conferences held by professional associations, people who offer distance learning courses can frequently share information about their institution and programs with other educators and administrators. Most professional associations, whether they are involved with general education (e.g., boards of education; elementary and secondary education), a subject specialization (e.g., technical communication, engineering, physics, computer science), or a region (e.g., a state-based group of professionals, a regional council, a territory's board of directors), hold meetings, conferences, and workshops. Participants may meet as a group in a single location or they may have teleconferences and videoconferences in lieu of travel. Nevertheless, they present numerous opportunities for sharing information about new courses and programs, as well as what works and what doesn't work in distance learning.

Of course, promoting your distance learning courses and programs in professional meetings and conferences may be more beneficial for you than cost-effective for your institution. Because the people who attend these meetings are often involved with their own distance learning programs (which may compete with yours) or may be interested in starting their own programs, you might find yourself in demand as a colleague or an expert about distance learning. However, you may not gain many potential new learners for your courses. Nevertheless, if you are associated with high-quality courses and programs, and you can offer assistance or advice for other professionals working with distance learning, you and your institution build a good reputation in this growing educational area. This reputation may help you as you apply for grants or look for partners to support future distance learning initiatives.

Some industries hold trade fairs to introduce new products and services. If your courses provide innovative approaches to new technologies or help employees update their technical skills, you may benefit by sponsoring a booth at a trade fair.

Career fairs are another good way to showcase your institution or company and its distance learning programs. Communities and individual schools often host career fairs so that their students or adults in the area can learn more about further education and training. You may want to provide a demonstration of the types of distance learning capabilities you offer, as well as hand out brochures, calendars, and registration materials.

Another way to let your peers, as well as the larger community of potential learners, know about distance learning opportunities is to host an open house or to schedule workshops, demonstrations, or tours of your facilities. By bringing your colleagues and/or members of surrounding communities into your facility, you can showcase your use of technology, your personnel, and your programs.

Professional Publications

Another way to promote your programs among professionals, with the resulting benefits accrued from an enhanced reputation, is through publications. Again, most educators are at least encouraged to publish information, both electronically and in hardcopy, about their distance learning courses and experiences in developing distance learning materials. Some periodicals offer research-based articles, in which educators can illustrate the measured success of their distance learning programs. Both qualitative and quantitative research is and should be published about the efficiency of individual distance learning programs and their generalizations to wider distance learning applications.

Most professional associations have quarterly journals, as well as more frequently published newsletters, for which educators can write articles. With the advent of more scholarly e-zines or the simultaneous presentation of hardcopy and softcopy issues of journals, educators have more opportunities to promote their distance learning programs in print and electronically. Although some potential learners may first become familiar with your distance learning programs from reading about them in a scholarly publication, you benefit most from a positive association with a well-respected program or courses. As you apply for grants, for example, you are often asked to provide evidence of your knowledge and experience. The ability to show a series of publications about distance learning helps to establish your role as an expert, one to whom funds or materials should be granted.

Interviews, Press Releases, and Features

Yet another form of promotion can be in the form of news. Especially if your program is highly regarded or you or your institution (or company) have developed a reputation for excellence in distance learning, you might encourage promotion through interviews. You might be interviewed for an in-house publication, which can promote your program to other employees, administrators, or students, or to a community or regional publication or broadcast. During an interview, you can explain your programs and indicate changes in upcoming courses and technologies. This type of promotion receives wider recognition not only from colleagues and peers, but also from potential learners, who might first learn about your program through a newspaper article, special print feature in a local magazine, or a television broadcast.

You may also work closely with local media representatives to feature your participation in community events or special events sponsored by your company or institution. If you hold an open house, for example, you should invite local media representatives to cover the event. You might suggest that an area radio station run a live remote broadcast from your event throughout the day or evening, for example. Other features can involve taped news features that describe the event and when it will take place; these short features may air on local television news broadcasts once or several times on the day before the event. Always make the local media aware of special events taking place at your business or institution or your sponsorship and/or participation in community events. The more often that your business or institution is spotlighted, the more opportunities you have to mention your distance learning program, even if distance learning isn't the focus of the current feature.

In addition to interviews and features, promotion takes place through press releases and news stories that your company or institution generates. Most businesses and academic institutions have a public relations person or department to write and release information to the local media. If you haven't been approached by your in-house public relations department, try writing a news release or suggest a story about your distance learning program. Sometimes you have to take the initiative in making sure the right people in your organization know about your program. Then the public relations people can take the information and promote your courses.

Many institutions and companies also use videos generally to promote their services. If your organization regularly relies on videos as part of its ongoing promotion to community or professional groups, or during site visits, trade shows, or other public presentations, then you will want to develop video information describing your distance learning programs. You might even need a separate video to highlight the role of distance learning within your company or institution.

If your distance learning program is Internet-based, you should make sure that the Web address for your course information appears in all corporate or institutional literature and videos. For example, your in-house newsletter might list your Web address along with important phone and fax numbers and e-mail addresses. At the end of a corporate or institutional video, your Web address should be listed.

Word of Mouth

Keep in mind that word of mouth is an excellent form of promotion. If you show people how effective distance learning is, whether through an on-site visit or from their experience as learners taking a course, you effectively advertise your programs to other potential learners. By being responsive to learner needs and finding several ways to show people what distance learning is and how your programs operate, you can effectively (and inexpensively) develop the best type of promotion, through positive word of mouth.

A MARKETING PLAN FOR DISTANCE LEARNING PROGRAMS

As you plan marketing and advertising strategies, work closely with experts who understand your market and objectives, and can help you adequately and cost effectively promote your courses and program. To help develop a marketing plan, you should first understand some basic principles of how the plan works. Then you can work more efficiently with the experts who will put your plan into action. If you're responsible for the program's promotion, analyze the marketing plan very carefully and map a strategy for implementing it. A marketing plan usually consists of these steps:

1. Conduct a situational analysis of where your program is, how it got there, and where it's now headed.
2. Establish marketing objectives that clearly specify where you want the program to go.
3. Map a marketing strategy that explains in detail how you'll meet your objectives (e.g., what will be done, who will do it, when it will be done).
4. Analyze your target audiences (again)—what appeals to them, what their needs are, etc.
5. Determine the position you want in the market (e.g., you want to be known as a leader in business teleconferencing services; you want to be the only vendor in your area to offer an online degree program in a subject area; you want to offer the lowest cost Web-based courses for adults within your region).
6. Determine the mix of media and advertising you want (e.g., you want to use only print media throughout the year; you plan a 50-50 mix of television and radio advertisements of your courses three weeks before a new term starts).

A simple example of the way you might implement this procedure when you want to market your distance learning program includes evaluating the program, setting objectives, identifying personnel and equipment, analyzing the target audience, identifying your market role, and selecting media for marketing.

Evaluate Program

You've already conducted an audience analysis as you designed your distance learning courses and program. Use this analysis as a starting point, but then ask more general questions about the current status of your program: What is working well in your current program? Why does it work well? What hasn't been so successful? Why do you think it hasn't been as successful? Where do you want the program to be in one year? in five years? By taking the time to evaluate your program's successes and weaknesses, you learn what has made your program work in the past and what is likely to work in the future. By taking into account current trends in technology, education, and training, you also can anticipate where you want your program to be in the future. Analyze the types of programs that may need elimination, course areas into which you can expand, and new or different technologies that will be needed to continue to meet learners' demands.

Some companies and institutions are required to develop annual strategic plans, as well as plans for the next 5 to 10 years. The analysis you conduct at this stage of your marketing plan can help you work with larger strategic plans. Conversely, if you understand where your business is headed and the areas of emphasis that will be important for the next few years, you can determine where distance learning initiatives fit into the scope of the whole business.

Set Objectives

Set objectives that are as precise as possible. A general objective like "We want to increase the number of learners in courses" won't help you develop a series of steps for action. An effective objective is detailed enough so that you can measure whether you achieve it and it gives you a good idea of the steps to take to ensure that you meet it. A better revision of the general objective might be, "We will increase the number of adult learners by 25 percent in the five business communication courses offered online during fiscal 1997 through two open houses at our corporate training center and a series of television ads broadcast throughout a four-state radius."

The detail in this objective shows how you can measure the outcome: Adult enrollment in five business communication courses must increase 25 percent within the fiscal year. The objective also indicates how you plan to achieve this: by hosting two open houses at the corporate training center and broadcasting a series of TV ads within your region. Objectives can be even more specific; you may create several, depending upon the scope of your program and the changes you want to make to keep it marketable.

Identify Personnel and Equipment

Once you've set objectives, you need to determine who will work together to complete the tasks required to meet each objective. Your team's responsibilities should be broken down into manageable tasks. Then you can create a timeline to indicate when each step will start and end. You'll also need to figure the costs to achieve each step, the equipment and facilities needed for each task, and any additional personnel, whether in-house or contracted, who might be assigned to assist with each task. Now you have an approach to implement your marketing ideas and meet your objectives.

Analyze Target Audience

At this point, you should analyze your target population(s) of learners again. If you've offered distance learning courses before, you should have evaluations from learners and educators/trainers. Use these evaluations as one method of learning what your audience likes, dislikes, needs, and wants. You also might survey potential learners to see what appeals most to them about distance learning courses. If you're working with an in-house training group, you also might survey supervisors and managers to learn what they would like their employees to gain from a distance learning program and how such a program would work best for their department or division. Knowing as much as you can about your market of potential customers/learners helps you fine tune the marketing strategy and, later, develop an advertising campaign and individual ads that appeal to your market.

Identify Market Niche

Determine exactly how you want to be viewed by your learners, as well as by other vendors, your colleagues, and your industry, business, or community. Your program can't offer everything to every learner, so you need to emphasize a market niche. When you envision your role in distance learning, you're more likely to work toward that goal, and set and meet objectives to help you work toward that goal.

Select Appropriate Media

Your company's or institution's budget and the availability of media may have a big influence on the media you employ for marketing. If you have a low budget, you may have few ads, but you may rely on low-cost promotional activities and professional associations to spread the word about your program. If you have a large budget, you might target several broadcast media, as well as print, in an ongoing ad campaign to build awareness of your program and conduct periodic motivational campaigns to encourage learners to register for courses. Your emphasis should be specific, so that you know which media will best present your program within the budget allowances you've set (or that have been set for you).

PLANNING ADVERTISING FOR YOUR DISTANCE LEARNING PROGRAM

When you have a marketing plan in place that outlines your approach to promoting your program, you can develop more specific advertising strategies to implement the marketing plan. Determine the purpose for each advertisement within your advertising plan. For example, you may want some ads to make people aware that your institution or business offers distance learning courses and to explain why distance learning is so important. You may develop ads that show your institution's or company's distance learning facilities and typical learners taking a course. The visuals, voiceovers, and/or text (depending upon the medium used for advertising) explain who you are. They subtly persuade listeners or viewers that distance learning is important for continuing skill and knowledge development for a better career and life. They illustrate how easy it is to take a distance learning course and show satisfied learners benefiting from your program. These ads can create a positive impression of your program, and distance learning in general, so that learners will remember your program when they need additional training or education in the future. This type of advertising increases your market's awareness of your institution or business and its programs. It can be used throughout the year to build an understanding of who you are and what you do.

You might decide that action-oriented ads are needed. Action ads motivate learners to do something, such as take a course or visit an open house. These ads prompt learners to act immediately; thus, this type of advertising may be best used immediately before a course or series of courses begins. You might use a harder selling approach in these ads. For example, you might emphasize registration procedures, cutoff dates, and fees in some ads, and describe new courses in others. In distance learning, these ads may have a limited life span, but they get across a specific message to motivate potential learners to act— before it's too late.

Other ads are targeted to learners who have already taken at least one distance learning course from you. Reinforcement advertisements remind learners what they liked about taking distance learning courses and how they benefited from their education and training. Although reinforcement ads can motivate learners to act (e.g., to take another course), they primarily remind previous customers of your business or institution and the courses you offer. At some point in the future, this reminder may prompt learners to take another course or to recommend your courses to others.

In addition to targeting types of ads and the media needed in the campaign, an advertising plan also indicates how you want the target market to perceive your program. The message for each ad within an advertising campaign should build an image of your company or institution and your courses; individual advertisements can be developed to create and enhance this image.

You should work with advertising or marketing agencies or consultants as ads are developed. These experts can help you (or complete the jobs to) create copy, develop storyboards, produce the ads, and buy advertising time or space to best highlight your program. They can help you develop theme campaigns or implement different advertising strategies throughout the year. Each ad should help develop your image as a high-quality vendor of distance learning programs and help you meet your advertising and marketing objectives.

MARKETING AND ADVERTISING CHECKLISTS

When you (preferably as part of an advertising/marketing team) begin to plan direct advertising, as well as promotional activities, to feature your distance learning courses or programs, you should ask yourself several questions. First, you should pull together the people who will make up the marketing team. Then you can later delegate individual tasks to people with the appropriate expertise. You also have to ask questions about the marketing strategy. Once you have a strategy in place, your team can develop individual pieces, such as television ads, print ads, and promotional articles. The following questions provide you with a starting point. As you develop a marketing strategy and implement the plan with advertisements and promotions, you will ask many more specific questions.

Questions about Your Team

- Who has experience developing a marketing strategy?
- Who has experience writing copy for print ads? radio spots? television spots? Web sites?
- Who has experience developing storyboards in preparation for production?
- Who has experience producing advertisements in print? radio? television? electronically?
- Should you rely on an in-house team, a hired consulting group, or a combination of in-house personnel and consultants?
- Who will be responsible for each task in the marketing strategy?
- Who will lead the team?

Questions to Help Develop a Marketing Plan

- What are the objectives for your program?
- How can marketing help achieve your objectives?
- Who is your target audience?
- If you have more than one market, who are your target audiences in general? for specific courses?
- Where is your target audience(s)?
- Which medium is/media are most effective in reaching your target audience(s)?
- What is the time frame for your marketing plan?
- What is your budget?

- Which type of marketing mix do you need (e.g., Should you use all print ads? Should you have a certain percentage of print ads and a certain percentage of radio spots?)
- How often should your strategy be updated?

Questions to Help Develop an Advertising Plan

- What is the theme or the focus of the advertisements in a campaign?
- How often do you need to advertise your entire program, company, or institution?
- How often do you need to advertise specific courses or programs?
- How do individual ads develop and support the entire marketing effort?
- What types of promotional activities can be used to supplement direct advertising?
- How will you evaluate the effectiveness of the advertisements?

SUMMARY

Marketing is an important part of distance learning. Although you can undoubtedly complete some advertising and promotional tasks yourself, you probably will need assistance with a broader marketing strategy. Seldom is one person, or even one in-house group, familiar with all media technologies as well as effective marketing strategies.

Like any other part of distance learning, advertising and promoting programs is crucial. These activities should be given the same consideration as other development aspects of your program. By developing an effective marketing strategy first, then designing individual advertisements, you can achieve the best results for your program.

Reconceptualizing Education and Training through Distance Learning

Educators and trainers are already good at their jobs. They understand that it's important to work with learners, to meet their individual needs as well as the needs of the group. They often are required to present a body of knowledge determined as important in the mastery of a skill and a subject area, but they also realize that education goes beyond the bounds of a daily lesson plan.

Educators/trainers who work with distance learning know how to work with the technology they use in their courses. Just about anyone can put together a Web site, write an e-mail message, learn which switches to flip to operate a console, and so on. The mechanics of creating a source of information and a method of transmitting it can be learned. Almost anyone can develop resources to be made available to others, then to explain what these resources are and where they are located. Anyone can make assignments or lead activities.

The starting point for distance learning should be where the mechanics of establishing information to be transmitted, transmitting the information, and leading activities meets educators/trainers with the interest and the desire not only to teach, but to teach a distance learning course. Not all educators enjoy working in a distance learning program; indeed, some are not as well qualified for this type of teaching. But the educators and trainers who are motivated to assist learners in a distance learning program, and also learn more about distance learning themselves as they continue to work with the technology, should be encouraged to participate.

Distance learning requires educators and trainers, as well as learners, administrators, executives, and others who play any role in a course or program, to take the best of in-person educational and training technologies and methods and find innovative ways to bridge the distance between learner and source of information. The most effective distance learning professionals are working not only to provide highly interesting and effective courses and programs on a daily basis, but also to help their colleagues, learners, and society in general reconceptualize education and training.

A distance learning program works well when four elements are in place:

- A dedicated, highly motivated group of educators or trainers (or a single educator or trainer)
- A dedicated, highly motivated group of learners (or a single learner)
- Effective educational materials designed specifically for the appropriate distance learning application
- Consistent, effective means of transmitting and receiving information

Without each of these elements, the distance learning program may exist, but it will not be worthwhile. In previous chapters, you've read about the technical components of a distance learning program; the type of educators, trainers, and learners needed for the program to be a success; and the types of courses, distance learning applications, and materials that are best suited to a distance learning program. When these elements work together, true education can take place.

TEACHING AND TRAINING IN A VIRTUAL CLASSROOM

Teaching and training via the Internet requires special skills of educators and trainers, just as receiving instruction through the Internet requires different types of preparation and use by learners. However, the institution or company offering distance learning also must understand how a distance learning program stems from its mission and goals. An effective distance learning program is an integral part of an institutional or a corporate approach to education and training. Simply having the capability to offer distance learning courses or programs is not a good objective; meeting the continually changing educational or training needs of learners by providing high-quality materials and services should be part of the company's or institution's mission.

High-quality distance learning is the result of a good combination of qualified educators/trainers, appropriate technologies, effective materials designed for the Internet, and learners who appreciate and need this type of instruction. Each element requires the company or institution offering distance learning programs to plan not only to meet immediate learning needs, but also to enhance the type of program they will offer in the next term, next year, and next century.

Offering distance learning through the Internet requires a forward-thinking approach to education and training, and a sense of the basic importance of additional knowledge and skills. When administrators and executives, in collaboration with technicians, educators, and trainers, design distance learning programs, they should first answer this series of questions:

- How does technology fit with our vision of our institution or business?
- How does technology relate to education or training?
- How can you teach more efficiently with technology?
- How can you better meet learners' needs through a distance learning course?
- How can the institution support the distance learning program, including its instructors?

These five questions not only help determine if the particular institution or company should offer distance learning, but how the courses or programs should be designed, if distance learning is, indeed, a worthy objective.

HOW DOES TECHNOLOGY FIT WITH YOUR VISION OF THE INSTITUTION OR BUSINESS?

Many people want to develop distance learning courses or programs because they are currently in vogue. They can be lucrative and garner prestige for your organization if they're done well. These courses also can help institutions remain marketable in a changing academic environment and help them to train, retrain, and retain employees. Although these are wonderful benefits your institution or business may receive if distance learning initiatives are successful, they aren't good reasons to enter the education business. You should create a distance learning course or program only because it's the best way to provide a service to an untapped group of learners.

Some institutions or businesses do very well in a low-tech environment; the nature of their business and the types of learners they serve don't need to work with much technology to receive the knowledge and skills they need. There is nothing wrong with your institution or business if you don't need to use all the Internet's many services or if basic technology is all that's required to provide instruction to your learners. You should match the technology with your institution's or company's abilities and needs, as well as those of the potential learners in your market.

Institutions and businesses that offer distance learning programs must be comfortable in using technology. They should have the funds and technical support readily available to meet today's needs for technology, but they should also have the resources to expand their technical capabilities as the Internet expands its services. For example, most institutions offering distance learning through the Internet at least offer e-mail services to learners and provide browsers that make using the Web easier and more enjoyable. They maintain one or several Web sites and regularly upgrade software and hardware to accommodate changing expectations for the Internet. In addition, they offer enough technical support so that users have as much access as they need (but not necessarily as much as they ideally would like or would use) to the Internet. If your vision includes expanding technology and you have the resources to meet continually growing technical expectations and needs, you are a good candidate to offer distance learning.

HOW DOES TECHNOLOGY RELATE TO EDUCATION OR TRAINING?

As you read in earlier chapters, some courses and subject matter require little technology for presentation to learners or for learners to practice. Some course materials are better suited to Internet use than others.

For example, a writing course may include some segments in which learners gather information through the Internet. They might ask questions of subscribers to mailing lists dealing with the subject about which they'll write or conduct research through online databases and e-zines to find facts and examples they'll use in their discourse. Learners might send drafts of their work electronically to the educator or other learners, then discuss the assignment via e-mail messages, a newsgroup, or a discussion group. However, the act of writing probably won't require the use of the Internet. Learners who use desktop publishing or word processing to complete their assignments might then attach their work to an e-mail message or link their documents to a course Web site, but the writing itself requires very little technology and would not have to involve the Internet.

Trainees in an automotive course may use desktop videoconferencing or classroom teleconferencing to share ideas, discuss techniques, observe what the trainer shows them, or complete tasks that the trainer can see and comment on. This type of educational experience can take place electronically, as well as in person in a traditional training setting, but neither videoconferencing, teleconferencing, nor traditional classroom training requires the Internet to meet the group's instructional needs. An automotive course may be offered via distance learning, but the appropriate type of distance learning does not necessarily require the use of the Internet.

Other courses rely on the Internet as a means of pulling the class together, as well as disseminating information. An Internet-based biology course might, for example, require activities such as reading texts online—probably through links to Web sites, taking interactive quizzes, and "virtually" dissecting invertebrates in an online simulation. Individual learners might discuss problem areas and further their research interests in private e-mail discussions with the educator. They might conduct research through the use of specialized online databases and mailing lists. Many different Internet services and resources can enhance this type of course, but the activities have to be carefully matched to the skill being developed or the type of learning reinforcement needed at this stage of the course.

Online HTML courses have been particularly effective for learners who expect no course credit but do need to learn about HTML and how to use it to create Web sites. Some courses are free, offered by individuals, institutions, or companies as a service; other courses have been offered through subscriptions to an HTML-generating software. These courses, because they relate to the Web and require the use of a computer, are perfect examples of Web-based courses. The instructions, course materials (usually the HTML generator), examples, and exercises are all geared for the Internet, specifically the Web.

As you determine if and how your institution or business should offer distance learning programs, you need to conduct, course by course and need by need, an analysis of the way technology meshes with the type of educational or training offerings you provide. Using the Internet to enhance instruction is a worthwhile objective, not only for distance learning courses, but for traditionally offered courses. The technology must support your objectives for each course, but the course should not revolve around the use of the technology.

HOW CAN YOU TEACH MORE EFFICIENTLY WITH TECHNOLOGY?

If you can offer instruction to learners in a convenient location, at a convenient time or variety of times, and when the education or training is needed—all without the aid of technology—you don't need a distance learning program. After all, corporations have been offering on-site and in-house training to employees and customers for years, and traditional educational institutions thrive on offering a variety of courses at one or several locations at differing times of the week and year.

Sometimes it's more cost effective to hire more educators or trainers to work with more learners than it is to invest in the technology required for a single instructor to transmit information to a wide audience. It may even be more cost-effective to pay the travel expenses of educators or trainers to go to widely dispersed sites or to bring employees to one location for a comprehensive series of training sessions. When you determine if distance learning is needed, you have to determine the cost-benefits ratio for your business or institution.

Some elements of traditional courses may be taught more efficiently via the Internet. For example, educators or trainers may be able to offer more guidance, answer questions, or make comments on performance more efficiently through e-mail. However, the entire course may not require Internet use or be best designed for the Internet as the primary means of communication. The whole course must be considered to see if teaching with technology is more efficient.

Keep in mind, too, that the educators and trainers, and possibly the learners, must have the skills needed to work with the Internet and the tools required to use it efficiently. As educators or trainers develop new materials, learn to work with new tools, and design courses specifically for the Internet, they may not be as efficient initially as they will be when they have more experience with distance learning through the Internet. Consider these short-term and long-term efficiency rates when you plan a distance learning program.

HOW CAN YOU BEST MEET LEARNERS' NEEDS THROUGH A DISTANCE LEARNING COURSE?

Distance learning courses should be designed with learners in mind. The learners who most need distance learning programs are those with special needs. A special need might be a specific type of training not currently offered nearby and learners would have to travel long distances to receive the required instruction.

Another special need might involve the learners' different physical abilities. A homebound learner, for example, may not be able to commute, participate in a traditional classroom, or work easily with standardized equipment. Learners with limited mobility might find it difficult to take several courses in a traditional classroom but can take courses at home via computer. A different style of keyboard or monitor may help learners read or send information more easily, but these customized pieces of equipment may not be used as readily in a traditional educational setting.

Special needs might involve the learners' personal needs to go over material several times to master it. The time needed to review material and repeat activities may not always be possible in the limited time allotted for a single traditional class or lab session.

Distance learning programs can make education and training more accessible to more people. It can make education and training more desirable and convenient. However, its greatest strength may lie in the way information can be presented in many different multimedia formats, so that learners' preferences can be met. For example, some people prefer to read texts, but others need the hands-on experience of doing. Online documents and simulations can present the same information in different formats so that each learner's preference is met.

Before you determine how distance learning can help individuals and groups, you should analyze your current target population and the possible market you want to reach with your program. Then you can determine if you can offer a unique, or at least highly competitive, course or if you're merely duplicating the efforts of other educational vendors.

HOW CAN THE INSTITUTION SUPPORT THE DISTANCE LEARNING PROGRAM?

Distance learning programs require a great deal of support: financial, technical, educational, and professional. If any type of support is lacking, the program suffers.

Educators and trainers who develop, update, and teach via the Internet require as much, if not more, preparation time and resources than their colleagues who deliver instruction through traditional methods. Course materials must be designed specifically for the Internet, because the medium is electronic. Also, the Internet's resources change daily, and the hardware and software used to access it change frequently. These constant changes require educators and trainers to update their materials and approaches to the subject matter frequently: A good distance learning course will never be offered the same way twice.

Although good teachers vary their methods and materials with each class, instructors who work with the Internet face the ongoing challenge of updating materials. If a course is offered during a traditional term, such as 10 or 15 weeks, the resources the educator requires learners to access may change drastically from the first day to the last. If, for example, at the beginning of a course the educator prepares a list of Web sites offering resources, those sites may change, may not be available, or may no longer be appropriate by the end of the course. Courses that are offered on a continuing basis need to be updated regularly for the same reasons, requiring the educator or trainer who maintains the site to be aware not only of what's needed for a particular course, but what's taking place on the Internet in general. Since a benefit of electronic information is its immediacy, distance learning educators and trainers need the time and resources to keep their course materials and instructional methods current.

Most educators and trainers lack the control they'd like to have over technology and budgets. Therefore, they need the support of technicians who can keep the system running smoothly and who can assist or train the people who design the course materials and content and offer instruction. There should be a good working relationship among the people with technical expertise and the people with the educational design expertise. It's better if these groups don't consist of the same people, so that individual technicians, trainers, and educators are not overwhelmed with work.

Because distance learning programs can become expensive, and technology needs tend to be ongoing, your institution or business must be committed financially to the program. Planning for future funds, including the use of grant moneys and shared resources, is a necessity.

Educational support is necessary for educators and trainers. Their area of expertise includes the design of appropriate course materials, then the presentation of those materials. They should be the persons allowed to design the course. No matter how well-meaning their intentions, technicians, executives, administrators, and others who have other areas of expertise should leave the course design to the people with the educational expertise. Designing an online course should be as individual as the educator/trainer, the course, and the institution or business offering the course.

Finally, professional development should be an ongoing requirement for persons involved with distance learning. They must be aware of the way technology is evolving and how distance learning programs are changing the nature of education and training. Professionals must be allowed to share ideas with colleagues and learn from others involved in distance learning initiatives. Therefore, they should be given the support to attend conferences, participate in seminars, read periodicals, collaborate online with colleagues, and experiment with new technologies. They may need specific training to learn to use new tools or to use them more efficiently. If your institution or business can provide these types of support to educators and trainers, you can design an effective distance learning program.

PRINCIPLES FOR EFFECTIVE DISTANCE LEARNING

If your institution or company is or may be getting into the business of distance learning, you should be aware of some important educational and training concepts. Without an understanding of these caveats, you and the learners you want to reach may not be as successful with distance learning.

Educators and Trainers Must Stimulate Change

The people who teach the courses and work with the learners should be the agents of change. Innovation in distance learning works best from the ground floor upward, from the educators/trainers and designers of the distance learning courses and programs up through the administrators and executives who may approve programs and oversee budgets. The people who work daily with learners and understand which technologies work best and why they work best in certain combinations are the people who should be determining the future of distance learning. They must be the ones who plan expansion of programs and more effective methods of presenting educational and training information.

Because these educators/trainers are the ones who will design the materials and deal with the daily realities of the distance learning program, they have to experiment with technology and educational methods and continually upgrade their knowledge and skills. They need to keep abreast of changes on the Internet and structure their courses accordingly, not only to keep themselves and their course materials up-to-date, but also to inform their administrators and executives about what's current in distance learning. Because these educators/trainers know best how to develop different materials to meet different learners' needs, their ability to do their job will rest with the support provided them.

Educators and Trainers Must Be Supported by the Technology

Educators and trainers must be part of a team with administrators, executives, and technicians to select the hardware and software to be used, the rules governing their use, and the timing of updates. The technology must be selected to provide the resources and methods of interaction required in a particular course; the course, and the instructional methods and materials, should not be designed because the institution or business wants to use a particular type of technology.

The Nature of Education Must Be Reconceptualized

Research, not teaching or training, fosters innovation. Teaching and training typically are conformist activities and too often are repetitive. A good distance learning program is based on the premise that the subject matter is not fixed, but malleable, and that educators/trainers, as well as the learners, are learning together by sharing information and developing new skills as each course progresses. Many educators in traditional academic institutions are accustomed to working in tenured positions, where it may become easy to rely on what's worked before, instead of experimenting to find new approaches. Although some institutions encourage educators to conduct research and/or require a certain number of research publications each year for promotion and merit-pay increases, other colleges and universities are primarily *teaching* institutions that provide little time for educators to conduct research. Instead, classroom teaching is the emphasis of the workload. When instructors teach four or more courses per term, or multiple sections of the same course, they may have little incentive to vary their teaching methods or materials from term to term.

In a similar way, many corporate trainers are encouraged to use programmed materials that they may not have developed, so that large numbers of employees may be trained efficiently and cost effectively. Using the same course materials, from tutorials to software to simulations, among many training sessions may be the traditional way to train employees. In fact, such consistency is usually encouraged, because the process ensures that all trainees received the same amount and type of instruction.

Although these educational and training practices are common, they stifle innovation and creativity, which are needed if distance learning courses are to be more than electronic storage spaces and lecture halls. Distance learning materials can and should be creative, innovative, and interactive; they should encourage learners to explore further. To realize the potential of distance learning, educators and trainers need time and support for research.

Every course must include elements of research. Educators, trainers, and learners must be researchers who keep seeking for new information and better ways of completing tasks to update their knowledge and skill base. Educators/trainers should encourage feedback from learners so that they can determine which materials and methods were most effective and which must be modified. Learners should share their knowledge and expertise during the course, so that their experiences and ideas can be incorporated into the course design.

The days of an all-knowing instructor giving an agreed-upon body of knowledge to passive students are, or should be, over. Distance learning should be innovative, not repetitive. It should use the Internet's strengths, not just make traditional texts available online. It should be dynamic, not static. It should be interactive, not passive.

Distance Learning Turns Teaching and Training into Publication and Presentation

Teaching and training are interactive; educators/trainers work individually and with groups of learners to develop a personal approach to the course. Because distance learning, by its nature, physically separates educators/trainers from learners, there is a chance that learners can feel isolated and the instruction can become impersonal and mechanical. However, good distance learning programs include components that bridge the geographic distance and bring together learners and educators/trainers, as well as other professionals.

The potential for sharing information and "talking" with more people is greater with the Internet than within a classroom or training center. Teleconferences and other types of broadcasts can be used to communicate directly with learners in real time. The Web and Internet services, such as e-mail, should invite interaction and be designed to meet individual learners' needs and preferences. Each distance learning course must be carefully designed to create a personal learning experience. Even though presentations are part of teaching and training in traditional settings, presentational skills are especially important in some forms of distance learning in *virtual* classrooms. Most obviously, teleconferencing and desktop videoconferencing require educators/trainers to hone their presentation skills.

Although educators/trainers may seldom, if ever, work with learners face-to-face in the same classroom, their presentation skills should be highly developed so that they nonetheless get to know learners and build professional relationships with them. Many distance learning technologies require a presentation personality, which requires more energy, smoothness in delivery, and projection of gestures and voice than presentations made within a classroom. Because distance learning sessions may be taped, the quality of the presentation should be uniformly high for every session. During a traditional classroom presentation, an instructor's "Ums" and "Uhs" or distracting mannerisms or hesitancy may not be remembered; during a virtual classroom presentation, an instructor's words and actions are broadcast to many more learners and/or recorded to be viewed and reviewed many times. To be an effective educator/trainer in a virtual classroom requires practice, preparation, and the ability to present information smoothly and clearly to a camera, as well as to a group.

In addition to flawless presentations as an important component of high-quality distance learning courses, educators'/trainers' materials are "published" each time they appear on the Internet, especially the Web. Information stored in a Web site is open to view and criticism (as well as use, whether authorized or unauthorized) by the masses. E-mail messages, especially those sent to a mailing list group, discussion group, or newsgroup, are read and critiqued by many readers and may be downloaded and printed for others' use. Bulletin board messages may be downloaded and shared. Educators/trainers who work with distance learning materials on the Internet are thus forced to "publish" their work more formally than they might in a traditional classroom. Their work has the potential to be viewed, as well as downloaded, by millions of people.

Even in light of copyright restrictions, many Internet users pirate online information. Educators/trainers have no guarantee that their information won't be "published" formally or informally without their knowledge or permission. They may be quoted (or misquoted) and their work may or may not be attributed to them. The Internet has the capability of making important materials, including articles about distance learning, widely read and used; the authors can become well known internationally. The payment for their publication may be low or none, but their recognition may be great.

As publishing through the Internet—whether through your own Web site with materials designed for learners or more formal publications designed for e-zines and electronic scholarly journals—becomes more common, the value of these electronic publications should be increased. Many academic administrators or corporate executives are unsure of the importance of electronic publications, because almost anyone can "publish" something on the Internet. Unlike refereed or edited articles or books accepted for print publication, electronic publications currently don't have the same degree of status offered by formally printed documents. The quality of a publication and its importance should be judged individually, not by its appearance in print or online. The status of electronic publications is currently being debated, but distance learning professionals can demonstrate the value and significance of electronic information. This is just one more area in which distance learning educators/trainers can enhance their profession and further an understanding of the value of the Internet in teaching and training.

Distance Learning Changes Education from a Linear to a Nonlinear Process

When learners use the Web, for example, they can access information in the order in which they choose. They may or may not follow the path that educators/trainers expected them to take. Learners may locate more sources of information and leap from link to link in a random order. The order of using materials is usually nonlinear, although learners can follow a predetermined sequence (if one is indicated) if they really want to use a linear order.

This ability to access as much or as little information as the individual chooses, in whatever associational order he or she desires, changes the nature of education from a linear to a nonlinear process. Of course, educators/trainers can develop a more linear organization for their course by numbering or dating materials, or by limiting learners' access to materials to a certain time period. However, even then, learners still can gain access to much of the information stored in a Web site in whatever order they choose; the Web's reliance on hypertext and hypermedia prohibits a purely linear approach to gathering information.

Therefore, educators/trainers who develop Web sites must make sure that each linked piece of information makes sense and is useful alone, but that the Web site also provides related pieces of information. If an order of presentation and use is required, the structure must be explained so that learners know how they're expected to access the information.

What is exciting about a nonlinear approach to education is that learners can follow their thought processes. They can learn as much about a subject as they need or want and their interests can prod them to find additional links to more information. They might follow tangents relating to their specific interests or questions, and thus be encouraged to learn more and relate it to what they already know or hope to learn. Associational thinking, as illustrated through Web links, can promote learning.

Learners May No Longer Need to Own the Tools of Their Education or Training

For better or worse, the *tools* of education and training are becoming more public, and they change the way learners perceive paper-based information. When texts and materials are available online, learners don't have to buy books, for example. They may not need to purchase CDs or videos, if they have access to music and video libraries online. Furthermore, learners may see these more "permanent" forms of information storage as outdated. Who needs to purchase textbooks, notebooks, or CDs when they become outdated rapidly and take up space? Learners who are members of a virtual academic community, for example, may never visit a "real" campus with a "real" bookstore. They may work with a virtual campus or training center and therefore be expected to have access only to electronic materials.

Electronic information can be up-to-the-minute. Although it's temporal and may not be important after it's used, the information also is the most current available and therefore has a special importance. Learners whose primary source of education or training takes place via the Internet may have a different appreciation of books as reference works, for example, because they know that they can get more recent information online. They may question the need for having information that is older, when they only want to know what's current. The importance of understanding the context and background of current information is being lost in the drive to work only with what is new, hot, or revised.

Thus, learners' reasons for buying books will change, as textbooks and similar reference works (e.g., magazines, journals, workbooks) are superseded by information available electronically on bulletin boards, in discussion groups, and on Web sites. Learners may decide that some "classics" or "standards" are worth purchasing, but more temporal items, like newspapers, journals, and reports, which indicate only the current state of research and knowledge, may not be perceived as worth storing for future use.

The materials used in a course may not always be available to learners, however, if they don't download them or save them electronically while they still have access to the materials. Since they may not need to refer to these materials, long-term access may not be a problem. If, however, learners do need to return to previously used electronic materials after they take the course, they may have limited or no access to them. Therefore, as educators/trainers develop online materials, they should help learners recognize the resources they may need to keep as references for future use and which resources have an immediate value only.

KEEPING INFORMED AND FURTHERING DISTANCE LEARNING

It's up to you to determine the effectiveness of your courses and programs and, on a larger scale, the future of distance learning. To help you keep up-to-date, to share your experiences and ideas, and to develop innovative teaching and training methods and materials with distance learning technologies, you should complete as many of the following activities as possible:

Initial Activities (when you first work with distance learning)

- Subscribe to distance learning mailing lists.
- Join or participate in distance learning discussion groups, MUDs, and newsgroups.
- Develop a Web site.
- Develop a bulletin board for your learners and/or organization.

Daily/Weekly Activities

- Browse the Web to check out new distance learning courses and resources.
- Actively participate in mailing lists.
- Participate in discussion groups, newsgroups, and MUDs.
- Lead or design a MUD for learners.
- Be an active Internet user.
- Research distance learning topics among Internet search engines.
- Subscribe to electronic and/or print publications dealing with distance learning.
- Evaluate your current materials, courses, and program.

Ongoing Activities for Professional Development

- Participate in a distance learning or education/training-related teleconference.
- Attend a distance learning conference.
- Write articles for e-zines, electronic journals, and print journals about your experiences with distance learning, technology, tools, or your specific courses and program.
- Write grant proposals.
- Take a distance learning course.
- Visit other vendors to learn about new technologies.
- Suggest and work to develop a distance learning consortium among representatives from business, industry, and academia.
- Revise evaluation tools for learners, executives, administrators, educators, and trainers to use in critiquing courses, materials, instruction methods, instructors' effectiveness, etc.
- Work with marketing and advertising personnel to create or update a marketing and advertising plan for your program.
- Write or suggest that someone write promotional pieces about your programs and supply the information needed to make others aware of your program.
- Keep an open mind and take up the challenge of designing more innovative, creative, and enjoyable courses for your virtual classroom.

RESOURCES FOR LEARNERS

If you're considering taking a distance learning course, browse the Web frequently. Look at the sample materials provided by vendors. Read the descriptions of the course content, educators'/trainers' credentials, institution's or company's credentials, and types of distance learning technologies and activities used within a course. You might start by looking at the Web sites listed in Appendix E, although there are many more Web sites created by distance learning vendors. But before you take a course, shop around. The Web provides descriptions of many distance learning opportunities and can help you match your interests and educational/training needs with the right vendor and course.

RESOURCES FOR EDUCATORS AND TRAINERS

Appendix A lists selected printed articles dealing with distance learning. Appendix B offers information about newsgroups and mailing lists. If you're interested in learning more about grants and grantors, check the resources listed in Appendix C. Appendix D lists e-zines about distance learning and Appendix E provides a list of online resources for people interested in knowing more about distance learning and visiting sites offering distance learning courses. Web sites relating to copyright issues, especially for fair use and educational copies, are listed in Appendix F. These appended materials can provide you with a starting point for your further education.

One site you should visit is the Distance Learning Association's Web site; it lists regional and national conferences about distance learning and can direct you to additional resources. You should check this site periodically, then participate in as many conferences and teleconferences as possible.

SUMMARY

Developing a distance learning program is a worthwhile objective, but for your program to be successful, you must carefully plan it. The challenge of developing effective distance learning programs is to be at the forefront of education. Its highest goal is to provide everyone with the information they need to live more fully. The Internet is only one way to help us reach for this goal, but it can be an effective tool if used wisely. When the Internet is used in conjunction with other tools for distance learning, you can create an effective educational or training environment.

11

International Education Issues

Distance learning can bridge international boundaries, as well as the boundaries formerly more strictly imposed by space and time. Through distance learning technologies, we can broaden or breach cultural, social, and political boundaries, within a country and across nations. Distance learning programs and activities can help us create a global schoolroom or lab; they can help us as educators, trainers, and learners share information and gain a broader perspective on a specific subject as well as on the world in general. Very positively, distance learning can help create an international, multicultural educational center that enhances collaboration among scholars and business people, and coordinates educational resources and teaching/training techniques.

Nevertheless, when you work with technologies that make information accessible to millions of people worldwide, you naturally wonder about the ways the information will be used or misused. Because satellite technology and electronic computer networks are venues that can be easily accessed by people who may or may not have been given permission to use the information transmitted along them, issues surrounding copyrights, patents, and trademarks have incited heated debates, nationally and internationally. The legalities involved with copyrights, patents, and trademarks vary among nations, and the laws frequently change. In addition, tracking down persons who infringe on the fair use of protected information across national borders may be more than frustrating; it may be next to impossible, unless the misuse of the originator's expression of an idea or a concept is brought to his or her attention.

However, the sharing of information across cultures has more implications and requires more careful thought than a fairly straightforward consideration of how the information will be used. As information for distance learning courses is planned, developed, and updated, educators and trainers must be aware of other cultural, social, and political issues beyond the legalities of working in an international marketplace. When a distance learning program is offered to learners outside a locality, and especially to learners from other countries, the types of distance learning available, the technologies required of students and educators/trainers, and the way course content is structured and presented all need to be planned with a multicultural, multinational audience in mind.

Worldwide courses also present different problems for administrators and businesses or institutions offering programs across countries. If courses are taken for credit, the amount and type of credit, the equivalency of degrees and certifications within different nations, and the methods of evaluating and verifying learners' participation pose very different problems than if learners take noncredit courses. If courses are taken for a fee, cost issues can include the conversion of currency, as well as the practicalities of receiving payment in an acceptable form (via credit card, bank note, check, or cash). Administrative issues for global distance learning must also be considered if you plan to enter a global marketplace.

Finally, although global collaboration among educators/trainers and learners can benefit all the participants and expand each person's global view, distance learning technologies naturally increase an institution's or a business's competition for "customers." When the competition takes place globally, many institutions throughout the world can potentially offer the same types of courses as your institution or company and be a competitor in your market. Collaboration and competition are closely related in distance learning.

COPYRIGHTS AND FAIR USE

Because many distance learning courses involve use of the Internet, especially the Web, educators/trainers are often most concerned about copyright issues for electronic information. The type of information sent electronically is often difficult to regulate and most Internet users fear censorship of what ideally can be a wonderful conduit for the open sharing of information internationally. Because laws regarding copyrights, patents, and trademarks vary among nations, everything from registering for legal protection to citing electronic sources to downloading and using the information may be treated differently, depending upon the country's legal system. Enforcing the laws that do exist may be difficult, although there are more efforts being made to enforce copyright violations, for example. Determining how to categorize electronic information and regulate its use are difficult issues still being debated and the situation is in a state of flux.

A fact or an idea can't be copyrighted. The expression of an idea and the structure of information can be copyrighted. Copyrights are designed to protect the authors and owners of works so that they can obtain commercial benefit from them and generally to control how their works are used. Copyright protection encourages the creative endeavors of authors, artists, musicians, and so forth by giving them the exclusive right to reproduce works and derive income from them. Companies, such as publishing houses, may own the copyright for works created for them or by their employees, including contract employees.

A trademark differs from a copyright. A trademark usually refers to a word or a phrase that identifies a brandname product or a generic product or service. The word (e.g., Apple, TV) isn't owned—which is especially important when you consider the number of common words that also are part of product or service names—but the context of the word in relation to the product or service is trademarked. When you're citing someone else's electronic works or protecting your own, you're more likely to work with copyrights than trademarks.

The following sections provide basic background information about copyrights, patents, and trademarks as used in the United States. Appendix F lists additional sources, including Web sites with information about Canadian and European copyright laws, that you should consult for a broader picture of the changing world of electronic information and its protection.

COPYRIGHT NOTICES

In the United States, documents (the term *documents* is used in very broad terms to include music, graphics, blueprints and designs, paper-printed information, electronic information, handwritten notes, etc.) created privately and originally after April 1, 1989 are copyrighted and therefore under copyright protection, whether the document contains a copyright notice. It's wise to assume that another person's (or company's or institution's) work is copyrighted, even if the word "Copyright" or the © symbol doesn't appear on the document. The format for a copyright notice is the following:

Copyright (date or dates, e.g., 1990-1992) by (author or owner of the copyrighted information)

or

© (date or dates, e.g., 1990-1992) by (author or owner of the copyrighted information)

You may place the correct copyright form on your works, but the works are automatically protected as soon as they are created. An author or owner of the copyrighted information may make it available to the public by providing a written notice to the effect that "I (author or owner) grant (this document) to the public domain." E-mail messages, Usenet new items, and so forth are not public-domain information without the expressed permission of the author or owner.

REGISTERING A WORK

Electronic information, such as e-mail messages, news postings, and Web sites, are protected by copyright when they're created. You don't have to register your work officially for it to be protected. However, if your company or institution wants to bring suit against an individual or a group who violated your copyright, you will have had to register your work and you should post a copyright notice on the work. Registration should take place as soon as you've created the work you want especially to protect; don't wait months or years and register works only when a copyright question arises.

If your site or work doesn't generate income, you probably won't want to register it, especially if you create lots of electronic works. The cost of registration may be prohibitive if you're a prolific Internet user! Sometimes a series of related works can be registered as a collection; consult copyright experts if you have a series of works to register.

Registration involves a fee and you'll have to officially submit the registration to the U.S. Copyright Office. In-house legal and publishing departments often handle the copyright issues for employees working for the company.

FAIR USE

Fair use is a legal license to use other's work, even if the work's creator is unaware of your use. Educational or "public good" uses of works typically fall under fair use, if the source of information is cited and the use is deemed "reasonable" (usually fewer than 10 copies are made and the intent is in the public's interest or for the advancement of scholarship). Fair use of copyright information includes commentaries, parodies, news, and research about copyrighted works without getting prior permission to use them from the author or owner. Some educational uses of information also fall under the fair use category.

Short pieces of a copyrighted work, such as an excerpt, are considered fair use, but you must attribute the source of the information. You can't copy even a short section of a work and allow readers, listeners, viewers, and so on to assume that it's your work. Cite the sources of information you didn't originally create.

Your intent in using copyrighted works and the way you use the work also determine if you're allowed fair use. For example, you can't damage the work's commercial value. If you reproduce and distribute photocopies of a book, for example, so that people no longer need or want to buy that product, you've damaged the work's commercial value.

Most writers of e-mail messages, for example, won't care that you copy their message and forward it to others without their permission. However, the work is protected; if you change the context or meaning of the original writer's work, you have, in effect, damaged the writer's reputation and the original work.

To avoid confusion about electronic information and its use, list owners may want to post notices stating that people who submit e-mail messages to the list retain their copyright and that messages may not be reproduced without the writer's permission. Some Web site owners state at the site that an e-mail message sent to the site may be used in a testimonial or a FAQ. Reminding users about uses of copyrighted information, whether in a Web site or on a mailing list, for example, is a good idea.

Web designers may not copy another's graphic, for example, and place it in their Web site, without the express permission of the creator. It's much smarter to use original graphics than to copy or use someone else's on your Web site.

CITING COPYRIGHTED INFORMATION

The Alliance for Computers and Writing has endorsed a citation format developed by Janice R. Walker. The format for a Web site is as follows:

- Author's name in reverse order
- The referenced work's title (e.g., the title of the Web page/screen within the whole Web site)
- The full work's title (e.g., the title of the Web site)
- The URL
- The date you accessed the information

For example, a citation may take this form:

Porter, Lynnette. "List of Preferred Distance Learning Sites." *Porter's Distance Learning References.* http://_____ (1 Nov. 1996).

The format for citing information from a Telnet site is similar:

- Author's name in reverse order
- The referenced work's title (e.g., the title of the Web page/screen within the whole Web site)

■ The full work's title (e.g., the title of the Web site)
■ The Telnet address and any additional instructions needed to access the information
■ The date you accessed the information

For example, a citation may take this form:

Porter, Lynnette. "More Distance Learning Links." *My In-house Newsletter* Issue 1. Telnet _____ (1 Nov. 1996).

The format for citing an e-mail address is shorter but contains the important referencing information:

■ Author's name in reverse order
■ Subject line
■ The words "Personal e-mail"
■ The date of the e-mail message

The format for an e-mail message looks like this:

Porter, Lynnette. "Distance learning courses." Personal e-mail (1 Nov. 1996).

Other associations and style manuals may suggest different citation styles. If you follow the Modern Language Association's or the American Psychological Association's style guides, for example, you may find slightly different formats for citing electronic information.

In short, when you work with copyrighted information, be safe, ethical, and businesslike. Cite sources of your information. Request permission to use copyrighted works when you want to copy information or use it in a work for hire, or another use that falls outside the fair use guidelines.

When you submit information electronically or make information available online, know that your work is protected by copyright law. If you need more formal protection, register your works.

COURSE DESIGN CONSIDERATIONS FOR A GLOBAL AUDIENCE

When you plan a distance learning course for an international audience, you still consider all the design and pedagogical issues discussed throughout the book. However, in addition, you need to be aware of cultural, social, and/or political differences among a group of learners, educators, and trainers. What you may take for granted as an "accepted" view about social structure, political structure, gender, race, ethnicity, age, religion, region, nation, or profession, for example, may not be considered in the range of acceptable beliefs or customs for persons from a different background. Although distance learning provides the opportunity for persons with different world views to exchange ideas and information, and thus learn from each other, in course design, you must be particularly sensitive to meeting all learners' needs without forcing one view or one opinion in lieu of others.

Subject Matter for Courses

Keep in mind that some subject matter, or approaches to it, may be taboo in some cultures or countries. Although the information is acceptable politically, it may be inappropriate for learners within a specific cultural or social group.

Age is another factor that can determine how participants in a distance learning course determine if information is appropriate. Some older participants may feel that certain subjects are off limits or just shouldn't be discussed, because these subjects were not discussed, or were discussed privately, when they were younger. Some younger participants may feel that certain subjects are unnecessary to discuss or may want to advocate a particular point of view. Audience analysis of the educators/trainers and the learners involved in a course can help you determine if subjects may be difficult to discuss or present within a class.

Some information within a country or political unit may be formally censored or deemed inappropriate for dissemination within a nation or among a certain group. If you're working with training programs within a country, for example, some information may be classified and require approval before it can be shared with others. It's a good idea to know as much about the multicultural, multinational audience as you possibly can as you design the course content, design, and structure.

Organization of Information

The structure of chunks of text may need variety to meet the expectations of learners from different countries or cultures. Readers in some countries are used to a deductive organizational structure, in which more general information is presented first and specific conclusions come later. This structure is popular in many Eastern countries. Readers in other countries prefer "sound bite" chunks of information, in which the main point is presented immediately. Later, if readers want to know supporting details, they can read background information. The inductive approach of presenting the thesis or main idea first is popular in many Western countries. Depending upon the learners who are taking a particular course, the structure of the information within a document—video or live presentation—and on a Web page, for example, may need to be varied to meet the needs of learners with very different expectations about the most effective way for presenting information.

Of course, the subject matter and the objectives for the course or lesson also have a bearing on the way information is organized. When educators/ trainers illustrate a process or train learners to perform a task, for example, they use a sequential order, with one step following another. If categorizing items is an important part of a lesson, a hierarchy (e.g., most to least important, least to most expensive, first to last in preference) may be created. In addition to meeting learners' preferences and expectations, you also have to gauge whether the subject matter has an inherent structure in which it should be presented.

Language Considerations

Language presents other challenges. For example, should you offer course materials only in one language or in several? Which languages are used primarily by your target group of learners? Which languages are required (for example, in a bilingual nation)? Which languages should be included if you plan to expand your marketing base for a particular program or course? If you offer course materials and descriptions in more than one language, you must make sure that a native speaker or someone fluent in idiomatic as well as formal usage translates or writes and edits the information. You may need to work with several people to prepare linguistically suitable Web sites, documents, and videos, for example.

You should carefully choose the words you use in your materials and presentations. What is a common term in your profession or country may not be understood by others who share your language, but not your national or professional idiom. Instructions for repairing an *elevator* may be understood in the United States, but instructions for repairing a *lift* may be more appropriate for the United Kingdom, for example. In presentations, be careful to enunciate so that your accent, inflection, or even use of gestures and eye contact is appropriate for your audience. You need to be understandable to everyone, whether through spoken, written, or body language.

Even within the use of one language, idioms and connotations can vary among social strata, region, and culture. Slang may not only be inappropriate, but also incomprehensible outside of your culture. For example, a U.S. learner who uses the phrase that he or she is "toast" to refer to being unprepared for a situation or exterminated by a situation may not be understood by an Australian learner reading the e-mail message; the Australian may use "cactus" to refer to the same unfortunate state of being. Slang, and other idiomatic uses, probably should be eliminated from your materials, if not your speech, during a distance learning course. At the very least, you should explain any appropriate slang that may not be understood by all your audience.

An important example of idiomatic, as well as cultural or social differences, is the use of humor. Some subjects should not be made humorous, whatever the nationality or culture of your learners. However, in many courses, you can inject humor appropriately. If you're designing information for a multicultural, multinational audience, you should be aware that what strikes some people as funny in one culture may not translate well to another culture. Humor can be idiomatic, but it can also be judged as humorous or not based on social and cultural norms. You should be aware of the nuances of language, especially in the connotations and denotations of words, as well as in the use of humor. Nuances of language in translation must also be checked to ensure that the appropriate inference is made for each word and phrase.

Information Design

The design of graphics and use of color, music, and special effects may differ in effectiveness and appropriateness across cultures and nations, too. For example, some colors may have different connotations, depending upon the learner's background. In the United States, for example, learners who regularly work with money on the job may be alarmed to see red used in a graphic depicting finances, because they don't want their finances to be "in the red." Similarly, the use of green in a financial diagram may signal growth, prosperity, or money. Outside the United States, or other Western nations, the color symbolism may not be the same.

The use of symbols is also important. Some symbols may not be acceptable for use in another culture or they may take on a different meaning than the one you intended. For example, the concept of a "home" button or icon may be readily understood in one culture if the symbol looks like a building with a slanted roof, a chimney, and a front door with windows. However, in another setting, this building may not resemble homes with which learners are familiar. Even the concept of "going home" to a starting point or place of origination may be different, as "home" may take on different connotations for different learners.

In addition, popular culture "icons" may not have the same meaning. Although *Sesame Street* may have made Big Bird an internationally recognized character, the primarily U.S.-based Barney may not be as commonly recognized outside of North America, or even the United States. Using popular references can be an effective educational or training tool, but you should check to make sure that everyone will understand the reference.

Personal and Business Expectations and Experiences

Other cultural differences can involve day-to-day expectations of what is "normal" in business or education. A home office, complete with fax machine and computer, may be typical for learners in some cultures, but other learners may have had little experience with a public or a business computer only, and the concept of working at home in a business office may be difficult to grasp. You may take it for granted that learners can get an e-mail address, but this may be difficult for some learners.

Business etiquette is another area where cultural differences are extremely important. The roles of men and women, the norms for working in groups or individually, the role of an individual within a business, corporate loyalties, and the protocol of meetings, for example, may differ dramatically across companies, cultures, and countries.

These course design considerations are important if you plan any course, but are especially crucial in the effectiveness of designing international distance learning course materials. In addition to these design considerations, you also need to anticipate any practical difficulties in presenting the information you've so carefully designed.

Practical Course Considerations for Day-to-day Operations

Working with learners across many time zones or even the date line may determine the type of distance learning technology you use. For example, you may need technologies that can be accessed at any time by any learner or educator/trainer (e.g., e-mail, bulletin boards, Web sites). If you plan teleconferences or desktop videoconferences with an individual or a group, you have to establish convenient places and times, which may be rather challenging.

You should know the significance of important dates within a country where you offer distance learning courses. Legal, religious, and cultural dates of importance should be listed so that you can plan start and end dates for assignments, courses, teleconferences, and so forth. You can more effectively judge when materials need to be sent or received and learners' social, business, and familiar responsibilities in preparation for special days. In addition, you can learn a great deal about a nation or a culture by understanding which dates are important and why.

Knowing which technologies are even possible within a region is important. Some learners may have little or no access to computers; others may find international mail difficult to send and receive quickly and economically. Still others may need videos formatted in a specific style to meet local equipment or broadcast standards. Although many electronic technologies are theoretically available worldwide, the day-to-day realities of setting up a course and establishing frequent communication networks still may be difficult.

OPEN UNIVERSITIES AND COLLEGES

Distance learning across national boundaries presents different challenges, but it is also an exciting prospect. Many universities and colleges offer courses in international business or other topics using international resources, but the *open universities* established in many countries are leading the way to the further collaboration among scholars, in particular. Although some "open" institutions primarily offer courses to learners within their country, others have truly opened their virtual doors to learners anywhere in the world.

Some educational institutions encourage international partnerships and consortia to help design curricula and offer courses. The following institutions are only a sample of those dealing in different ways with international distance learning:

- Washington State University's International Education Partnership Program, according to its Web site, encourages distance learning through seminars and cross-cultural collaborations in Asia. Faculty expertise and international resources are also available to K-12 educators. (You can learn more about the International Education Partnership Program, as only one example of an international program, through the Web site currently at (http://134.121.112.52/case/coe07.html). Washington State University's home page is found at http://www.wsu.edu.).
- Another interesting site for information about international courses, conference, and policy issues is the Center for International Business Education and Research (CIBER). The Center is located physically at Georgia Tech, but its cyber address is (http://www.inta.iac.gatech.edu/ciber.html).
- Information about Fulbright scholarships and programs can be found through the International Education Administrators Programs (http://www.cies.org/www/ieaprograms.html) and the Council for International Exchange of Scholars (CIE) (http://www.cies.org/www/index.html).
- National (U.S.) and international services and resources for K-12 educators can be found at (http://kalama.doe.hawaii.edu/upena/Pilot/training/niiaward.html), for example; the distance learning programs described there were designed to create a "global schoolhouse" for children in Hawaii, but the descriptions and site lists can help educators everywhere.
- Worldwide resources and issues about special education are listed and described at the Special Education Distance Education Resources site (http://141.218.70.183/speddistedwww/internationalsped.html). This resource list is provided by The Open University's International Centre for Distance Learning; the resources are divided geographically worldwide and also listed by institution within a country.
- Athabasca University is building an online list of international distance learning programs at (http://ccism.pc.athabascau.ca/html/ccism/deresrce/institut.htm).

These and other Web sites offer a growing body of knowledge about opportunities to develop international distance learning courses and programs, and the number and types of international programs currently available. You should check as many as possible, as well as conduct ongoing Internet searches for more recent courses, programs, and sites.

If you plan to offer a course internationally, you may want to check some mailing lists and Web sites to learn about the way different institutions are tackling the challenge of multinational, multicultural programs. Appendix G provides a starting point for your exploration of international distance learning.

ADMINISTRATIVE ISSUES

Administrative educational issues can include ways to market programs internationally, registering and receiving payment from learners, verifying that participants taking the course for credit have actually completed the course, and meeting international or national standards for providing credit or certification. In addition, the costs of working with an international audience daily must be figured in the usual administrative tasks, such as budgeting distance learning programs and planning the types of technology that will keep the institution or business current in the business of distance learning.

If you plan to market a course internationally, your marketing plan and individual advertising strategies as part of the marketing plan may include a multilingual format. You may decide that some types of advertising, such as broadcasting through radio or television spots, are more costly and less effective on a broader scale. However, you may want to emphasize print media or you may decide that use of the Internet and Web are the best ways to make more people aware of your institution or business and the courses you offer. Participation in international distance learning meetings, conferences, and seminars may be an effective way for you to share information with colleagues and generate interest in your programs.

If you plan to expand your marketing and advertising efforts in these directions, you should enlist the help of a professional advertising or marketing agency that specializes in both education and international sales. These professionals can alert you to the needs of your potential learners, the best marketing strategies for a given nation or region for your product (distance learning courses), and the legalities and practicalities of marketing and advertising in another country.

Other practical matters to consider include ways of registering learners for courses. If you're offering noncredit, free courses, you may not be as concerned with the number of people who take the course, unless you need to send or receive materials by phone, fax, or surface mail. However, if you plan to offer a for-credit course, especially one that leads to a degree or a certification, you need to consider the amount and type of credit you offer and whether that credit, diploma, degree, certification, or other proof of achievement is readily transferred for use in another country. Educational standards for levels of achievement, types of degrees, and requirements for certifications may vary dramatically across countries. Therefore, you may need to work collaboratively with other institutions or businesses in a second (or third, etc.) country to be able to offer for-credit courses that will be understood and accepted across boundaries.

If you accept payment for courses or materials outside the country, you should have a procedure for determining exchange rates, figuring any additional out-of-country or overseas charges for processing or handling materials, and receiving payment. If you'll be conversing directly with persons who may not speak your native language, you should have a means for providing information or resources in translation.

If you plan to offer materials for sale, or if educators/trainers require learners to receive information other than through e-mail, bulletin boards, and Web sites, for example, you should determine the amount of time and the cost of sending information by surface mail or through voice mail or fax. Some information may need to be available in more than one language or format. For instance, videotape formats vary by nation; a format playable on VCRs in Europe differs from a format playable on VCRs in North America. You should determine how many formats or languages are appropriate for your materials, then make learners aware of the availability of the materials they need. If taxable materials are sold, you also need to determine which taxation laws apply to your materials, institution, and level of international trade.

SUMMARY

Distance learning, especially at the international level, offers more opportunities for professional collaboration. If you'll be designing a distance learning course for an international audience, you may want to seek partners at similar institutions in the country (or countries) where you plan to offer the course. This can be especially important for research-oriented courses or degree-related courses. Not only do you receive assistance in establishing a course, meeting any legal or professional standards in another country, and gaining insight into the appropriateness of information and formats within a different culture, but you also establish a global network for your own educational development. If your business plans to expand courses, you may prefer to hire consultants to help you with the legal, social, and political issues involved in international trade or you may need to work closely with your company's legal department.

Just as distance learning technologies open new markets for your company or institution within a region or country, so do they help you enter an international marketplace that you may previously have never been able to enter. However, as more learners gain access to the Internet and Web and learn about education and training offered globally, there is also more international competition for your current market. You need to establish your niche in distance learning, then determine if your program really needs to be international in scope. You may decide instead to add more information about international issues to courses currently available only within your region or country and to encourage collaboration among professionals and learners worldwide; however, your course is available only to a limited national market. When you think of an international marketplace, determine where your place should be within it, so that you can maximize the effectiveness of each distance learning course and target a specific part of the potentially global market.

Appendix A

Bibliography of Printed Sources

If you check any database dealing with education, training, computer science, telecommunications, and so on, you'll find thousands of articles about some aspect of distance learning or distance education. The following list is by no means inclusive or indicative of the quality of articles; it simply provides a starting point for your additional research into some applications of distance learning. The following articles come from a variety of educational, trade, and popular media journals; they were selected to show the breadth of sources available about a variety of educational and training subject areas and types of distance learning. They should be consulted in addition to journals dealing specifically with distance learning (e.g., *The International Journal of Distance Education*, *The American Journal of Distance Education*).

Ahuja, Sudhir R., H. Fred Haisch, and Ram S. Ramamurthy. 1995. "Multimedia Collaboration." *AT&T Technical Journal* (September/October): 46–53.

Anderson, Erik T. 1996. "Distance Education Classroom Design: Some 'Rules of Thumb.'" *The Agricultural Education Magazine* (May): 17–18.

Armstrong, Sue. 1996. "Farming for Distant Degrees." *New Scientist* (May 25): 14–15.

Ashworth, Kenneth H. 1996. "Virtual Universities Could Produce Only Virtual Learning." *The Chronicle of Higher Education* (September 6): A88.

Baird, Marcia. 1995. "Training Distance Education Instructors: Strategies that Work." *Adult Learning* (September/October) 24–26.

Berleant, Daniel, and Byron Liu. 1995. "Robert's Rules of Order for E-mail Meetings." *Computer* (November): 84–85.

Bernice, Rachel. 1996. "Distance Education: Beyond Correspondence Courses." *Canadian Social Trends* (Spring): 21–23.

Blumhardt, John H., and Larry R. Cross. 1996. "Making the Jump(s) into Cyberspace: A Discussion on Distance Learning Paradigm Shifts Required for the 21st Century." *Education at a Distance* (January): 13–21.

Bozik, Mary. 1996. "Student Perceptions of a Two-Way Interactive Video Class." *T.H.E. Journal* (September): 99–100.

Bruce, Mary Alice, and Richard A. Shade. 1995. "Effective Teaching and Learning Strategies Using Compressed Video." *TechTrends* (September): 18–22.

Bucher, Katherine. 1996. "How Are Television Networks Involved in Distance Learning?" *Technology Connection* (February): 14–15, 17.

Cantelon, John E. 1995. "The Evolution and Advantages of Distance Education." *New Directions for Adult and Continuing Education* (Fall): 3–10.

Care, William Dean. 1996. "The Transactional Approach to Distance Education." *Adult Learning* (July): 11–12.

Carter, Alex. 1996. "Essential Questions on Interactive Distance Education: An Administrators' Guide." *International Journal of Instructional Media* 23(2): 123–29.

Carter, Vicki. 1996. "Do Media Influence Learning? Revisiting the Debate in the Context of Distance Education." *Open Learning* (February): 31–40.

Chance, Edward W. 1996. "Electronic Field Trips: Using Technology to Enhance Classroom Instruction." *Rural Educator* (Spring): 11–13.

Chaptal, Alain, and Eric Briantais. 1995. "Some Thoughts on Digital Television and Interactivity." *Educational Media International* (December): 219–23.

Chute, Alan G., and Linda S. Shatzer. 1995. "Designing for International Teletraining." *Adult Learning* (September/October): 20–21.

Cohen, Andy. 1996. "Long-distance Learning." *Sales & Marketing Management* (June): 55–56.

Comeaux, Patricia. 1995. "The Impact of an Interactive Distance Learning Network on Classroom Education." *Communication Education* (October): 353–61.

Comerford, Richard. 1996. "Interactive Media: An Internet Reality." *IEEE Spectrum* (April): 29–32.

Cookson, Peter S. 1995. "Audioconferencing: Instructor and Participant Responses to Critical Conditions." *TechTrends* (September): 23–25.

Dalziel, Christine. 1995. "Fair Use Guidelines for Distance Education." *TechTrends* (October): 6–8.

Dede, Chris. 1996. "Emerging Technologies in Distance Education for Business." *Journal of Education for Business* (March): 197–204.

Durham, Tony. 1996. "Invisible Borders around the Elite: Global Scramble to Develop and Control Forms of Distance Learning." *The Times Higher Education Supplement* (September 13): 33.

Eddy, John Paul. 1996. "Internet, Computer, Distance Education, and People Failure: Research on Technology." *Education* (Spring): 391–92+.

Edwards, Richard. 1996. "Troubled Times? Personal Identity, Distance Education and Open Learning." *Open Learning* (February): 3–11.

Elsberry, Jeffrey, and Charles Lindsey. 1996. "Science and Math Curricula in the Twenty-first Century." *Journal of College Science Teaching* (March-April): 346–51.

Ember, Lois. 1996. "Learning Chemistry at a Distance: The South African Experience." *Chemical & Engineering News* (April 8): 45–48.

Evans, Arnold. 1996. "In a Virtual Class All of Its Own." *Times Educational Supplement* (June 28): SS17A.

Fetterman, David M. 1996. "Videoconferencing On-line: Enhancing Communication over the Internet." *Educational Researcher* (May): 23–27.

Flusfeder, Helena. 1996. "Each According to Need: Development of Distance Learning at the Open University in Israel." *The Times Higher Education Supplement* (September 13): 36.

Freddolino, Paul P. 1996. "The Importance of Relationships for a Quality Learning Environment in Interative TV Classrooms." *Journal of Education for Business* (March): 205–08.

Galbreath, Jeremy. 1995. "Compressed Digital Videoconferencing: An Overview." *Educational Technology* (January/February): 31–38.

___. 1996. "Interactive Television: The State of the Industry." *Educational Technology* (March/April): 24–35.

Garland, Virginia E., and Ann L. Loranger. 1995–96. "The Medium and the Message: Interactive Television and Distance Education Programs for Adult Learners." *Journal of Educational Technology Systems* 24(3): 249–57.

Geidt, Jonathan. 1996. "Distance Education into Group Areas Won't Go?" *Open Learning* (February): 12–21.

George, Rigmor. 1995. "Open and Distance Education as Social Practice." *Distance Education* 16(1): 24–42.

Gilbert, Larry. 1995. "Computer-based Audiographics for Distance Education: An Inexpensive, Interactive and High-quality Alternative." *Educational Media International* (March): 32–35.

Granger, Daniel, and Meg Benke. 1995. "Supporting Students at a Distance." *Adult Learning* (September/October): 22–23.

Ham, Rodney. 1995. "Distance Education." *The Technology Teacher* (March): 43+.

Havice, Pamela A., and Michelle H. Knowles. 1995. "Two-way Interactive Video: Maximizing Distance Learning." *The Journal of Continuing Education in Nursing* (January/February): 28–30.

Heidenreiter, Terrence J. 1995. "Using Videoteleconferencing for Continuing Education and Staff Development Programs." *The Journal of Continuing Education in Nursing* (May/June): 135–38.

Hopkins, Annis H. 1996. "Women's Studies on Television? It's Time for Distance Learning." *NWSA Journal* (Summer): 91–106.

Itzel, W. John. 1996. "Distance Learning through Wide Area Networking." *Media & Methods* (March/April): 6.

James, Waynne Blue, and Daniel L. Gardner. 1995. "Learning Styles: Implications for Distance Learning." *New Directions for Adult and Continuing Education* (Fall): 19–31.

Johnstone, Sally M., and Barbara Krauth. 1996. "Balancing Equity and Access: Some Principles of Good Practice for the Virtual University." *Change* (March-April): 38–41.

Jordahl, Gregory. 1995. "Bringing Schools Closer with 'Distance' Learning." *Technology & Learning* (January): 16–19.

Kearsley, Greg. 1996. "Structural Issues in Distance Education." *Journal of Education for Business* (March): 191–95.

Kinnaman, Daniel E. 1995. "The Future of Distance Education." *Technology & Learning* (January): 58.

___. 1996. "A Year for Debates." *Technology & Learning* (May/June): 94.

Krasilovsky, Peter. 1995. "What's New in Desktop Videoconferencing?" *Electronic Learning* (April): 16.

Laney, James D. 1996. "Going the Distance: Effective Instruction Using Distance Learning Technology." *Educational Technology* (March/April): 51–54.

Lawrence, Betty Hurley. 1995–96. "Teaching and Learning via Videoconference: The Benefits of Cooperative Learning." *Journal of Educational Technology Systems* 24(2): 145–49.

LePage, Denise. 1996. "Distance Learning Complements a Pre-service Mathematics Education Model." *T.H.E. Journal* (August): 65–67.

Lewis, Ted. 1995. "Living in Real Time, Side B (Where Will the Brain Power Come From?)" *Computer* (October): 8–10.

Littman, Marlyn Kemper. 1995. "Videoconferencing as a Communications Enhancement." *The Journal of Academic Librarianship* (September): 359–64.

Lowery, Bennie R., and Felicie M. Barnes. 1996. "Partnering to Establish a Distance Learning Program That Is Responsive to Needs." *T.H.E. Journal* (February): 91–95.

Lucas, Allison. 1996. "A Virtual Business Degree." *Sales & Marketing Management* (March): 14.

Martin, Barbara, and William J. Bramble. 1996. "Designing Effective Video Teletraining Instruction: The Florida Teletraining Project." *Educational Technology Research and Development* 44(1): 85–99.

Martinez, Reynaldo, Jr., and Bill Sweger. 1996. "Plugged In." *Vocational Education Journal* (March): 30–31.

Mather, Mary Anne. 1996. "Cutting-edge Connectivity: ISDN and Beyond." *Technology & Learning* (May/June): 28–30+.

___. 1996. "Resources for Learning at a Distance." *Technology & Learning* (May/June): 29.

Maxwell, Leigh. 1995. "Integrating Open Learning and Distance Education." *Educational Technology* (November/December): 43–48.

May, Susan. 1996. "Distance Learning: Its Impact on Women." *The Delta Kappa Gamma Bulletin* (Winter): 39–44.

McDevitt, Margaret A. 1996. "A Virtual View: Classroom Observations at a Distance." *Journal of Teacher Education* (May/June): 191–95.

McMahon, Teresa, and Walter Gantz. 1995. "Interactive Technology and Interuniversity Team Teaching." *Journalism and Mass Communication Educator* (Summer): 62.

Moller, Leslie, and Darryl Draper. 1996. "Examining the Viability of Distance Education as an Instructional Approach." *Journal of Continuing Higher Education* (Winter): 12–21.

Murphy, Tim. 1996. "Agricultural Education and Distance Education: The Time Is Now." *The Agricultural Education Magazine* (May): 3+.

Musial, Gloria G., and Wanita Kampmueller. 1996. "Two-way Video Distance Education: Ten Misconceptions about Teaching and Learning via Interactive Television." *Action in Teacher Education* (Winter): 28–36.

Nichols, Elizabeth G., and Janice E. Beeken. 1994. "Teaching on Compressed Video: Helpful Hints." *Nurse Educator* (May/June): 7–8.

Ohzu, Hitoshi. 1996. "Behind the Scenes of Virtual Reality: Vision and Motion." *Proceedings of the IEEE* (May): 782–98.

Opitz, Margaret. 1996. "What's New in . . . Interactive Distance Learning: Implications for the Classroom Teacher." *The Clearing House* (July/August): 325–26.

Pucel, Joanna. 1995. "Interactive Two-way Television: A New Frontier for Higher Education." *The Delta Kappa Gamma Bulletin* (Spring): 49–54.

Rees, Fred J., and Dennis A. Downs. 1995. "Interactive Television and Distance Learning." *Music Educators Journal* (September): 21–25.

Rose, Ellen Cronan. 1996. "'This Class Meets in Cyberspace': Women's Studies via Distance Education." *Feminist Teacher* (Fall): 53–60.

Russell, Anne L. 1995. "Stages in Learning New Technology: Naive Adult Email Users." *Computers & Education* (December): 173–78.

Russell, Thomas L. 1995. "What is Your Faculty-recruiting Attraction/Retention Quotient?" *TechTrends* (October): 31–33.

Salomon, Kenneth D. 1995. "A Primer on Distance Learning and Intellectual Property Issues." *West's Education Law Reporter* (March 9): 305–13.

Salvador, Roberta. 1996. "'Vision Athena' connects Indiana Schools." *Electronic Learning* (March): 9.

Sanchez, Raynette. 1996. "Star Schools: A Constellation of Distance Learning Resources." *Principal* (September): 46–47.

Schrum, Lynne. 1996. "Teaching at a Distance: Strategies for Successful Planning and Development." *Learning & Leading with Technology* (March): 30–33.

Schwartz, Rachel A. 1995. "The Virtual University." *ASEE Prism* (December): 22–26.

Shapard, Rob. 1996. "Information Superbyways: Cities and Counties Get Plugged In." *American City & County* (February): 20+.

Shields, Jean. 1995. "Connecting Classrooms with Today's Technologies." *Technology & Learning* (February): 38–40+.

Silva, Pamela Urdal, Mary Elaine Meagher, and Marlin Valenzuela. 1996. "E-mail: Real-life Classroom Experiences with Foreign Languages." *Learning and Leading with Technology* (February): 10–12.

Simonson, Michael. 1995. "Does Anyone Really Want to Learn . . . at a Distance?" *TechTrends* (October): 12.

Smith, Constance Ridley. 1996. "Taking the Distance Out of Distance Learning." *Training & Development* (May): 646–47.

Smith, Richard C., and Edwin F. Taylor. 1995. "Teaching Physics On Line." *American Journal of Physics* (December): 1909–96.

Sopova, Jasmina. 1996. "Distance Education in the High-Tech Era." *UNESCO Courier* (April): 27–28.

Stewart, Robert D. 1995. "Distance Learning Technology." *New Directions for Adult and Continuing Education* (Fall): 11–18.

Thach, Liz. 1995. "Instructional Design and Adaptation Issues in Distance Learning via Satellite." *International Journal of Instructional Media* 22(2): 93–110.

Thomson, W. Scott, and Parmalee P. Hawk. 1996. "Project DIST-ED: Teleconferencing as a Means of Supporting and Assisting Beginning Teachers." *Action in Teacher Education* (Winter): 9–17.

Thornburg, David D. 1994. "Why Wait for Bandwidth?" *Electronic Learning* (November/December): 20–21+.

Touchstone, Allison J. L. 1996. "A Technological Solution in Search of an Instructional Problem." *The Agricultural Education Magazine* (May): 4–5+.

Twigg, Carol A. 1996. "Is Technology a Silver Bullet?" *Educom Review* (March-April): 28–29.

Van Horn, Royal. 1996. "Sorting It Out: Distance Learning, Video Conferencing, and Desktop Video Conferencing." *Phi Delta Kappan* (May): 646–47.

Verrecchia, Felice Philip. 1995. "Distance Learning & Teleconferencing Fever." *Media & Methods* (March/April): 26.

Wagner, Ellen D., and Barbara L. McCombs. 1995. "Learner Centered Psychological Principles in Practice: Designs for Distance Education." *Educational Technology* (March/April): 32–35.

___. 1995. "Distance Education Success Factors." *Adult Learning* (September/October): 18–19+.

Wang, Shousan. 1994. "Basic Considerations of Distance Education Programs." *International Journal of Instructional Media* 21(1): 53–60.

Wang, Shousan, and Lawrence Buck. 1996. "A Practical Setting of Distance Learning Classroom." *International Journal of Instructional Media* 23(1): 11–22.

Weaver, Sherrill. 1995. "Distance Learning Resources for Distance Educators." *New Directions for Adult and Continuing Education* (Fall): 71–77.

Whitaker, George W. 1995. "First-hand Observations on Tele-course Teaching." *T.H.E. Journal* (August): 65–68.

Wood, Joan B., and Iris A. Parham. 1996. "Distance Learning: Videoconferences as Vehicles for Faculty Development in Gerontology/Geriatrics." *Educational Gerontology* (January-February): 105–15.

Yager, Robert E., John A. Dunkhase, and John W. Tillotson. 1995. "Science-technology Reform via Distance Education Technology." *TechTrends* (October): 19–22.

Distance Learning Newsgroups and Mailing Lists

Newsgroups provide yet another means for you to share information about distance learning, ask questions, and learn about new resources. You should contact the *listserv*'s e-mail address for specific instructions about subscribing to a mailing list. You can read messages on and subscribe to newsgroups through most browsers' Newsgroups menu.

Newsgroups

alt.education.alternative
alt.education.distance
alt.education.email-project
alt.education.research
alt.literacy.adult
misc.education
misc.education.adult

Mailing Lists

Adult Education Network	listserv@alpha.acast.nova.edu
Adult Education and Literacy Test Literature	listserv@cunyvm.bitnet or listserv@cunyvm.cuny.edu
Alternative Approaches to Learning Discussion	listserv@sjuvm.bitnet or listserv@sjuvm.stjohns.edu
American Association for Collegiate Independent Study	listserv@ecnuxa.bitnet or listserv@bgu.edu

Audiographics in Distance Education	listserv@cln.etc.bc.ca
Canadian Adult Education Network	listserv@uregina1.bitnet or listserv@uregina1.uregina.ca
Canadian Association for University Continuing Education	listserv@uregina1.bitnet or listserv@max.cc.uregina.ca
Discussion Group for Vocational Education	listserv@ucbcmsa.bitnet or listserv@csma.berkeley.edu
Distance Education Evaluation Group	listserv@unlvm.unl.edu or listserv@unlvm.bitnet
Education Net	listserv@nic.umass.edu
Educational Policy Analysis	listserv@asuacad.bitnet or listserv@asuvm.inre.asu.edu
Forum for Teaching and Learning in Higher Education	listserv@unbvm1.bitnet or listserv@unbvm1.csd.unb.ca
Higher Education in Latin America	listserv@bruspvm.bitnet
International Discussion Forum for Distance Learning	listserv@psuvm.bitnet or listserv@psuvm.psu.edu
Interpersonal Computing and Technology	listserv@guvm.bitnet or listserv@guvm.ccf.georgetown.edu
Latin American and Caribbean Distance and Continuing Education	listserv@yorkvm1.bitnet or listserv@vm1.yorku.ca
Learning Styles Theory and Research List	listserv@sjuvm.bitnet or listserv@sjuvm.stjohns.edu
New Patterns in Education List	listserv@uhccvm.uhcc.hawaii.edu
National Literacy Advocacy List	majordomo@world.std.com
Research SIG of the Open and Distance Learning Association of Australia	listserv@usq.edu.au
Teaching Effectiveness	listserv@wcu.bitnet or listserv@wcupa.edu

Appendix

C

Online Resources about Grants and Granting Opportunities

As you work with the Web, you'll find several links to the same online documents, databases, and Web pages that have information about granting opportunities, current grants, solitication notices, changes to granting procedures, applications, awarded grants, and federal agencies that grant resources. The following links provide starting points for locating the federal government's and nonprofit organizations' Web resources about grants and granting opportunities. Remember, too, that the design of Web pages and the location and availability of sites frequently change; these links are current at the time of publication.

Many organizations publish hardcopy documents that may not be duplicated on the Web and some grantors don't have a Web site. You should also check print publications, such as grants directories and federal agencies' documents, to make a complete search for grant information.

Adult Distance Education Internet Surf Shack, list of resources	http://www.helix.net/~jmtaylor/edsur.html
Alberta Distance Learning Centre	http://www.lrdc.edc.gov.ab.ca/upi/28531301.htm
Alberta Learning Resources Distributing Centre	http://www.lrdc.edc.gov.ab.ca/lrdchome/htm.lrd
Apple Computer Corporate Giving Program	http://www.apple.com or http://education.apple.com

AT&T (grantor for educational programs)	http://www.att.com/foundation/ or http://www.att.com
BellSouth Foundation Grant Guidelines	http://www.bsf.org/bsf/grantguide/index.html
BellSouth Foundation Grant Guidelines— Application	http://www.bsf.org/bsf/grantguide/docs/application.html
British Columbia's Distance Education Branch	http://www.etc.bc.ca/
California Distance Learning Project, resources list	http://www.otan.dni.us/cdlp/cdlp3/cdlpadultlist.html
Coca-Cola Co. (grantor for educational programs)	http://www.cocacola.com
Commonwealth of Learning	http://www.col.org
Digital Equipment Corporation (grantor for educational programs)	http://www.digital.com/info/community/contrib.html or http://www.digital.com
Distance Learning Funding Sourcebook	http://www.technogrants.com
Edith Cowan University	http://www.cowan.edu.au/ecuwis/docs/foundation/ remote.html
Education World (guide to online resources, including grant information)	http://www.education-world.com/db/grants.shtml
EduWeb	http://www.netspot.unisa.edu.au/eduweb/eduweb.htm
European Open University Network	http://pressure.engr.utc.edu/library/DE-Web-l.html
Far West Laboratory for Educational Research and Development	http://www.fwl.org/edtech/dlrn.html
Federal Register	http://gcs.ed.gov/fedreg.htm
Federal Register (link provided through the Community of Science site)	http://cos.gdb.org/repos/fr/fr-intro.html
Federal Register Database	http://www.access.gpo.gov/su_docs/aces/aces140.htm
General Education Resources, Vose School Education Resources site created by Beaverton Schools, Oregon)	http://elaine.teleport.com/~vincer/general.html
Global Network Academy	http://www.calpoly.edu:80/~delta/

GrantsNet http://www.os.dhhs.gov/progorg/grantsnet/index.html

IBM Corporation Contribution
Program http://ike.engr.washington.edu or
http://www.training.ibm.com/usedu

Microsoft Online Training http://www.scholars.com

National Institutes of Health
Database (link provided
through the Community of
Science site) http://cos.gdb.org/best/fedfund/nih-introlhtml

National Institutes of Health,
currently funded grants http://www.nih.gov/grants/ora/crisp.htm

Online Distance Learning, University
of Twente http://www.to.utwente.nl/isn/Online95/
campus/living/procee95/m0600319.html

Rio Salado College http://www.rio.maricopa.edu

Seattle Central Community College http://seaccd.sccd.ctc.edu/~ccoresp/corres.htm

Small Business Administration
Phase I application (link provided
through the NIAID/National
Institutes of Health site) http://niaid.nih.gov/newsletter/maya/sbir/phase.htm

Sun Microsystems project in
Kansas http://www.sunlabs.com/research/distancelearning/
kansas.html

Sun Microsystems video project http://www.sun.co.jp:8080/960201/cover/learning.html

TeleEducation New Brunswick,
list of Web sites http://ollc.mta.ca/teleedds.html

U.S. Department of Education http://www.ed.gov

U.S. Department of Education's
Grants and Contracts Information site http://gcs.ed.gov

University of Maryland, list of links http://nova.umuc.edu/~erubin/de-gen.html

University of Wisconsin,
list of resources http://www.uwex.edu/disted/home.html

E-zines about Distance Learning

These online publications are not the only ones available about distance learning, but they can provide a starting point for your online research into distance learning. You might read these sources in addition to print sources, such as those listed in Appendix A. Most journals are refereed. You should contact the *listserv*'s e-mail address for instructions to subscribe to the e-zine.

American Center for the Study of Distance Education (ACSDE) and American Journal of Distance Education	listserv@psuvm or listserv@psuvm.psu.edu
Commonwealth of Learning (COL) and the International Council for Distance Education (ICDE) COL-ICDE Distance Education Research Bulletin	colicde-request@unixg.ubc.ca
Distance Education Online Symposium	listserv@psuvm.bitnet or listserv@psuvm.psu.edu
Educational Uses of Information Technology	listserv@bitnet.educom.edu
Electronic Journal of Communications	comserve@rpitsvm.bitnet or comserve@vm.its.rpi.edu
Electronic Learning	http:/199.95.184.10/EL/index.html

Interpersonal Computing and Technology: An Electronic Journal for the 21st Century	listserv@guvm.bitnet or listserv@guvm.ccf.georgetown.edu
Journal of Computer-Mediated Communication	http://www.huji.ac.il/www_jcmc/jcmc.html
Journal of Extension	almanac@joe.uwex.edu
Journal of Technology Education	listserv@vtvm1.cc.vt.edu
New Horizons in Adult Education	listserv@alpha.acast.nova.edu
Online Chronicle of Distance Education and Communication	listserv@alpha.acast.nova.edu

Instructional Web Sites

The following sites describe distance learning or provide distance learning courses or programs. They represent only some sites dealing with distance learning; this is not an inclusive list, as some sites' content (or address) is changed, new sites are created, and others are deleted. Because the location of the site, whether national or international, is unimportant for distance learning, only the institution's or organization's "basic" title is provided.

When you use a search engine, such as Yahoo, Altavista, WebCrawler, Magellan, or Excite, for example, you can find lists of online resources about distance learning. By using keywords like *distance education* and *distance learning* along with other delimiting descriptors, you can access hundreds more sites. For example, Christina DeMello has compiled a list of educational institutions offering distance learning courses; her list now contains more than 3,000 entries! For an update on her list, visit (http://www.mit.edu:8001/people/cdemello/univ.html). Another good list of resources to supplement this short list is a directory of resources at (http://www.academic.panam.edu/~travis.dist.html). As you search the Web, you'll find many other such listings of distance learning resources and sites.

Acadmia University, Nova Scotia	http://dragon.acadiau.ca/~conted/conted.html
Africa Growth Network	http://www.agn.co.za/
Alexandria Education/ Entertainment Center	http://ourworld.compuserve.com/homepages/alex_theater/homepage.htm

Arlington Courseware   http://www.crl.com/~gorgon/distance.html

AT&T Center for
Excellence in Distance
Learning   http://www.att.com/cedl/

Athabasca University   http://www.athabascau.ca/

Bastyr University   http://www.bastyr.edu/distance_learning/distance.html

Black Hills State
University   http://www.bhsu.edu/academics/distlrn/dl1.html

Brevard Community
College   http://www.cww-eun.com/bcc/index.html

Butler Communica-
tions, Inc.   http://www.bucx.com/BUCX_web/newbut5.htm

Butte College   http://www.cin.butte.cc.ca.us/media_services/distance

CALCampus   http://calcampus.com/

California College for
Health Sciences   http://www.cchs.edu

California Institute
of Integral Studies   http://www.wcc-eun.com/eun/phd.html

California National
University   http://www.cnuas.edu/

Center for Networked
Information Discovery
and Retrieval   http://k12.cnidr.org/

Central State
University   http://www.university.edu/

Chemeketa Community
College   http://www.chemek.cc.or.us/Chemeketa/emergency-
services/distance-learning.html

Chrysalis School   http://www.wolfe.net/~chrysalis/

City University,
Seattle, WA   http://www.wcc-eun.com/city/index.html

Colorado State
University Business
School   http://cobweb.cobus.colostate.edu:80/html/disted/surge.
html

Columbia Southern
University   http://www.colsouth.edu/

Common Lisp
Programming for
Artificial Intelligence,
The Open University   http://kmi.open.ac.uk/courses/dmzx863.html

Community Learning Network (British Columbia)	http://www.etc.bc.ca/tdebhome/cln.html
CurriculumWeb	http://www.curriculumweb.com/curriculumweb/
Cyber High School	http://www.webcom.com/~cyberhi/
Dennison Online	http://www.dennisononline.com/
Distance Learning Help System, Quebec	http://www.quebectel.com/saad/indexAng.htm
Distance Learning: Designing Systems and Materials, The Open University	http://www-iet.open.ac.uk/iet/distance.html
Distance Learning Network	http://www.dlnetwork.com/
Economic Development Institute, World Bank	http://www.worldbank.org/html/edi/learning.html
eMail Classroom Exchange	http://www.iglou.com/xchange/ece/index.html
Entrepreneurs International, Inc.	http://www.ist.net/ei/
ERIC Clearinghouse on Elementary and Early Childhood Education	http://ericps.ed.uiuc.edu/
Federal Training Network	http://www.nmaa.org/member/ftn
Fraser Valley Distance Education School	http://www.fvrcs.gov.bc.ca
Gallaudet University	http://www.gallaudet.edu/~cceweb/disted/de.html
Georgia Technological Institute	http://www.conted.gatech.edu/
Globewide Network Academy	http://uu-gna.mit.edu:8001/uu-gna/index.html
Grand County School District	http://www.grand.k12.ut.us
Greenleaf University	http://www.greenleaf.edu
Health School, Australia	http://www.about-australia.com/hsa.dep.htm
Health University, The	http://www.healthy.net/univ.index.html
Heriot-Watt University	http://lynn.efr.hw.ac.uk/TEFRC/mba/works.html
Howard University, School of Continuing Education	http://www.con-ed.howard.edu/

Humber College On-line	http://hcol.humberc.on.ca/
ICS Learning Systems	http://www.icslearn.com/
Indiana University, Bloomington, Division of Extended Studies	http://www.extend.indiana.edu/
Institute for Distance Education, University of Maryland System	http://www.umuc.edu/ide/ide.html
Kathleen Gilroy Associates	http://www.kga.com/
LearnersWeb	http://www.innercite.com/~rklimes/learners.htm
Logipac and Concordia University	http://www.logipac.com/
Miami Bible Institute	http://www.fiu.edu/~wgreen01/mbi.html
Miami University's Index of Distance Education Sites	http://miavx1.muohio.edu/~cedcwis/Distance_Ed_Index.htmlx
Michigan Information Technology Network	http://www.mitn.msu.edu/MITN.htm
Michigan State University, College of Engineering	http://www.cps.msu.edu/~forsyth/GradDisEd.html
Mind Extension University	http://www.meu.edu/meu/catalog/catalog.html
Minneapolis College of Art and Design	http://www.mcad.edu/academic/DL/distance.html
Mohawk College	http://www.mohawkc.on.ca/dept/disted
NAU Star Schools Project	http://star.ucc.nau.edu/starschools/index.html
National Distance Learning Center (NDLC), University of Kentucky	http://www.occ.uky.edu/NDLC/NLCexplain.html
National Institute for Paralegal Arts and Sciences	http://law.net/~nipas/index.htm
National Science Foundation SUCCEED DT-5 Demonstration Projects	http://fiddle.ee.vt.edu/succeed/distance.html
New Jersey Institute of Technology	http://www.njit.edu/njit/Department/CCCC/VC/index.html

Newcastle Schools	http://www.netlink.co.uk/users/itcentre/
NIIT NetVarsity	http://www.niitnetvarsity.com/
Oberlin College	http://www-ts.cs.oberlin.edu:80/rooms/distlearning.html
Ontario Institute for Studies in Education, University of Toronto	gopher://porpoise.oise.on.ca/11/resources/IRes4Ed/ resources/distance
Open University (England)	http://www.open.ac.uk
Open University of British Columbia	http://www.cyberstore.ca/ola/openu/inst.html
Open University, Orlando, Florida	http://www.openu.com
OpenNet	http://www.opennet.net.au/
Oregon Community College Distance Education Consortium	http://www.lbcc.cc.or.us/occdec/chart.html
Project Diane (Diversified Information and Assistance Network, Tennessee)	http://www.diane.tnstate.edu/
Purdue University, Cooperative Extension Service	http://info.aes.purdue.edu/acs/disted.html
Rochester Institute of Technology	http://www.rit.edu/Academic/Dist_Learn/
Salve Regina University (RI)	http://www.wcc-eun.com/salve/index.html
Satellite Educational Resource Consortium	http://www.scsn.net/~serc/
School District of Philadelphia	http://libertynet.org/education/schools/lion/dept-distnc-prof.html
Shenandoah University	http://www.su.edu/west/calcmath.html
Simon Fraser University, Centre for Distance Education	http://www.cde.sfu.ca/Default.html
South Carolina ETV (educational television)	http://www.scetv.org/
Southern Alberta Institute of Technology,	

Energy and Natural Resources	http://www.sait.ab.ca/calendar/distance/correspdenr.htm
Southern California University for Professional Studies	http://www.scups.edu/
TEAMS, Los Angeles County of Education	http://teams.lacoe.edu
TeleEducation, New Brunswick	http://tenb.mta.ca/whatis.html
Texas A&M University	http://www.isc.tamu.edu/FLORA/tfphome1.html
TI-IN Network	http://www.tiin.com/
Travel Study Programs	http://pw2.netcom.com/~stash3/small.html
United States Distance Learning Association	http://www.usdla.org/
University of Alaska, Anchorage	http://www.uaa.alaska.edu/
University of Berkley	http://www.uofb.com/
University of British Columbia	http://www.videos.cstudies.ubc.ca/
University of Calgary	http://www.ucalgary.ca/
University of Hawaii Distance Education	http://www2.hawaii.edu/deit/
University of Louisville	http://www.louisville.edu/groups/distance-www
University of Maryland	http://www.umcp.umd.edu/TeachTech/itech.html
University of Minnesota	http://www.cee.umn.edu/disted or http://cda.mrs.umn.edu/~itvumn/delinks.html
University of Missouri	http://www.missouri.edu/~wleric/writery.html
University of North Carolina at Charlotte	http://www.coe.uncc.edu/~jonewby/notes.html
University of North Dakota	http://www.und.nodak.edu/sem/cedp/
University of Phoenix	http://www.uphx.edu/center
University of Southern Queensland, Distance Education Centre	http://www.usq.edu.au/dec
University of Texas	http://www.utexas.edu/world/instruction/index.html

University of Texas, Dallas	http://www.utdallas.edu/dept/mgmt/mims.html
University of Toledo	http://131.183.61.190/eqDial/Intro
University of Waterloo	http://www.uwaterloo.ca
University of Wollongong	http://www.uow.edu.au/health/phn/page.html
Utah Education Network	http://www.uen.org
Vancouver School Board Adult and Continuing Education	http://www.NerveCentre.com/VSB-Adult-Ed/
Village Learning Center	http://www.snowcrest.net/villcom/vlchp.html
Virginia Satellite Educational Network	http://www.pen.k12.va.us/go/VDOE/Technology/VSEN
Virtual Art School	http://dspace.dial.pipex.com/town/plaza/ad370/
Virtual Hospital, Department of Radiology, University of Iowa College of Medicine	http://indy.radiology.uiowa.edu/VirtualHospital.html
Virtual Language Lab, University of Pennsylvania	http://philae.sas.upenn.edu/
Walden University	http://www.wcc-eun.com/walden/index.html
Washington State University	http://www.eecs.wsu.edu/~cs445/
Wentworth Worldwide Media	http://www.classroom.net/
Westcott Communications	http://www.westcott.com/
Western Michigan University	http://www.wmich.edu:80/sip/
Wright-Patterson Air Force Base, Ohio, Civil Engineer and Services School	http://www.afit.af.mil/Schools/CE/dist.htm

Appendix F

Copyright, Trademark, Patent, and Intellectual Property Web Sites

The following sites provide some basic information about copyrights, patents, trademarks, and other intellectual property, with a special emphasis on information designed for use on the Internet. Several sites include information about educational and fair use of information, in the United States, as well as other North American and European nations. Because laws are in the process of change, and copyright issues in particular are heavily debated, you should check with these sites often to learn the latest information about intellectual property and legal requirements and restrictions.

Site	Address	Information
Benedict	http://www.benedict.com/register.htm	Copyright registration
	http://www.benedict.com/newsgrp.htm#newsgroups	Copyright information about newsgroups
British Columbia's Ministry of Education	http://www.etc.bc.ca/provdocs/copyright.title.html	Copyright information
Canadian Government's Copyright Board	http://www.gc.ca/copyright_board/	Updates and reports regarding Canadian copyright issues
CANCOPY	http://www.cancopy.com/	Canadian copyright information

Columbia University	http://www.ilt.columbia.edu/projects/copyright/index.html	Copyright information and links
Consortium for Educational Technology for University Systems (CETUS)	http://www.cetus.org/fairindex.html	Fair use
Copyright Clearance Center	http://www.copyright.com/	Copyright information
Cornell University	http://www.law.cornell.edu/usc/17/501.html	U.S. copyright act
Creative Incentive Coalition	http://www.cic.org/	Copyrights and resources
Dalhousie University	http://www.dal.ca/~copyrt/copyright/dalcopy.html	Canadian copyright information
EFF Intellectual Property Online: Patent, Trade-mark, Copyright Archive	http://www.eff.org/pub/intellectual_property	Copyright, patent, and trademark information
European Commission's project about intellectual property and networks	http://www.imprimatur.alcs.co.uk/	Intellectual property online
Franklin Pierce Law Center	http://www.fplc.edu/tfield/order.htm	Emphasis on small business, entrepreneurs, and individual artists
Industry Canada	http://infolic.gc.ca/ic-data/info-highway/ih-e.html	Reports about changes regarding intellectual property and the Internet

Intellectual Property Center	http://www.ipcenter.com/	Copyright, patent, and trademark information; newsletters, e-zines with updated information
Stanford University	http://fairuse.stanford.edu	Copyright and fair use information
U.S. Copyright Office	http://lcweb.loc.gov/copyright/	Government copyright resources
U.S. Patent and Trademark Office	http://www.uspto.gov/	Government patent and trademark resources
World Intellectual Property Organization	http://www.wipo.org/ http://itl.irv.uit.no/trade_law/documents/ i_p/wipo/art/wipo.html	WIPO's home page Copyright information

International Distance Learning

The following mailing lists are only a few available to help you learn more about international distance learning issues.

Name	Description	Address
ACPACOMX	An international learner discussion list	listserv@mitvma.mit.edu
APEX-L	A list for college or university educators who are developing international programs for Asian cultures	listserv@uhccvm.uhcc.hawaii.edu
INTED-L	A list for learners, educators, trainers, interested in international education	listserv@uwwvax.uww.edu
INTER-L	A list for learners, educators, trainers, interested in international education	listserv@vtvml.cc.vt.edu

These Web sites for "open universities" can provide you with an idea of the number and types of courses available and whether the courses are designed primarily for an international or a national audience. Many sites have links to pages dealing with international educational issues or documents describing international distance learning conferences, seminars, and collaborative activities. (See also other appendices for more international universities, college, or businesses offering Web courses.)

University	*Address*
Open Learning (Australia)	http://www.ola.edu.au/
Athabasca University (Canada)	http://www.athabascau.ca
The Open Learning Agency (Canada)	http://www.ola.bc.ca/
Universidad Abierta y a Distancia (Colombia)	http://gnuibe.unarino.edu.co/www/cread.html
Universidad Nacional de Educacion a Distancia (Costa Rica)	http://www.upv.es/~jlhueso/uned.html
Northern Finland Learning Network	http://oyt.oulu.fi/~nofwww/eng/nofhome.html
Open Learning Institute of Hong Kong	http://www.ol.hk/
East-Hungarian Regional Centre of Distance Education	http://www.kmrtk.klte.hu/kmrtk1.htm
Open University of Israel	http://www.openu.ac.il/
Open University of the Netherlands	http://www.ouh.nl/ou/homepage.html
Allama Iqbal Open University (Pakistan)	http://www.undp.org/tcdc/pak3029.htm
University of South Africa	http://www.unisa.ac.za/
Sukhothai Thammathirat Open University (Thailand)	http://www.stou.ac.th/index.htm#Contents
The Open University (UK) (Other addresses for the Open University's many Web pages are listed throughout the book and in other appendices.)	http://hcrl.open.ac.uk/ou/ouhome.html
Universidad Nacional Abierta (Venezuela)	gopher://arenal.uned.ac.cr/

Glossary

analog signal. An audio or video signal, like those currently used for television, radio, and some telephone lines, used in broadcasting and is represented with measurable physical quantities (e.g., voltage).

bandwidth. The amount of information that can be sent through a channel.

baud. A unit that signals speed; in telecommunications, represents the number of discrete elements that are transmitted in one second.

broadband. A high-capacity communication circuit with a speed (usually) higher than 1.544 Mbps; a channel that can carry much of the electromagnetic spectrum and can accommodate all media.

browser. A program used to read hypertext or hypermedia information.

CATV. Cable television or closed-circuit television.

chunk. The smallest meaningful piece of information.

client. The program that makes use of a resource from the server.

codec. A coder-decoder of video and audio signals that converts analog signals to digital signals, then compresses digital signals for outgoing information, then decompresses incoming information and converts digital signals to analog signals.

compressed video. Compression of the normal amount of information transmitted so that it can be transmitted over a smaller carrier, with the resulting loss of some information, which in turn means a lower quality of picture and/or sound.

desktop videoconferencing. A way to connect participants in a teleconference conducted through personal computers.

digital signal. An audio or a video signal that is represented by discrete variations (e.g., in frequency, amplitude, voltage) and that can be transmitted faster than analog signals.

distance education. Education or training offered to learners who are in a different location than the source or provider of instruction. Also known as *distance learning*.

distance learning. Education or training offered to learners who are in a different location than the source or provider of instruction. Also known as *distance education*.

DVC. *See* desktop videoconferencing.

e-mail. Electronic mail messages sent across a network to an individual or a group.

e-zine. Electronic magazine presented only on a network.

fiber to the curb. A type of cable used to create an ITV network.

file transfer protocol. A service/program that lets you copy a file from one Internet host to another.

FTP. *See* file transfer protocol.

FTTC. *See* fiber to the curb.

gopher. A client or a server program that allows you to make choices from menus.

graphical user interface. A way of working with (interfacing with) a system using icons and other visual and audio aids.

GUI. *See* graphical user interface.

hertz. A unit of frequency values representing cycles per second.

HFC. *See* hybrid fiber/coax.

HTML. *See* Hypertext Markup Language.

http. *See* Hypertext Transport Protocol.

hybrid fiber/coax. A type of cable used to create an ITV network.

hypermedia. Information presented as prose, sound, video, animation, static graphics, icons, and/or other formats connected by hyperlinks allowing access from one linked chunk of information directly to another.

hypertext. Prose connected to other related prose sections by hyperlinks allowing access from one linked chunk of information directly to another.

Hypertext Markup Language. A series of codes used to format information such as Web pages, hypertext, and hypermedia links, etc.

Hypertext Transport Protocol. Hypermedia information that can be uploaded or downloaded, usually abbreviated as the first part of a Web address (e.g., http://www.address).

Integrated Services Digital Network. A digital network that provides seamless communication of voice, video, and text between personal computers and group videoconferencing systems; anticipated to replace telephone-line communication in the future.

interactive television. So that users can play games, use video phones, receive educational programs, etc., by interacting with the television to work with a variety of services.

interactive video network. A telecommunication method to connect users via interactive television.

intranet. An internal or in-house network; a type of local area network to link people within an organization or an institution.

ISDN. *See* Integrated Services Digital Network.

ITV. *See* interactive television.

IVN. *See* interactive video network.

LAN. *See* local area network.

listserv. A program that administers a mailing list.

local area network. Two or more computers connected directly, as by cables, within a local (small) area.

mailing list. A list connecting users with similar interests to post notices and send messages about a topic or interest area.

modem. A device to connect a standalone computer with a network, usually via telephone lines; a device to convert digital signals to analog signals and back.

MUD. *See* multiple-user dimension or domain.

multiple-user dimension or domain. A virtual reality site where users take on roles and discuss issues, direct events, meet other users, etc.

narrowband. A low-capacity communication circuit with (usually) a speed of 56 Kbps or less.

network. Two or more computers that are connected.

newbie. A new subscriber to a mailing list.

newsgroup. Another name for a discussion group, a series of articles about a topic that is readable with a newsreader program.

server. The program that provides a resource; also called a file server.

SGML. *See* Standard General Markup Language.

Standard General Markup Language. A series of codes used to format information for use across many platforms.

T1. A dedicated digital circuit that makes point-to-point connections; a carrier that allows users to send several applications in a single data stream (including voice, video, or data) over a dedicated transmission line.

T3. A dedicated digital circuit that makes point-to-point connections, but with a greater carrying capacity than T1; a carrier that allows users to send several applications in a single data stream (including voice, video, or data) over a dedicated transmission line.

telnet. A program that allows you to connect to the Internet from your computer (the local computer) through another computer (the remote computer).

uniform resource locator. The technical description of the information's location on the Internet.

URL. *See* uniform resource locator.

user. Someone who has access to the system.

WAIS. *See* wide-area information service.

WAN. *See* wide-area network.

Web. *See* World Wide Web.

wide area information service. A system to search the text of sources you specify by keywords you've selected and to present the relevant information from the search.

wide-area network. Computer network in which the computers are connected through less direct links, such as telephone lines and satellite hookups.

wideband. A medium-capacity communication circuit with (usually) a speed between 64 Kbps and 1.544 Mbps.

World Wide Web. Information available in hypermedia through the Internet and accessible through a variety of interconnected links.

WWW. *See* World Wide Web.

Index